Problems of Higher Education

Problems of Higher Education

T.K. Hemchand

CRESCENT
PUBLISHING CORPORATION

[The responsibility for the facts stated, conclusions reached and plagiarism, if any, in this book is entirely that of the Author. And the Publisher bears no responsibility for them, whatsoever.]

Problems of Higher Education

First Published : 2009

ISBN 978-81-8342-143-0

Published by :

CRESCENT PUBLISHING CORPORATION
4831/24, Prahlad Street,
Ansari Road, Darya Ganj,
New Delhi - 110002
Ph. : 23272541, 23257835
Fax : 91- 011- 23257835
e-mail : campusbooks@hotmail.com

Printed at :

Roshan Offset Printers
Delhi

Preface

Higher education today is widely recognised as most desirable and important educational endeavour, serving not only as a means to a degree or vocational skills, but also as an important index of the developmental process. For long, primary education, especially in developing countries where illiteracy is a major issue, has been the most important, or in some cases, the sole recipient of governmental support and action. However, as the global economic, political and social contexts evolve, primary education no longer suffices as resourceful enough. As the plethora of options and opportunities provided by education increase, higher education offers students to avail themselves of the best in education services and stretch themselves to the best of their abilities.

Availing overself of higher education option is, however, better said than done. A myriad number of problems persist in higher education, all of which serve to hinder the smooth flow of the higher education process, and prove to be a source of immense consternation. This book has been designed as an incisive manual which looks into the issue of higher education problems, taking into account such issues as evolving social contexts, teachers and infrastructure, finance and resources, quality maintenance, etc. It explores these matters through numerous perspectives aiding a multi-dimensional view of the issue, and analyses its implications. In addition, it studies higher education as it is within different social contexts, providing a model for improvement of higher education within the Indian context, as well as fostering a deeper understanding of the issue.

It is hoped that the erudition and insight of the book serve well for the readers.

Prof. T.K. Hemchand

Contents

1

Technological Influence on Higher Education

Technology in higher education affords the opportunity to create a learning environment that is learner-centric, individualised, and interactive. Technology will greatly expand access to higher education and fundamentally change the models of education with which we are familiar. In particular, technology will enable education that is learner-centric, individualised, and interactive, making education far more relevant to the needs of individuals. It will allow for anytime, anyplace learning, which will be particularly attractive to working adults, and it will enable true lifelong learning in a formal sense. These new forms of educational delivery will require new ways to measure and credential learning.

Although modern technologies may have a place in helping students visualise real-world phenomena or, through distance delivery, in providing classes that might otherwise be unavailable, they are primarily linear, passive presentations of material in the tradition of classroom instruction. They represent distribution of current models of education, but they offer no new educational paradigm.

Specifically, online education enables us for the first time to put knowledge and learning within reach of all those who have access, at the time and place where such knowledge is needed. Internet-based education offers the potential of thousands of classes on hundreds of subjects available anytime night or day, at any place, at the convenience of the student. Although post-secondary education has been both place-bound and time-bound, we now have the opportunity to truly have anytime, anyplace learning. Although the source of knowledge and learning has traditionally been the professor, knowledge and learning is now available over the Internet.

Teachers in traditional models perform as a "sage on the stage." What new paradigms help create is a "guide on the side" model. These two phrases describe succinctly the difference between teacher-centric classrooms and learner-centric classrooms. In the former, teachers are presumed to be the font of all wisdom and knowledge. Their job is to move that wisdom and knowledge from their own brains to the receiver brains of their students.

Almost nothing is taken into account regarding the personal context, knowledge, or experience that each learner already brings to the learning situation. Students are seen primarily as empty vessels or passive receptacles waiting to be filled. The availability of thousands of classes over the Internet enables learners to select their own learning choices from the offerings of many sites, order them the way they want, and pursue the outcomes that are important to them. This shift to learner-centric education has already begun, and it will take on added momentum as high-quality instructional content becomes available over the Internet. High-quality instructional modules will enable individuals to access the knowledge they need when it is needed, moving to "just-in-time" education rather than "just-in-case" education.

Technology-Based Education

The research and service contributions of universities are

an important component of our free and innovative society. There is significant evidence that research universities have positive economic effects in their communities. Campus-based universities and colleges also serve as an important "transition point" for young people graduating from high school, who are not yet prepared to enter the workforce and serve as fully participating citizens. The social aspects of the campus experience are important elements of learning at this stage of life, though they receive no credit or grade.

The model of existing universities and colleges is based on the idea that postsecondary education is an opportunity, generally for 18- to 25-year-olds, to dedicate several years to learning and preparation to become fully functioning adults ready to enter the world of work. Technology will impact, to some degree, our traditional campuses and students.

Universities will teach technology use and will have ongoing requirements to have the latest technology available. Professors will increasingly require students to use the Internet for research and supplemental information and sometimes for communication and collaboration. Some universities will develop a "brick-andclick" approach by offering a combination of classroom courses, online courses, and hybrid courses that combine online teaching with classroom discussion, as well as offering online courses through their continuing education departments to reach out to other learners.

However, the use of technology does not change the fundamental distinctions between our traditional educational system and the new models of online learning. Those distinctions are in the role of the student, the role of faculty, and the role of the institution. Most institutions, especially educational institutions, have difficulty in reinventing roles, so it is likely that new institutions will take the leadership role in online learning. The new models of online education serve different functions than our traditional universities. Fundamentally, online education is more applicable to lifelong learning than to education as an event, and it is more applicable to working adults than to students just out of high school.

Student's Role

Online learning implies learner-centric education, where learners take responsibility to choose learning activities of most value and relevance to them. Traditional-aged students (18 to 25) are generally not able to take such responsibility. They do not yet have the experience in work and life to know which learning is most important. Moreover, many of these individuals benefit from the social interactions of a campus.

In contrast, adult learners generally have full-time jobs, families, and a good idea of the additional education they need. They have little patience to sit through long lectures of information that may or may not be relevant. These students are able to take responsibility to define the learning that is important to them, and they will be demanding consumers of educational content. Many of these individuals simply cannot participate in formal education that is place or time specific. They require the anytime, anywhere learning afforded by online education.

Faculty's Role

In traditional institutions, faculty members are perceived as the sources of knowledge, and their role is to communicate that knowledge to their students. With students who have little experience, there is arguably a common body of knowledge that needs to be taught and is relevant for most students. However, in the information age, the amount of knowledge and information is doubling every few years. It is no longer possible for professors to master more than a small slice of the current knowledge in their field.

Research and researchers will continue to be vitally important to our society. Yet, with the increasing amount of content available over the Internet, the challenge for students is not access to information and knowledge. Understanding what is most important to know and where the best source of that knowledge lies are the challenges. Consequently, the role of faculty in online education shifts to mentoring—directing students to appropriate content; helping them learn how to learn and to find, sift, and judge the quality of information; and encouraging their progress.

Role of Institution

Our universities and colleges are set up to define the learning that is required. They do this through required courses, prerequisites, and a specified number of credit hours. They also do this at the course level, with each professor deciding what he or she will teach in a given semester. Institutions certify learning by having professors assign grades to student performance and by counting credit hours completed toward a degree.

Generally, an institution certifies only the learning that is done there, with some provision for the transfer of credits from elsewhere. In online learning, learning experiences may be from anywhere, not only from other universities and colleges but also from personal study or corporate training and work experience. The role of institutions will be to certify learning regardless of where it is done. This will change the institutional role from mandating classes and credit hours to developing measurements of knowledge and skills.

Effective Technology Use

The potential of online learning cannot be realised without addressing some significant challenges.

The quality of instruction is paramount. Many of the current online courses are of very poor quality, amounting to little more than professors putting their lecture notes online. To the extent that courses are simply text-based, electronic correspondence courses, they will be no more effective than those same courses in print form. The two most significant priorities in developing online courses governors can support are that they be modular and interactive.

Modular content enables students to individualise their learning experience by skipping parts that they already know and focusing on modules that are relevant to their individual needs. New online content should be developed as learning objects, each addressing a particular objective, that can be linked to form modules and courses. New standards are being developed for learning objects to make them interchangeable. Effective online content is also highly interactive, utilising the power of the computer to process student responses, provide specific feedback, and modify instructional paths based on student performance.

Developing high-quality online courses is expensive. A typical development team would include, at a minimum, an instructional designer, a subject-matter expert, a graphic artist, a programmer, and an editor. Although faculty members are often the ones tasked with putting courses online, few if any of them have all of these skills. A few universities are organising to support faculty development efforts, but this is not widespread, partly because of the high cost of doing so. The only way for institutions to afford the cost of high-quality course materials is to amortise the cost over many students by sharing courses.

The current model is for every institution to develop its own set of online courses. However, from a national or state perspective, it makes no sense for an institution to be funding another English 101 course if there are already 10 good ones available from other institutions. There is no reason for 10 institutions to each develop a course in a particular subject, if they could pool their expertise, share the costs, and generate one really excellent course for all to use. Although the idea of sharing courses in many ways goes against the tradition of our universities as individual silos of learning where faculty design their own classes, there is a precedent in the use of nationally published textbooks.

The concept of sharing online content, in the form of courses or simply individual learning objects, raises the issue of intellectual property rights. The issue is most often framed as to whether the faculty or the institution owns the course, but the issue is more complex. Developing high-quality online courses is beyond the capability of most faculties. It requires the skills of a team and the corresponding investment, and the challenge is to have adequate incentives for faculty, other team members, and the institution to participate in the development and wide distribution of online courses.

The revenue-sharing model is more important than the ownership question, but both must be addressed to enable the maximum sharing of content. At the same time, if states are funding online course development at state universities and colleges, they should be insisting that these courses be used across the state, and perhaps shared among states, rather than the same courses being developed at each state institution.

The major challenges to distance education during the past 50 years have been low student completion rates and the lack of collaboration one would experience in a campus environment with both faculty and other students. However, Internet-based education can potentially address both of these issues. Collaboration over the Internet, using chat rooms, threaded discussion groups, message boards, and other tools, may be even richer than the interactions on campus.

Increased collaboration leads to a sense of a learning community, and as a result, higher completion rates. The addition of faculty mentors to work with and encourage students has a further positive effect on completion rates. Nevertheless, these elements of e-learning are not present in many models and require thoughtful implementation.

Technologically mediated learning means new roles for students, faculty, and institutions. These new learning models also produce new roles for state policies and new opportunities for governors to harness this powerful tool.

Assuring Quality

The governments have the opportunity to frequently and compellingly convey the need for new models for assuring quality and credentialing learning. Post-seondary education has long been self-regulated, through regional accrediting bodies, and more recently, through various national accrediting groups. The departments of education, corporations, government entities, and other universities accept accreditation as a certification of quality education. Accreditation is required for central financial aid, for government and corporate tuition reimbursement, and generally to attract students to institutions of higher education.

Traditionally, accreditation has looked at the quality of institutions and the qualifications of their people and processes. More frequently, quality assurance processes are beginning to assess the quality of learning at an institution. For example, the National Council for the Accreditation of Teacher Education is reforming its quality assurance process to include a demonstration by teacher candidates that they can connect theory to practice and be effective in the classroom. Pass rates on a content knowledge test will be used in the accreditation decision.

Although institutional quality assurance is moving toward recognition of skills and knowledge obtained, technology-based education will enable learning to take place in many ways and many places outside of traditional higher education institutions. If learning is directed by the individual and not by an institution, and if that learning is unique to each individual and may be accomplished either through formal classes, by independent study, through work experiences, or in other ways, then the measuring and credentialing of that learning become critical. Perhaps the most important impact of the Internet on education is that it transfers authority from learning institutions to individuals. This trend, at least for adult learners, will lead to some surprising consequences.

Individualised education will lead to individualised accreditation or certification of learning achieved. This trend is already well underway in the technology field, with industry certifications. This trend will spread to other disciplines. As a result, the role of our education institutions must expand to measure and credential learning regardless of where that learning occurs, or new institutions will be formed to provide this function.

There will be a greatly increased need for, and acceptance of, competency-based certifications rather than traditional grades on transcripts. Historically, universities have held the position that "the only learning that counts is the learning you do here." Learning is measured in credit hours, and the degree of learning is measured by attendance, classwork, assignments, and tests, which are created and assessed by instructors and reflected in grades.

Although this system will continue to be used with traditional campus-based students, it is inappropriate for the new models of online learning. Where learning may have been done anywhere, and in a variety of ways, the measurement of learning will move to measuring outputs—what one knows and can do—rather than activity. Ultimately, there will be a preference for independently determined competency assessments *instead* of grades. This preference is already being expressed by employers and is demonstrated in the technology certifications developed by industry.

In the end, if students can define, obtain, and validate their own learning, and employers find the validation reliable, then the meaning and value of a college degree is redefined. Although accredited universities and colleges largely control access to higher education today because they control the credentialing of learning, the higher education landscape of the future will be more open with different kinds of acceptable credentials and different forms of accreditation and validation of learning.

In addition to calling for new models of assuring quality and credentialing learning, governors can help articulate the need for swifter quality assurance processes. Regional accreditation is typically a five- to seven-year process, which is a huge barrier to entry for new participants in the education market. Even after accreditation, new degrees must be individually approved, which can take three to six months after the degree is developed.

Although appropriate in past societies of limited change, the slow pace of traditional accreditation is not responsive to the New Economy requirements for education. For example, because of changes in technology, many programs of technology instruction have an effective life of only two to three years. Essentially, new programs in postsecondary education must circumvent traditional accreditation, as is the case with the burgeoning demand for technology certifications.

Implications for Government Policies

Governments and institutions should support online education as an alternative to traditional campus-based education, particularly for working adults, but also for rural students who may be unable to attend a traditional college or university. Online education has the potential to make a significant difference in workforce development and economic competitiveness. To make this happen, the authorities can take the following actions.

— *Ensure that Internet access is widely available.* This includes ensuring access to computers and infrastructure among those who might otherwise not have such access. It also includes giving all individuals the basic knowledge to use the access provided. Knowledge of computers and the Internet is essential in the New Economy, but this knowledge is made exponentially more important because these tools will be key to all kinds of learning.

— *Support financial aid eligibility rules to support study in qualified e-learning programs.* To promote online learning, adminitstrators can advocate for changes in government policies. They can also put e-learning on an equal footing with more traditional classroom education by recommending changes to state financial aid programs and policies that promote online education.

— *Recommend that state and industry tuition reimbursement provisions include e-learning.* States should actively utilise e-learning for the ongoing training and development of state employees. States should also include and even encourage e-learning solutions in their requests for proposals for workforce development programs.

— *Support the development and acceptance of alternative measures for assuring quality education.* Historically, both government and industry have relied on traditional accreditation for assuring quality in education. As a result, only courses from accredited institutions are eligible for tuition reimbursement, accreditation is a requirement for central financial aid, and accreditation is a requirement to bid on many government education and training jobs. Both government and industry need to measure quality by measuring the knowledge and skills acquired by their employees; such measurements will enable new and innovative programs, as well as technologies, to demonstrate their practical worth without a lengthy formal accreditation process. States need new processes to license alternative providers that can demonstrate the effectiveness of their programs, rather than leaving this task to traditional accrediting processes.

— *Shift public post-secondary education funds from institutions to individuals.* While continuing support for existing state universities and colleges, governors should carefully assess the need for more campus buildings in a learning environment that may increasingly be online. Over time, the funding of higher education should shift to financial support of individuals rather than institutions. Money will then flow to educational providers that best meet student needs, encouraging and increasing competition in higher education and empowering students to choose learning experiences that are most relevant to them.

Access and Equity in Higher Education

Terms such as 'access', 'equal opportunity', 'equality of outcomes', 'affirmative action', and 'equity' are frequently encountered in the area of higher education policy and analysis. The key umbrella or organising concept, however, is 'equity' conceived as: fairness; equality of treatment where comparable features and conditions pertain; and opportunity to participate and contribute, without hindrance through prejudice and discriminatory customary practice.

Equity in this sense, need not connote equality in any precise or mathematical sense, e.g. fixed quotas for under-represented groups proportional to overall population, lotteries for admission to popular courses or institutions, etc, although as strategies these may sometimes be attempted. Nor does it imply uniformity whether of institutional provision or entry and study requirements. On the contrary, it is now widely accepted that, rather than sameness, substantial diversity and fitness to individuals and groups, and their circumstances, are appropriate if the varied needs of students are to be met. The notion of "fitness" has its roots in Platonic and Aristotelian ideas which give prominence to ideas of distinctive differences requiring individual treatment or the recognition of categories of people for which collective action is appropriate. They have always been relevant in educational provision.

Historically, in educational practice, these ideas have at times been associated with exclusion and privileged access and treatment rather than a fair chance for all. By contrast, contemporary liberal democratic and ethical theories support different ideas about 'fitness', 'fairness' and 'justice'. Most notable, perhaps, are those developed by John Rawls in his theory of justice and, in different ways, by a considerable body of philosophers, social theorists and economists, and resoundingly expressed in the Universal Declaration of Human Rights and the European Convention on Human Rights. Considerateness and concern for the well-being of all people feature strongly in modern intellectual theories and declarations.

The crucial point behind the Declaration and the Convention on Human Rights and by this body of theoretical literature is that equity is put at the centre of discourse and policy: everyone in the community should be given equal consideration and the opportunity to develop human capabilities. Inequality, for example, according to Rawls' 'Difference Principle', in access to primary goods, is acceptable only when it can be conclusively shown that ultimately it gives rise to greater benefits for everyone. More precisely, inequalities above a (low) threshold can be tolerated only when they function to help more people move across it. This of course does not preclude forms of inequality reflecting 'special conditions' and there is considerable debate about the implications of these conditioning factors. Sen, for example, prefers the concept of freedom for all to achieve, or capability.

Despite the differences it is clear that system-wide policies, structures and institutions and their procedures can be expected to submit to the claims of justice, fairness and equal opportunity. Discussion of these concepts and reflective analysis of their educational implications would seem to be an important role for staff and students in higher education.

In modern political analysis, equity is often subsumed under the concept of democratisation – the recognition that all individuals have rights and needs, that these considerations require and have a central role in policies and action strategies. Through participative procedures, whereby all have a voice and an impact, more general concepts are translated into practical action. Decisions should not be pre-emptive, by one group on behalf of another, but should be shared, giving rise to a sense both of individual freedom and of a community of interests and values.

Universities in several countries rather sharply experienced the impact of democratic ideas following the radical student movements of the late 1960's. They are now embedded in national policy frameworks and institutions' decision-making procedures, as well as more generally in such international conventions as those of the United Nations.

In higher education the challenge now is both to fully embrace the concept of equity and with determination to integrate it with the long-established traditions of excellence and merit and the more recent policy preoccupations with standards, quality, efficiency and relevance to social and economic needs. The need for this reconciliation is implicit in the legislative requirements that have been set in Ireland in recent years and in policy proposals designed to strengthen higher education and its role in national development.

Policy must take account of such considerations as quality and suitability of qualifications for specific study programmes, economic and socio-cultural needs, human capital needs, financial and other considerations. Practical issues include the systems of assessment and certification at secondary school level, procedures for managing alternative entry routes which include non-formal learning methods for determining specific qualities for particular higher education programmes. In this regard, OECD countries, until relatively recently, could be classified into 'supply-driven' (e.g. the highly competitive selection procedures in the UK and Irish universities); demand driven (e.g. Italy, Germany, Belgium, The Netherlands) and student market driven, whereby government leaves access to market forces (U.S.). Admission procedures for students fall broadly into one of two approaches, or some combination of them: system-wide right of entry to all who are deemed qualified; institutional selection according to determinations made for particular programmes and courses. For either approach variations can be and often are made under special entry schemes for under-represented groups, for example though the ways points for entry are allocated for specially targeted groups.

In practice, across the OECD membership there are now strong and reasonably consistent moves towards opening up access opportunities for tertiary education to ever wider and more diverse groups. More precisely, 'equity' refers comprehensively to policies, procedures, strategies and everyday actions designed to improve the higher educational, employment and advancement opportunities for those of low socio-economic status, women and girls, ethnic and other minorities, the people with a disability and others denied previous opportunity to enter higher education or discriminated against in various ways. The wish to study and the aptitude to succeed are determining factors but it cannot be assumed that there is some definite standard or level which acts as a threshold. The notion of some fixed quantum of talent, a 'pool of ability', is no longer acceptable. On the other hand, it would scarcely be equitable to offer particular kinds and levels of study opportunities in the certain knowledge that potential students would be quite unable to meet the requirements. Procedures are needed to ensure every opportunity, from early childhood onwards for students to demonstrate their aptitudes and interests rather than depending on the selection role of upper secondary education. Also required are second chance opportunities, especially for mature age students.

'Educational opportunity' refers to circumstances affecting selection and entry to programmes; conditions of study which include curricula, teaching procedures, learning resources and financial considerations; criteria for successful performance and graduation and conditions governing assessed performance; and factors affecting entry into the work force over which higher education has some control or influence.

There is of course a distinction between access for students and equal employment opportunities for staff; nevertheless they can be viewed as part of a single 'equity continuum'. Of particular relevance for present purposes, is employment in academic institutions: opportunities for under-represented groups and those actively discriminated against not only to freely enter the academic labour market but to be promoted fairly and to advance to positions of responsibility and influence.

'Equity' in its broadest sense would refer to all stunts and staff or prospective students and staff – that opportunity and provision should be such as to sustain and advance the interests of everyone. However, such an interpretation, important as it is for overall policy making, would embrace all aspects of higher education whereas the focus here is, as indicated, on particular categories of potential and actual students and staff, traditionally and still often typically under-represented in universities and other tertiary institutions.

'Equity', thus defined, forms a significant element in the extension into many aspects of higher education of notions of justice and fairness and liberal democratic ideas, policies and practices. Although often associated with particular political movements and campaigns the range of issues arising for broad-based equity policies in education goes well beyond the concerns and actions of particular special interest groups.

Great advances have been made over several decades in advancing equity in higher education, for both students and staff. For the 1981 OECD Conference on Policies for Higher Education in the 1980's, access to higher education was one of the four main themes. In many countries, in the fields of equal opportunity employment and anti-discrimination, there are now well-established legislative frameworks and often also a commission and/ or other agencies responsible for implementing legislation, monitoring and reporting on compliance and handling complaints and disputes. Their scope normally includes education at all levels.

Specifically in higher education, and throughout the OECD region, there is a continuing movement to advance equity through these and other means. Unquestionably there has been very considerable progress, through the substantial quantitative growth of university places that has occurred during the past three to four decades.

No less important has been the establishment of a greater diversity of institutions and programmes, facilities and arrangements to meet the needs of individuals and groups previously given scant attention. Success has been achieved in improving access and study opportunities for disabled students; women have made substantial career advances; and universities generally are much better able –and willing – than in the past to construct and implement broad-based equity policies. Increasing participation rates at all levels are one indicator of progress in achieving equity objectives.

Driving Forces of Equity Agenda

In addition to and partly as a result of the impact of

education democratisation movements, and the pressure of special interest groups extending over several decades, the current equity agenda may be said to derive from five main sources:

— determination by governments, public agencies and a variety of policy makers and Non—Governmental Organisations and community action groups to advance the needs and interests of specific categories of under-representation, both students and staff;

— a large and cumulative body of legislation particularly relating to human rights, equal employment opportunities and anti-discrimination, leading to many innovative organisational practices in institutions;

— a growing volume of research evidence on, amongst other things, the limited effectiveness or slow results of many of the legislative and policy measures that have been taken;

— sensitivity of policy makers, system managers and institutions to reports of persistent inequity, and breaches of legislation conventions, regulations, etc.;

— continued representations by special interest groups.

Progress of a substantial kind cannot be gainsaid. These gains have, however, served to identify shortcomings and highlight further needs. The more widespread the experience of upper secondary and tertiary education becomes, the greater the likelihood that those who do not acquire qualifications risk being socially and economically marginalised.

Equity Shortcomings

The fundamental goals of the human rights movement, and policies formulated in many countries for improved access to higher education for under-represented groups and greater equity in academic employment, have not been fully or in many instances even adequately achieved or implemented. Strong evidence for this has been provided in the Council of Europe international study which has recently resulted in a firm and comprehensive Ministerial Recommendation.

For many researchers and commentators, there are genuine grounds for concern, indicating amongst other things weak policies, inadequate implementation procedures and the ignoring of legislative requirements and agreed procedures. Although not possible to quantify in all respects, these weaknesses are sufficiently widespread and well documented as to be the target of continuing criticism and agitation. Even so, there is still a view that the concern in the sphere of education is exaggerated, that there is insufficient recognition of substantial gains already made, too much special pleading and not enough attention to the basic requirements of upholding standards in academic life, of the tradition of excellence.

Some members of minority groups, 'some women' may have had fewer past opportunities. But these are transitional and marginal problems that can be handled within the academic tradition" Unfortunately, the transition is proving to be a very extended one and it is precisely aspects of 'the academic tradition' as embedded in customary practice and institutional structures that have been held up by many researchers and scholars as a cause of continuing difficulty in achieving equity objective. Academia, as perceived by critics, is characterised as traditionally elitist, male and patriarchal in its culture, values and structures. Men, it is claimed, are encouraged by their professors, women not. The valued tradition of collegial decision-making, it has been claimed, can actually inhibit equity, causing senior administrators to hold back from enforcement.

The barriers in the eyes of some critics, are compounded by other factors than gender: "Academia, too, has a class structure: its hierarchy of professors, assistant professors, and part-timers is not solely a ladder based on merit, but a track based on a number of gender, racial/ethnic, and socio-economic factors. The degradation many working-class women experience in academia replicates that of the larger classed society".

The striking image of the 'glass ceiling' has been adopted by women's groups to explain why it is that for some people in higher education there is no great problem in career progression, whereas for others there is a continuing sense of injustice. For men, looking down, there is nothing to see; but women, striving to go forward find themselves hard up against the glass ceiling. There were several reported instances of the strength of tacit resistance to the implementation of equity policies; reports from national equal opportunity commissions also provide many examples of breaches of regulations and laws.

There are conflicting perceptions and points of view. On the one hand, the belief that while there may be problems, procedures are in hand to manage them and, on the other, that there are barriers still to shatter, changes to be made in the academic system itself. There are also questions to raise about categorisation. 'Social class' for example must be defined with reference not merely to patterns of income distribution and their traditional occupational correlates, but to the changing composition of society and indeed to the role of education as itself a nominator of social class. Comparisons over time of rates of participation may not be of like with like.

The issues are complex and warrant careful elucidation. The desire to open up admission procedures must be tempered by a realistic appraisal of student capabilities and the readiness and capacity of institutions to provide suitable study environments. Very high dropout rates in some European countries where access is open are scarcely equity-positive. It is arguable, of course, that still the most effective 'strategy' for achieving equity objectives is expansion, the wave effect that carries all before it. Certainly expansion has broadened opportunities, but these opportunities for higher education are still unequally distributed, even on the strictest interpretation of the traditional merit principle.

Indeed a large part of the rationale for a major international study, by the Council of Europe, is precisely "a concern that this expansion has not fully met the hope placed in it for greater equity between all potential students and for the inclusion of those belonging to social groups historically disadvantaged in respect of access to education". The Council of Europe and other sources do not confine the concerns about exclusion to certain social groups. In access to higher education institutions, iower socio-economic groups, however defined, are indeed under-represented; but women, too, having succeeded in gaining access as students and progressing well, including employment in academic institutions, have not had the success they seek and expect in climbing the career ladder.

Since women are now enrolling in many academic subjects at higher levels than men, the need is for women to accept the challenge of "stepping out of the shadows to take over leadership responsibilities, and believe in their future". These are not the only unfulfilled goals. There are significant barriers facing various categories of students with a disability; some ethnic minorities are very poorly represented either as students or staff; financing arrangements often confer unequal benefits or impose hardships in inequitable ways; and higher education – universities in particular – still tends to advance those already more socially, culturally and economically favoured. Prejudice and discrimination are reported in relation to sexual orientation; adolescent boys are an emerging equity category not yet fully recognised, and so on. These are generalisations, they have different force, impact and significance across and within different societies but they present a generally valid picture of unequal representation and participation across a wide spectrum of countries.

The challenge is real, but policy responses are not straightforward. There are cultural and social norms at stake, political interests and active pressure groups at work pursuing diverse ends. To be equitable, education policies and practices need to satisfy a very wide and varied set of criteria and they require to be negotiated, tradeoffs included. Moreover, they are not, of course, the only relevant criteria.

Higher education must satisfy scholarly standards of excellence or quality, be financially sound and accountable, connect with major developmental needs in the economy and society, meet a variety of community and family expectations, contribute positively to the advancement of knowledge and the education of the professions, and so on. What is not at issue, however, is the obligation, both legal and moral, that increasingly falls upon higher education institutions to demonstrate that equity features prominently and consistently in their stated policies and their practical actions.

Significant progress, like the increase in women's participation in undergraduate education which now, in a number of countries, exceeds men's, is welcomed as is the steady increase in women's employment in academic positions once the exclusive preserve of males. But such changes have not been sufficient for policy makers and many members of the academic community who seek more evidence of progress in achieving goals.

Not only have explicit goals and targets not been met (or even set) in several areas, but the concept of equity has often been defined too narrowly. An obvious example is the widespread acceptance of the principle of applying the same access rules to everyone. This, on the face of it, seems equitable, but in practice it has not assisted in improving access for some poorly represented groups. Awareness of this led to what has been criticised in a Council of Europe study as a 'symbolic model of equal opportunity'

In this model, while limited numbers of students from under-represented or 'non-traditional' groups have been admitted under special arrangements, the basic fabric of the rules of admission remains intact. What is perhaps more important, it is now recognised that the special arrangements, commendable in themselves, need to be part of a much broader strategy which treats 'access' as but one step or stage in a policy process that should start in the early years of schooling, since it is schooling that, unless reformed, reinforces unequal opportunity. Where interpretation does not extend quite as far as this, it does embrace considerably more than 'entry' or 'participation'.

In the Council of Europe project on Access to Higher Education in Europe, access was defined as:

— greater participation in higher education of good quality;

— the extension of participation to include currently under-represented groups;

— a recognition that participation extends beyond entry to successful completion.

There is a growing realisation that further critical analysis and more substantial measures including closer monitoring and detailed reporting are required to achieve equity goals for both students and staff. In the area of disability, there is, as a result of persistent effort, a much better understanding than in the past of the often subtle barriers that stand in the way.

Regarding women's employment in universities, several decades of experience with programmes of equal employment opportunity have resulted in a much deeper understanding than hitherto of the cultural and organisational boundaries or barriers, that may militate against employment equity, reinforcing discriminatory practices and beliefs. 'Equity' needs to be further elaborated, its frame of reference extended, from specific procedures relating to fair practice in employment or study opportunities, to include the fundamental norms, values, ethos and way of life of academic institutions. Such extension can be quite problematic and is often contested, covertly if not explicitly.

From time to time, governments are alerted to the need for rather more strenuous measures than have flowed from equal opportunity legislation, or they are urged to take a more forceful approach to developing the implications of legislation and giving greater impetus to equity goals in higher education. As the Council of Europe recognised, the legislative approach is itself an important step in advancing equity in higher education, but not sufficient.

Financial obstacles can of course be a considerable barrier, even in regimes where tuition fees are low or non-existent. Costs for supporting non-traditional students, for example, are often high both for institutions and the individuals and these can be critical when they reinforce other socio-economic factors. Tuition fees, even in schemes which are specifically designed to greatly alleviate hardship, may have a negative, discriminatory impact on enrolments. Targeted initiative schemes can be highly beneficial at the tertiary level, particularly in support of labour market policies, but their equity significance may be in question and is in any case lessened if incentives and support for study from an early age are insufficient.

A single institution will be responsible for only part of what might be termed a generic or developmental strategy for equity in higher education, and individual public agencies and government departments will have only partial policy responsibility. Nevertheless, there is an accumulating body of research findings and experiential evidence that supports the need for a more systemic approach in which the roles and responsibilities of various elements and agencies are brought together, into more coherent, co-ordinated policy initiatives.

Barriers of Access to Higher Education

Despite the many improvements that have been made and the wide range of policy instruments that have been deployed, there remains a formidable array of barriers. They are summarised below.

Barriers to Student Access and Progression

— Characteristics of primary and secondary schooling which favour academic advancement of some groups of students but not others; high dropout and failure rates at secondary school level; lack of transparency in educational provision, of guidance and orientation, and of suitable ways of recording, acknowledging and enhancing achievement and progression for students with learning difficulties or 'school resistance';

— Socio-economic – financial and cultural factors in family and community; growing income disparities and 'poverty pools'; unequal cultural capital across social groups; inadequate forms of liaison and communication;

— Geographic factors that militate against knowledge of availability of programmes and ready participation in them;

— Financial constraints on family and prospective/ actual students; inadequate incentives to continue studying;

— Difficulties facing public authorities and institutions in meeting additional costs for equity purposes in era of declining per capita budgets;

— Legislative gaps; weak policy approaches including procedures for monitoring, evaluation and follow-up; inadequate research-based knowledge of 'what works';

— Rigid application of merit principle and one-sided pursuit of narrow concept of excellence in education including particularist concepts of 'the idea of a university';

— Weaknesses in teacher preparation, supervision and professional development;

— Amongst staff in higher education, a continuing prejudice towards, lack of understanding and willingness or ability to provide support for, the study needs of particular disadvantaged groups;

— Community hostility to consequences of affirmative action, e.g. quotas, heavy subsidies;

— Poor data on performance and inadequate procedures for identifying 'at risk'students;

— Bafflement over/ lack of clear research findings about and understanding of why policy measures have not worked, notably in seeking to improve the ratio of low socio-economic groups in upper secondary and higher education.

Barriers to Staff Recruitment and Career Advancement

— Cultural assumptions, values, institutional structures and procedures favouring traditional patterns of staff recruitment and advancement;

— Lack of knowledge by potential and actual staff of opportunities for careers in higher education;

— Over zealous and confrontationist prosecution of affirmative action programmes;

— Lack of or failure by individuals from under-represented groups to participate in support structures, networks etc. that assist in developing knowledge of opportunities, self esteem and confidence.

— Difficulties, especially for women, of multiple socio-cultural-personal role expectations and requirements;

— Tacit or explicit discrimination against candidates with a disability, members of particular ethnic and minority groups, etc;

— Weak or non-existent policies, structures and procedures designed to overcome inequities in all aspects of staffing at the institutional level;

— Inadequate system-wide policy frameworks including inadequacies in incentives and sanctions;

— Lack of institutional policies and procedures focused on career advancement.

Barriers to Staff and Student Advancement

— Displacement or dilution of the equity agenda by other policy preoccupations e.g. quality bench-marking, economic performance, globalisation and internationalism;

— Deja-vu: a sense that much having been achieved, equity issues are being over-emphasised;

— Ignorance, lack of information about both deficiencies in the present situation and opportunities for improvement;

— Macro-features or changes in society which militate against the pursuit of equity as a major objective. A most interesting example, in some central and east European countries, is the association of equity in the minds of politicians and in society more generally, with the now discredited communist ideology;

— Financial difficulties and resource allocation procedures.

Equity Target Groups

This section addresses the five main equity groups which have been the subject of considerable attention in the policy arena and research literature in many countries in recent decades: low socio-economic status; women and girls; mature age and part-time students; ethnic and other minority groups; persons with a disability. These are not the only under-represented groups in higher education, nor the only groups subject to discrimination in society – for example members of the gay and lesbian communities, members of rural and isolated communities. Also, relevant equity categories may well shift over time as targets for some groups are achieved or nearly so, and as new categories become relevant. A further point is that it is not uncommon for individuals to belong to two or more equity categories at the same time, thus compounding disadvantage.

Low Socio-economic Status

Socio-economic factors affecting educational access and progression have been a policy preoccupation in OECD member countries for decades. In the concern over educational equity arising from the international democratisation movements of the 1960's, there were several strands. In the post war period, and into the 1970's, a major concern was the under-representation of low socio-economic groups in higher education. The economic rebuilding of Europe under the Marshall Plan extended to embrace social reconstruction, with a prominent role for policies aimed at reducing inequality of opportunity. In the USA, there was a revival of the 1920's and 1930's movements to redress social and economic deprivation, strongly reinforced by the Civil Rights movement of the 1960's.

Rates of attrition from formal schooling and low standards of attainment in secondary school examinations have been the subject of decades of research, advocacy and policy initiatives. What must be borne in mind, however, is that while there was a common concern over under-representation of low socioeconomic groups across OECD countries, there were significant variations according to local circumstances.

In Belgium, for example, economically and socially disadvantaged students were the target of policy initiatives, but, equally, so were girls. In practice, regional disparities were marked and this, as in some other countries, led to regionalisation of institutional provision with an emphasis on first cycle (short) programmes. Region and socio-economic status in this instance were to an extent overlapping categories. Despite multiple policies in Flanders, including financial support, the less well-off groups have continued to be (relatively) disadvantaged. Much of the critical literature has been directed at schools' response to socio-cultural factors influencing student performance, and the class bias of schooling.

Both national governments and international bodies in the immediate post World War decades gave a prominent place to socio-economic factors in policy making and analysis. While this has continued, the oil shocks of the 1970's, recession and then the international drive towards liberalisation of markets, the rapid development of new communication and information technologies, economic globalisation and persistent high unemployment levels especially among youth have given rise to other policy preoccupations. The educational agenda has become very crowded, public funding is subject to heavy constraints and the needs of those whom opportunity appeared to pass by have come into competition with many other concerns.

These considerations on the one hand, and the deeply embedded, complex structural factors in society on the other must largely explain the apparent inability of countries to make significant progress in increasing the proportion of people from low socio-economic groups in higher education. However, the issue is not as straightforward as it might seem at first glance. First, it would be a mistake to assume that the category 'low socio-economic' is static, as already mentioned. Note should also be taken of the hopeful trend of inter-generational changes in relative incomes – a function of increased participation rates in upper secondary and higher education. A second, related point is that, while the proportion of students from the lowest socio-economic categories are not in general improving, the overall numbers are, as a consequence of the great increase in numbers of students enrolled. Third, there is need for considerable caution in interpreting figures – not all countries or institutions record socio-economic status and those that do use different definitions and procedures.

In most countries inequalities feature in relations between socio-economic groups. Despite continuing economic support to underprivileged groups, the development towards equal access is believed to be stagnating. This has more to do with 'cultural capital' than with 'economy in a narrow sense'.

Increasing participation is a necessary consequence of realising the stated aim of 'achieving equality of opportunity for access to all forms of education Schooling can serve both as a conduit and a barrier: increasing enrolment rates and diversified routes provide a conduit but, at the same time, can act as a barrier for some families and students.

The differentiated secondary school system is seen to present a series of four thresholds for students gaining access to higher education in Germany: the first is the transition from a common primary school to one of three secondary school systems, only one of which *(Gymnasium)* provides a standard route to higher education. Transitions within the secondary school and qualifications for higher education further whittle down the pool of students whose qualifications will enable them to enter higher education.

In the international research literature, socio-economic conditions affecting student access to higher education have been a strong concern for several decades, greater in some countries than others, muted at times, but persistent. Research and policy measures have centred on: the disparity of opportunity among social classes, with a recurring emphasis on low socio-economic status family background, the concept of cultural as well as economic capital, rural areas and economically disadvantaged regions or areas, and the interactions among these factors. Sometimes, attention has focused on the 'second chance' principle, i.e. increasing opportunities for mature age students but this is quite variable across national higher education systems. But, access once gained, not all problems are solved.

A series of studies of the East and Central European socialist countries conducted by Dutch researchers documents the intergenerational transmission of inequalities – a counterbalance to the argument already referred to, that participation in higher education can effect a shift in the social balance. The Dutch studies have been carried out in the conceptual framework of 'New Class' theories which aim to show how political resources (party membership) displace traditional resource distribution (owners vs non-owners).

The socio-economic issue is fundamental since it goes to the heart of basic aspirations of the democratic society and the role of education in advancing the interests of all people. But its significance is all the greater in that often clustered around social class are issues to do with disparities between rural and urban areas, ethnic and minority discrimination, inadequate housing, health problems, family difficulties and others.

Expansion and diversification have indeed increased numbers in all socio-economic categories but overall the balance remains much the same even in those countries that have tried very hard, through government intervention, to create a more equal society. The very quest for greater social equality may now be in jeopardy as income differentials increase. A question inevitably arises, therefore, about the credibility and effectiveness of measures taken in many countries and sometimes over several decades in the educational drive for equity in social class terms. Powerful forces in the wider socio-economic setting must be more directly addressed if educational policies are to have the desired effect. What is true of education seems to be true also of other 'welfare'fields including health and social services, that resources made available to the underprivileged are also taken up by the middle classes, leaving the relativities unaffected.

Single issue policies, like direct measures to improve access to higher education are clearly insufficient, although they remain necessary. If, as often declared, the educational objective has been to change the balance, to achieve greater equality of access across the spectrum of socio-economic classes, as distinct from a numerical increase as part of a general wave of expansion, the overall conclusion is that the policies have either failed or had only a quite marginal impact.

Enduring Problems of Access and Equity

For the deep-seated problems, difficulties and barriers that are proving quite obdurate, special efforts, some of them long term, will be needed. They are variously described as structural, legal, attitudinal, organisational, financial or, more often, a complex mix of these and other factors for which the term 'cultural' is a convenient, if rather vague, blanket. Since educational policies and educational institutions form an integral part of modern society, drawing their goals, beliefs, practices and structures from society at large as much as from their own distinctive histories and modalities, it is necessary to take these broader social trends and values fully into account. Equity issues most intimately connect higher education with its wider social and cultural environment. Policies need to be both intensive and extensive.

If success in equity policies in higher education in countries of quite diverse political ideologies has been moderate or quite limited in some areas, and if rates of progress in achieving clearly defined – and sometimes well resourced – policy objectives is slow, it is necessary to reflect on underlying social dynamics which may not be susceptible to voluntaristic policy intervention. The realization of a societal goal requires introducing a change into societal relations and, as a rule, attempts to introduce change encounter some resistance. Unless this resistance is reduced, a course of action set will not be a course of action followed.

To minimise resistance, policies need to be well thought out, responsive to a variety of expressed preferences by groups and interested parties, clearly explained and justified, targeted, and resourced. Their implementation should be monitored and evaluated and adjusted if necessary to meet changing circumstances. Equity objectives directed at the advancement of particular groups—and procedures adopted in pursuit of these objectives—have been the most visible witnesses of the drive for greater equity in higher education. However, there have been two general developments which have had positive equity outcomes: (1) the massive increase in student enrolments and (2) the introduction or extension of institutional and programmatic differentiation in higher education (diversification). These developments, in addition to driving forward the equity movement, are in part an outcome of the broader community interest in a more equitable society.

Diversification in the province of higher education is the result of several factors of which efforts to equalize opportunity is but one – the separate, historical origins of more 'academic' and more 'vocational' institutions (often with a strong socio-economic class basis), demands of the industrial and service economy, finance (universities are usually more expensive), among them. However, inasmuch as differentiation not only of institutional type but also of programmes and ways of teaching and learning is a recognition of the different characteristics and needs of students and a determination to make higher education in some form more widely available, diversification can be an important factor in advancing equity policies. It ceases to be so when the channeling of students into different kinds of institutions is negatively discriminatory, when it reinforces existing inequalities. It then has the opposite, if unintended, effect of undermining the goals and values of equity.

Strategies to Promote Access and Equity

The gains already made in achieving greater equity provide platforms for further progress. The different aspects and dimensions of equity, and the varied national and local settings in which policies are formulated and implemented indicate that a variety of approaches is required. While international experience and viewpoints among policy makers, researchers and commentators converge on a number of key considerations, caution is needed when transforming these into strategies of wider general applicability. The circumstances and needs of the several major under-represented groups obviously differ: what may be suitable for increasing participation in higher education by ethnic minority students may not the same as the requirements for improving study career opportunities for people with a disability. Moreover, in the higher education community within as well as between countries there are different expectations, structures and value orientations, and at times divergent views about appropriate policy mixes.

A significant limitation in drawing general conclusions for future action on the basis of 'international good practice' is the dearth of evaluative research on the impact of established policies and programme initiatives. Such research, to be valid and carry conviction, would need to be long term and comprehensive, taking account of the multiplicity of factors which, over time, bear on access, performance and professional advancement. There appears to be little interest in or ready support at present for such research, which means that for many of the interventions and particularly the recommendations for policy change, explanations and expectations regarding effect must be to a degree provisional.

Legislation, Monitoring and Compliance

In those countries with robust equity policies and programmes there has been strong state intervention: comprehensive, coherent policy making; equal opportunity and anti-discrimination legislation; and an effective regulatory and monitoring structure. The establishment of monitoring and compliance authorities, and of agencies to support innovations, and of commissions or quality agencies to review and evaluate the performance of higher education testify to the importance of strong central initiatives. Standing commissions and Ministry divisions to fund institutions and overview policy are coming to use financial inducements, incentives and sanctions. Firm, well-focused policies at the state and regional levels are proving their value.

The huge growth of the tertiary education sector world-wide has extended opportunities in varying degrees to all of the under-represented groups, including opportunities for careers in higher education. Equity goals are not the only driving force; moreover, gains have been uneven with some groups left behind. Large enrolment increases can be accompanied by poor retention and success rates. Continued overall volume growth of the sector remains, however, one of the most effective ways to achieve inclusiveness. It needs to incorporate targeted growth, e.g. of mature age entry, ethnic minorities.

Achieving Flexibility

A greater diversity of institutions and flexibility of provision are seen by the OECD and the European Community among other bodies as necessary as demand for and participation in tertiary education increase. This means broadening the concept of higher education to make it more inclusive and the adoption of more flexible forms of teaching and learning, recognition of prior learning, credit transfer, etc. Diversification policies can be used to improve access and study opportunities, for example for part-time and mature age students, those who do not meet normal entry criteria, for students with strong practical interests, those on low incomes and so on.

A great strength of tertiary education in the United States is its diversity. The community colleges for example are valued – by students who work, have children, are of modest means—for their affordability, flexible scheduling, convenience and personal attention. Many structural reforms across Europe since the 1960's have resulted in a wide variety of post-secondary institutions either within or providing access to higher education. In Belgium, Germany, the Netherlands and the UK where existing vocational institutions have been transformed into non-university higher education institutions and new institutions established.

Responsiveness to equity requirements is being shown right across the higher education sector in more course options, greater support and guidance for students with special needs, flexible scheduling, part-time and distance education, and so on – a growing readiness to adapt the educational system to the characteristics and circumstance of non-traditional students.

In some instances – for example with minority groups – there is beginning to be an acceptance that distinctive cultural features including valued symbols and rituals should feature rather than be suppressed under blanket, system-wide policies and conventional institutional procedures. The customs of particular groups can, for example, enliven graduation ceremonies – as when Australian Aboriginal graduate students are 'danced' by their communities to receive their diplomas at graduation ceremonies, a visible symbol of the community's 'ownership' of success.

Policy Coherence

Policy, structural and vertical programme coherence across the levels of education from early childhood to tertiary education is still often weak. It is extremely difficult to achieve across the major social sectors of education, health, welfare, housing, employment, etc. There is growing recognition that equity problems in higher education cannot be solved only at that stage or by an exclusive focus on educational opportunities. Early identification and intervention are necessary and at the school level, if progress is to be made in increasing the proportion of under-represented groups seeking and eligible for access at the tertiary level. The importance of policy coherence across sectors is shown, for example, in the kinds of support that need to be mobilised when people with a disability or women with family responsibilities with a low income and living in isolated areas seek access to tertiary education.

Mutual Advancement

Especially in the areas of women's education, opportunities for people with disabilities and mature age study in distance education institutions, experience has demonstrated the value of self help groups, and of networks which draw upon pooled experience, provide support and encouragement, and monitor the performance of the education system against their own goals and expectations.

Advances have been made as a result of well-organised lobby and pressure groups which, while they may be uncomfortable at times for institutions and governments, have been instrumental in identifying shortcomings and mobilising support in overcoming them. The women's movement has been most active and successful both in pressing for changes in course content, teaching and learning and in pursuing career advancement for women, including confidence building and leadership training events. Encouragement can be given to selfdefined under-represented groups to provide mutual support and organise their own projects for advancement.

Focus on Institutions

National policies, legislation, monitoring and compliance agencies, networks and self-help groups are crucial, but the equity heartland in higher education remains the institution. Measures which are having an effect include the annual reports on equity performance which all public universities make to the national ministry. Policies, procedures, values and ethos and the way of life of the institution are decisive in determining whether equity is achieved in practice.

Equity is the province of the whole institution. An illustration of this is admission policy. It is now common for institutions in many countries to accept professional experience in lieu of some formal qualifications, and to provide bridging courses – which may be by distance education, for example, for adults. Assessment practices can vary, to take into account special needs, such as the language of indigenous people, disability and off-campus study: cultural biases can be reduced in assessment practices, course materials and teaching procedures.

The spirit of the equity enterprise and the day-to-day reality of enhanced opportunity are experienced by students and staff as members of institutions. Hence the pay-off from those systems where the policy framework provides for – or requires – a clear demonstration by institutions of their actual performance in developing and implementing comprehensive equity programmes.

Institutions can achieve much by examining their own structures to identify specific needs and establish mechanisms to address them; such as appointing a special adviser to the rector or women's affairs; setting up a committee to review and report on progress in advancing its own equity mission; establishing a diagnostic and tutorial support centre for students; allocating a tranche of new post doctorate positions to women; establishing a centre for research and promotion which provides a national service.

Mainstream support, if broadly developed, can provide for many equity needs, avoiding wasteful duplication of specialist services. The role of institution leaders and governing bodies is crucial: in providing direction and support for equity policies, prominence in launching them and in follow through. The regular administrative reporting of progress to academic and faculty boards and governing bodies, against clearly stated equity objectives is an important contribution to institutional awareness and solidarity. Institutional leaders need to be publicly identified with equity policies. It is, as has often been remarked, the pattern of life that the student experiences at the institution that can make the difference between success and failure.

Performance Improvement

Where equity is identified as an important element in the overall quality, efficiency and performance of systems and institutions, it can be incorporated within a broader set of strategies, not seen as something special, separate from the institutional mainstream of teaching and research – and potentially contentious. This is partly a matter of definition; partly of goal-setting and resolution in execution; partly of monitoring, reporting and evaluative procedures. Benchmarking— in the more precise form of quantitative comparisons among institutions or across systems or more loosely as the use of a variety of instruments and procedures to appraise performance against some kind of comparative standard—is gaining ground in higher education in the quest for improved quality and efficiency.

Performance against equity criteria and goals can form part of benchmarking as of the many other evaluation procedures now commonly used in higher education systems. Drawbacks in highly targeted, specialist programmes, such as the problem of self-identification by some disabled and ethnic groups, or apparent unfairness in affirmative action, could be lessened with greater emphasis on a broad concept of quality and delivery to include equity. Incentives for improved performance measured against the institution's own goals are likely to achieve more than sanctions. More attention needs to be given to implementation and follow-up when conducting reviews whether institutional, national or international.

Financing, Resourcing and Managing

One of the challenges for effective implementation of equity policies is to meet the call for additional resources – for facilities and materials for students with a disability, for aid to needy students, for additional tutorial, technical and administrative resources, for mentoring, staff development, and for monitoring, evaluation and compliance. Some of these costs can be streamlined, for example, by inter-institutional co-operation in the design and provision of facilities, by consolidation into regional or national bases, and by more flexible use of specialist staff including sharing among institutions.

There is scope to interrelate and mainstream the different equity structures and programmes. Conversely, institutions can avoid costly litigation (whose incidence is growing) by adhering to antidiscrimination and equal opportunity legislation, and can attract additional funding (or avoid penalties) by meeting performance targets – as in the Danish taximeter and the Australian performance funding formulae. There are also substantial financial benefits to systems as well as institutions where courses are not unduly protracted, completion targets are met and dropout and failure rates are kept to a minimum. Financial incentives are becoming more common.

It is important for equity purposes to ensure that, in strict performance regimes, low performing students—and staff—are not excluded, but provided with opportunities to do well. The maintenance of high standards and the quest for excellence need not stand in the way of a rethinking of performance in acknowledgement of the greater diversity of the higher education population. While there are financial implications, it is poor economy to admit large numbers of students and then to accept high failure and dropout rates.

2

ICTs in Higher Education

Globalisation and ICT applications place new demands on higher education establishments and hold important implications for their teaching and research functions, especially in light of the growing importance placed upon lifelong learning and upon more flexible forms of higher education delivery. The Centre for Higher Education Policy Studies (CHEPS) and the Faculty of Educational Science and Technology of the University of Twente in the Netherlands launched an international comparative study on Models of Technology and Change in Higher Education in 2001. The project was co-funded by SURF (the support agency for technology in higher education in the Netherlands), the Bertelsmann Foundation, Germany and the Norwegian Ministry of Education. The outcomes of the study are meant to be relevant for higher education leaders, managers policy makers at institutional and national level, national agencies, technical and pedagogical support units, and HRM managers.

The study applied an international comparative methodology and is carried out in the Netherlands, Germany, Norway, the United Kingdom, Australia, Finland and the USA. Data were collected through Web-based questionnaires tailored to three different response groups: decision makers, support staff and instructors. In total 693 persons responded to the questionnaire. This implies that between 20 and 50 percent of the institutions in the various countries responded (institutional data were also gathered), with the exception of the USA where the response was much lower.

The main findings of the survey were:

1. *Change is slow, and not radical*: Overall it seems that higher education institutions do not expect revolutionary change as a result from or related to the use of ICT. In general, there is not really a concern about being forced to change by external forces or developments. Rather, a "business as usual" approach is taken, without anticipating any real dramatic changes in mission, profile or market position. Nevertheless, institutions are gradually "stretching the mould"; they change their procedures and models as a process of change from within. These changes, however, are gradual and usually slow and may comply with the slight changes in needs and demands as perceived by the institutions. Small changes between countries, however, suggest that institutions that have a clearer view on their mission with respect to serving different target groups with ICT and on their position in that/those particular markets demonstrate higher levels of use of ICT.

2. *ICT in teaching and learning: Widespread but part of a blend*: ICT use, in terms of e-mail, word-processing, PowerPoint, and the Web, has become standard as part of the teaching and learning process. But this has not radically affected the nature of this process; rather, ICT has become part of the blend of on-campus delivery. This trend is seen in terms of ICT policy and objectives relating to ICT, as well as in the way that ICT use has been implemented into practice. In particular, Web-based systems are seen

as valuable and leading to more efficient practices. This second main theme emerging from the study is related to the first: ICT use, in terms of email, PowerPoint, word processing and Web resources, has become commonplace, but in a way that only gradually is stretching traditional on-campus practices. The lecture remains the "core medium", the instructional form, which is most highly valued. However, ICT has clearly become part of the blend, serving as a complement to already existing instructional tools.

3. *Instructors: Gradually doing more, but with no reward:* The third theme regards the instructors' role in the use of ICT, how this relates to their views on teaching and learning and on their actual workload and job satisfaction. Also here the "stretching the mould" theme is recognized. Overall, the instructor is still there, but doing more with technology with no particular reward. Instructors are less concerned/ interested in/hopeful about technology than those not on the "front line". Instructors are not particularly concerned about ICT, and not actually changing their ways of teaching even though they use ICT in different ways. Thus, the instructor is also "stretching the mould" with ICT use as part of daily practices. While there are no serious concerns about this, and a generally positive feeling about ICT's effect on personal work conditions and efficiency, there also are little or no systematic rewards to move instructors to do more than the gradual "stretching"

The findings of the survey are by and large consistent with the outcomes of various other international studies. The general picture is that in most cases institutions are now transferring from a period of rich and mostly bottom-up experimentation to a phase in which institution-wide use of ICT is being encouraged. In many cases the first stage of institution-wide ICT implementation, i.e. the establishment of institution-wide technological infrastructure, is now in place. However, the second stage, i.e. rich pedagogical use of this infrastructure, is in many cases still in development. The third stage, which could be labelled as strategic use of ICT with a view to the different target groups of higher education, has in most cases not been considered explicitly yet.

Furthermore, it was concluded that in general institutions are still by and large focused on their traditional target group (high school leavers). The main challenge for both institutions and governments is now to develop more strategic policies on how ICT can be used for the different target groups that higher education is expected to serve in the knowledge economy in the 21st century. These target groups include traditional learners as well as lifelong learners from both within or outside the country. It should be explicitly understood that especially the new type of learners constitute an attractive market on which higher education institutions will find themselves in competition from both national and international, traditional and new providers.

Explicit policies at both institutional and governmental levels will be required considering the challenges ahead. For enhancing the on-campus learning experience, institutions need to improve and extent the actual (richer) pedagogical use of ICT. In order to further enhance flexibility next steps need to be made in terms of system development, integration, accessibility, user convenience, etc. But in particular the strategic use of ICT for the diversity of higher education target groups will require explicit policy development.

Rationales

From many studies, it has become clear that:

— Due to their channging environment higher education institutions have to define clear and comprehensive strategies for ICT and have to make considered choices about the markets they can and wish to serve and by which type of technology use.

— The actual influence of these external conditions, however, is determined by the way in which the internal actors perceive the changes in their environment and by their ideas about the future.

— There is a gap between vision and reality. Or that the "Virtual University" works in theory but not in practice. Many institutions are still struggling to overcome the "pioneer" or the "1000 flowers blooming" phase, while trying to move into a phase of more mainstream engagement.

— In order to be successful, indeed, the commitment of some dedicated individuals will not suffice; the institution itself must make a commitment and has to develop a targeted implementation strategy.

— In order to progress both internally (involving more staff) and externally (better serving current and new students), we need to know more about the implications of technology use.

Building on these insights, the purpose of the international comparative project was to study factors that influence current models relating to technology use in higher education and which predict how institutions are likely to evolve, given their current conditions. Consequently, it explored the way in which higher education institutions perceive their changing environment in relation to their ICT strategies - i.e., which external factors are actually influencing the strategic decision-making of institutions in this area - and how they respond to these challenges. Furthermore, the study reviewed how strategic responses translate into internal policies and implementation plans and what effect they are perceived to have on teaching and learning practices.

Objectives

The objectives of the study were to:

— Gain a further *insight* in and understanding of the institutional, policy-based responses and initiatives with respect to the use of ICT in higher education.

— Further develop and *test* four scenarios on strategic choices of HE institutions with respect to the use of ICT in their education functions.

— *Predict* the different strategic pathways that higher education institutions may choose with respect to the use of ICT in higner education and the critical conditions and implications at various levels that are related to them.

Research Questions

The central question for the study was:

— Which scenarios are emerging with respect to the use of ICT in higher education and how can future developments be predicted and strategic choices be based on these scenarios?

Sub-questions are:

1. What strategic choices do institutions make with respect to the use of ICT in response to these external conditions and developments and how do they view their future missions, profiles and market positions?

2. Which external conditions and developments influence the choice of higher education institutions (HEIs) with respect to the use of ICT

and how are these perceived and analysed by key different actors?

3. What role does external collaboration play in achieving the strategic objectives ?
4. Which internal conditions and measures are being taken in order to achieve the strategic targets ?
5. What are the implications of the various strategic choices / models for:
   - Technology use, including course management systems
   - View(s) on teaching & learning and specific pedagogical models and dimensions
   - Time, workload and satisfaction of staff?

Conceptual Framework

The conceptual framework of the study consisted of a model predicting the variables that will have an impact on an institution's ICT and educational delivery approach.

There were many variables involved in an institution's decision to offer its educational program in a certain way to its students. These variables form a complex system, where each variable has an influence on the others, and where new impulses are continually challenging the system to make new responses. Such a dynamic system is difficult to capture and study. For the research, variables were looked at individually that in reality never appear in isolation but in combinations with other variables. A model to study variables that influence an institution's dominant approach to educational delivery and the use of technology in the delivery was by definition incomplete and overly simplistic. However, key variables can be identified that repeatedly have been shown to have a major impact on policy, implementation, practice, effectiveness, and eventually on an institution's general approach.

Environmental conditions and settings

Every university operates in a particular environment. Features of this background can be taken as the baseline upon which any eventual decision about scenarios and educational delivery will take place. In terms of the institution, its history, its culture, and its particular demographics have led it to adopt (perhaps implicitly) a particular mission for itself and a profile that distinguishes it from other institutions as well as markets it to its potential clients. The "mission and profile" of the institution will certainly be a key factor in its evolution toward one of the scenarios.

The profile of an institution is not only influenced by its history and demographics but also by its current leaders. Universities differ in the degree of centralized or decentralized leadership typical for decisions about ICT and educational delivery. Also, the unique characteristics of those in leadership positions in an institution have a clear impact on the operational scenarios. Thus "Leadership, internal power structure" is also an important background dimension in a university's change process with regard to educational delivery and ICT.

Students are the main clients of the university and directly or indirectly the main source of income. Their characteristics and needs steer the university in its programs and approaches. As more and more non-traditional students, such as working people, require new services from the university, their influence will be a substantial component on the change process. Parallel to them, the faculty in the institution are another critical variable affecting change.

Instructors bring with them their own histories with respect to change and technology in teaching and learning which in turn influence their willingness or capacity to adopt new forms of educational delivery. Thus student and instructor characteristics both are critical baseline conditions for the choice of a dominant scenario for the institution, currently and in the future.

While the institution is shaped and constrained by its own characteristics, it is also directly influenced by the outside world. This can occur in many ways. The society in which the university is based will have its own standards and ideas relating to a "good education" which must be respected. The policy of the national government or of other agencies that accredit and fund the university form critical constraints on its operating decisions. Two main sets of external pressures are those (a) related to new competitors for the university in terms of its target market, its status, and its funding; and (b) also with respect to ICT, the general and unavoidable movement toward technology provision, such as via e-mail, Internet, and Web access, that is now becoming standard to society itself. All of these aspects: "Social aspects of good education", "Increasing competition", "Technology push", and "External policy" need to be taken as environmental conditions influencing the eventual choice of a dominant scenario for a particular university.

All of the aspects mentioned under "Environmental Conditions and Settings" come together in various ways to steer the current policy of the institution relating to educational delivery and ICT. Most institutions do not make an explicit policy decision relating to one of the four scenarios shown in Figure 1, but instead establish a number of intermediate policies relating to ICT. These intermediate policies relating to ICT can be based on increasing the efficiency of operations, increasing the quality or teaching and learning, enhancing the flexibility to various educational services and options for the students, enhancing cost-related payoffs, and increasing access opportunities to both traditional and non-traditional students. Together, this cluster of variables could be seen as "Type of Policy".

Given the environmental conditions of the institution, and the policies that reflect those conditions, the next step in moving toward a scenario can be called "implementation" aspects. These aspects relate to the provisions made available in the institution to support instructors and students in their use of technology. They also relate to incentives for instructors to embark on a technology-related change process. Policy dictates the sorts of technical infrastructure available, ranging from hardware access, software licensing, and network access to types of software applications available.

The policy of the institution also dictates the types of flexibility in participation that can be offered to students. On another scale, the policy and environmental characteristics of the institution determine the sorts of new and external partnerships that the institution may commit to in order to carry out its mission and associated policy. Together these implementation aspects, taken as a consequence of environmental conditions and policy, suggest at least six "Implementation" clusters that will influence any eventual scenario for the institution. These clusters can be called "Instructor support", "Student support", ""Staff-related policies", ""New partnerships", "Software, hardware, and network infrastructure", and "Types of flexibility in terms of participation offered by the institution".

Even though an institution establishes various support structures or partnerships, it does not mean that they are all taken up into daily practice. Technologies may be available but little or never used. Instructional practice may or may not make use of technologies even if the institution supports these. Clearly, the combination of environmental characteristics, policies, and implementation support form an important precondition for use in practice, but use in practice is not an immediate consequence. Two clusters of variables related to use in practice, relating to technology practice and instructional practice, should also be included in a model predicting delivery scenarios.

The combination of environmental characteristics, policy, implementation support, and actual use in practice of technologies for educational purposes will lead to a perceived or verified set of results in the institution. These experiences and (perceived) effects will have an impact on the eventual commitment to a delivery scenario. A variety of different types of effects can be involved, such as the perceived importance of technology use on the strategic goals of the institution, the perceived effect on efficiency, the level of satisfaction, the perceived effect on institutional effectiveness, and the perceived effect on working practices. All of these should be taken into account.

Technology Mediated Higher Education

The phrase 'technology-mediated learning' represent a broad range of activities from the use of audio-graphic conferencing to three-dimensional simulated worlds. It can be defined as the use of networked computers for learning. This definition includes those instances where computers are used to enhance face-to-face learning or to deliver a course completely online—and everything in between.

The delivery of TML through consortia is identified as a recent innovation in distance education. The most high-profile recent developments in TML consortia are the Western Governors' University (WGU) and the California

Virtual University (CVU). Both offer access to Internet-based courses, as well as programs via satellite. The Western Governors' University is a distance learning consortium of universities in more than 16 US states and territories. It has been joined by some outside affiliates including the University of British Columbia and the China Internet Education Centre. The California Virtual University limits affiliation to California-based institutions. The CVU has created an online home for the TML offerings provided by state-affiliated public and private higher educational institutions.

Another important consideration is the prominence of for-profit educational delivery systems such as the US-based University of Phoenix. The University of Phoenix delivers courses using a combination of face-to-face and TML by opening up sites in different centres and through their Online Division. Magellan University is another example. Both of these institutions have opened online Web sites that advertise courses and programs delivered on the Internet.

Many commentators argue that the future lies in knowledge-based, high-tech industries, all highly competitive and global in scope. In this emerging economy, learning and training is both a key industry and a competitive advantage. Some have argued that it may surpass the traditionally dominant sectors of manufacturing and tourism.

World education markets are fragmenting, with numerous niche markets developing on an international and regional scale. A recent study from Australia finds that the higher education sector today is in the same position as the telecommunications and banking sectors when they first faced massive deregulation. Many of the study's interviewees reflected the view that universities are not meeting the needs of their stakeholders. Lifelong learning has become the new catch-cry, and has helped to create a growth in demand for new services. If traditional post-secondary institutions cannot fulfil this new demand, new suppliers will emerge.

The Australian study finds that the real threat to education from these new providers is in nontraditional undergraduate student education, an area that includes a variety of continuing and professional education programs and specialised training programs. These programs are potentially the most lucrative—leaving the possibility that traditional institutions may be left serving only the less-profitable traditional undergraduate market, with declining public budgets. In short, at a time when the public purse for higher education institutions is shrinking, the market for the profitable high end of higher education is becoming more competitive.

Emerging Models

There are two types of distance education (DE) institutions : single mode or dual mode. Single mode are those distance teaching institutions that are set up to teach using various media. Dual mode are campus-based institutions that also offer distance education courses and programs. Consortia are voluntary associations of independent institutions that share the costs and benefits in delivering distance education programs.

Large, autonomous, single-mode post-secondary institutions are still the most cost-effective means of providing standard education to large numbers of students. In countries such as India, China and Indonesia, where access to telephones and computers is limited, these institutions still have great value. However, in more developed countries in North America and Europe as well as Singapore, Hong Kong, South Korea and Malaysia, with the rapid rate of adoption of telephones and computers, the open universities and other institutions are beginning to make wider use of telecommunications to enable more interactive learning.

Since the late 1960s, institutions world-wide have been created with a distinct mandate for distance education. These institutions normally have no students on campus. The earliest in this modern rebirth was the University of South Africa, founded in 1963. Other examples are the Open University in the United Kingdom as well as the Universitat Oberta de Catalunya in Spain. Their mission is to deliver courses to adults who cannot or do not choose to attend traditional institutions. The mega-universities referred to above have achieved a per student cost of less than $350, compared to an average cost of $12,500 per student in US colleges and universities. Their practices will help keep education costs affordable in the next century. They operate primarily through correspondence but most also make heavy use of television and radio. They are all experimenting with technologymediated learning.

In the US, the University of Phoenix delivers courses using a combination of face-to-face and TML by opening up sites in different centres and through their Online Division. Magellan University is another example. They both have opened online Web sites that advertise courses and programs delivered on the Internet. Diversity University and the Athena University/Athena Academy (Virtual Online University) are among the first institutions to deliver courses exclusively over the Internet using MOO (Multi-user Object Oriented) technology. MOOs are online text environments using IRC (Internet Relay Chat) to facilitate synchronous conferencing using text. More advanced systems support a visual component and even three-dimensional environments. Spectrum University is a non-profit institution that offers free courses to students on the World Wide Web.

A recent innovation involves the delivery of TML through consortia. In this model, a number of traditional teaching institutions bands together to offer programs at a distance, linking institutions through a co-ordinating body. In the US, course delivery has been realised typically via satellite videoconferencing. One of the earliest attempts at creating a TML consortium was the University of Mid-America in the mid-1970s. Japan has followed the American model with the Inter-University Satellite Network. The oldest online higher education program comes from the US-based Electronic University Network (EUN), which began in 1983. The EUN is a consortium of over 20 academic institutions and businesses that provides courses (60 undergraduate, 30 graduate), degree programs (Ph.D. in Integral Studies, MBA, A.A. and A.S. degrees) and industrial training. It has served over 20,000 students.

The National Technological University (NTU) is a consortium of 40 university schools of engineering, headquartered in Fort Collins, Colorado. By the end of 1990, more than 1,100 distance education students were taking graduate degree programs in engineering, with active collaboration from their employers. After six years of operation it was expecting 1990-91 revenues of $13.5 million US, and enrolment trends indicated it would offer more Master's degrees in engineering by 1994-95 than any other American institution. In addition, the NTU had approximately 65,000 non-credit enrolments during the 1989-90 school year.

The most significant recent developments in TML consortia are the Western Governors' University (WGU) and the California Virtual University (CVU). Both offer access to Internet-based courses, as well as programs via satellite. The Western Governors University is a distance learning consortium of universities in more than 16 states and US territories. It has been joined by some outside affiliates including the University of British Columbia and the China Internet Education Centre. The California Virtual University limits affiliation to California-based institutions. The CVU has implemented an online home for the TML offerings provided by state-affiliated public and private higher educational institutions.

There is wide acceptance of online courses and degree programs in Europe. The Norwegian Association for Distance Education and FernUniversitat (Germany) are examples of institutions offering distance education programs. Others exist in Belgium, Portugal, Spain France, Greece, Turkey, Holland and Denmark. Nonetheless, studies by the European Union have found that Europe is lagging behind Canada and the US in online education. The problem is the relatively small numbers of homes, educational institutions and businesses that have computers with modems. This problem is amplified by line charges for local telephone calls. Unlike in North America, Europeans must pay for every second they use their telephone even when it is not long distance. This discourages users from staying online for sustained periods.

Moreover, the traditional fragmentation due to the multitude of languages and countries is a significant barrier although the growing acceptance and use of English as the lingua franca, and the further development of European integration is beginning to break down some of these barriers. A further complication is the entrenchment of US software products in most European markets. This market dominance has fuelled fears of losing unique European cultures at the hands of American software and educational industries.

The environment in Europe has changed dramatically over the last few years. In 1995, the European Union began two important learning technology programs aimed at education and training (SOCRATES and LEONARDO DA

VINCI), with EU 1 billion each over four years. Recently, many national governments have launched programs to connect schools to the Internet and equip them with better computers. A by-product of this has been the identification of the need for industrial training that has opened up major TML market opportunities for the delivery of training to unemployed and under-skilled workers and to the workplace.

The largest group of education and training CD-ROM titles on the European market are in language training, IT, business management and science. The best markets for attracting students and course providers appears to be in the UK, France and Germany. These countries have established multimedia industries, their governments are committed to training and education, and they have strong economies.

Deutsche Telekom launched its Global Learning range of services in early 1997. Working through partners, they offer three methods of individual learning: computer-based training (CBT) and multimedia applications for employees of a single company with tutors; training offered to both internal employees and those of other companies (e.g. Siemens Nixdorf) with self-testing and teletutors and; the Global Learning Institute, a learning and consultation forum to help transfer conventional courseware and train tutors, course developers and administrators. Several corporations have joined forces with universities in Europe to create EuroPace and the PALIO project, which offer courses electronically to employees.

The UK Open University (OU) has probably invested more than any other institution to reengineer itself into a global education provider. The OU's approach—large numbers of students and courses that remain the same for several years—would appear to be ideal; the OU can justify the high cost of developing high quality course materials by its lower per student cost and by amortising the costs over several years.

Open University Worldwide was established in 1996 to seek new markets abroad and reduce the university's reliance on government funding. Despite these efforts, Open University's approach is still mainly that of print-based, mass distance education. Early feedback on CD-ROM development shows that high-quality multimedia takes too long and is too expensive to be a viable alternative.

Open University Business School (OUBS) began offering the course, "The Capable Manager", to twenty managers at the United Nations in New York in February 1998 as part of the first stage of an MBA degree. OUBS viewed the launch of the course as a competitive bid for a part of the distancelearning business market. Competitors include Apollo Group in the U.S. and Online Education in Hong Kong. OUBS does not wish to offer the course in countries where tutored learning is available, which restricts its market. In the private sector, British Telecom launched Solstra, a net-based training system that allows companies and colleges to interact with students.

In Australia, enrolment increased 39 per cent between May 1997 and May 1998. In contrast, oncampus enrolment increased only 12.4 per cent over the previous year. The Ministry of Higher Education predicts that foreign student enrolment will bring $4.5 billion to the country by 2001. In anticipation of this, Australia will be spending $21 million on an overseas marketing campaign over the next four years, and Australian Education International has been created as a generic promoter of Australian distance education services. An example of an Australian distance education program can be found at Edith Cowan University.

Canada has experience in both single and dual mode institutions to deliver distance education. Canada's open universities include Athabasca, Télé-université du Québec and the Open Learning Agency of British Columbia.

Traditional universities and colleges can offer highly interactive education at a distance and still provide on-campus facilities that are costly and difficult for single-mode distance education institutions to provide. In the most common type, traditional institutions deliver courses using a variety of media to off-campus students through their external, continuing studies departments or through special programs. Some examples include the University of Waterloo, which is primarily involved in correspondence delivery. Ryerson Polytechnic Institute created an Open College section in the early 1970s. In BC, North Island College was conceived as an institution that would build on distance education as a core philosophy and methodology. The University College of the Cariboo has built a comprehensive outreach strategy utilising interactive videoconferencing and web courses.

Distance learning networks that facilitate the delivery of courses by different institutions at all levels have been initiated in Canada. These networks are formed by governments, institutions themselves, or by consortia. Initially based on audiographic teleconferencing technology (electronic whiteboarding), these networks serve a variety of institutions in their geographical areas. The TETRA network in Newfoundland was the first such Canadian network, launched in 1977 as a distance learning network in conjunction with Memorial University of Newfoundland's telemedicine project. Because the province has only one university with no internal competitors, TETRA, as a university initiative, quickly became a ubiquitous network serving university students around the province.

Contact North in Northern Ontario began as a consortium consisting of two community colleges and two universities, with representation from public schools, and involving northern communities and other organisations. TeleEducation NB serves residents in the province of New Brunswick. Another network, Alberta-North, is in place in northern Alberta. Recently, Industry Canada's Notemakers pilot project has encouraged TML development consortia.

One outcome has been the consortium centred at the University of New Brunswick among six universities in Atlantic Canada for the online delivery of first year university courses. The Toronto-based Telecommunications Learning Institute is a private sector consortium of telecommunications and banking companies that offers courses and programs to members online.

Contact South is a consortium of Ontario colleges for the delivery of online courses. Members share development and expenses related to the delivery of TML. Consortia such as Contact South are attractive options for Canadian community colleges and institutes. Their smaller size relative to the universities and the logic of scale often leads these institutions to participate in provincial or regional TML coalitions such as Contact South or TeleEducation NB. Nationally, the Association of Canadian Community Colleges (ACCC) is pooling resources and expertise for the purpose of institutional support and joint marketing of services.

Canada is an acknowledged world-leader in distance education, led by such organisations as the TeleLearning Network of Centres of Excellence (TL*NCE). Unique in the world, the TL*NCE is a $12 million national collaboration of Canadian researchers, private sector organisations and members of the public in the development, application and evaluation of TML with a focus on collaborative learning and knowledge building. Hosted at Simon Fraser University, the network plays an important role in researching and developing advanced networked learning environments for all levels of the education system and the workplace.

Two of its "beacon technologies" include the Virtual-U, is an integrated distributed learning environment and WebCSILE (Computer Supported Intentional Learning Environments) developed at the Ontario Institute for Studies in Education (OISE). Network researchers are also addressing associated questions such as the education of educators and the role of telelearning networks as the basis for a learning society. TL*NCE is now studying the creation of a Global TeleLearning Institute to provide leading edge research, services, technologies, and content in online learning in collaboration with organisations around the world.

A second important Canadian research initiative is EV-Net which is dedicated to the assessment of new learning tools for the information highway. EV-Net was funded by the Social Sciences and Humanities Research Council as part of the establishment of 5 research networks in training and education.

The Canadian Association of Distance Education (CADE) is also well known internationally and recognised as one of the leading organisations within the International Council of Distance Education (ICDE).

Canadian integrated distributed learning environments like First Class, WebCT, ShareLine, and Zebu, as well as instructional design tools such as Integreator and Télé-université's Campus virtuelle are leading the world into online learning.

Industry Canada and the Office of Learning Technologies have sponsored two studies of online educational delivery applications. The first was conducted by TeleEducation NB and Mount Allison University's Learning Technology Centre as a survey of "Integrated Distributed Learning Environments". The BC Standing

Committee on Educational Technology and the Centre for Curriculum Transfer and Technology (SCOET) conducted another more detailed investigation. This study established criteria for evaluating online educational delivery applications.

The University of New Brunswick (UNB) is the home of the WWW-DEV listserv which is the world's leading discussion group for online course developers. Every year UNB hosts the North American Web Conference, focusing on innovative and practical uses of the World Wide Web in education.

Online courses at Canadian universities and colleges are multiplying quickly. For example, The Southern Alberta Institute of Technology (SAIT) offers the first year of a two-year engineering technology program online. SAIT has partnered with a number of organisations to deliver the program, including Lethbridge Community College and the Northern Alberta Institute of Technology.

The East/West project, funded by Industry Canada Notemakers' pilot project, involves Canadian adult learners and learning professionals taking a full online course offered through the WWW. Titled Introduction to Information Technology & Telecommunications, the course consists of four modules. Available in both official languages, the course is accredited in four provinces (Alberta, British Columbia, New Brunswick and Newfoundland). The development of this course pointed to the need for a new paradigm for continually maintaining courses, i.e. finding ongoing financing as opposed to the traditional one-time development costs. The course and the course development standards established are being used by many institutions around the world.

The "California syndrome" refers to the increasing unwillingness of baby boomers whose children have left school to subsidise public education through their taxes. Private institutions like those mentioned below have started filling the breach. The main cost-saving measure employed by private universities is year-round teaching, offering four-year programs in two or three years. Students pay lower fees and start full-time employment earlier. A 1989 study at the University of Toronto showed that foregone earnings, after-tax, cost the average student more than four times as much as tuition fees. This ratio will only increase as the average age of students rises, including adults in mid-career positions.

In the San Francisco Bay area, Knowledge Universe, a publicly-traded company founded in September 1997, made $700 million in revenues in less than a year by purchasing Internet-based corporate training companies.

DeVry Institutes taught 28,000 students on 13 campuses across North America in 1996, including three in Canada: Calgary, North York and Scarborough. Listed on the New York Stock Exchange as a publicly traded company, it charged about $21,000 for a three-year Bachelor of Science degree at the time. DeVry made a profit of $15 million US in 1995 on revenues of $229 million US. The university's professors can share in the profits by participating in an employee share-ownership plan. The DeVry example demonstrates the potential viability of undergraduate education as a profitmaking business. It has been estimated that a virtual university with a basic undergraduate curriculum could cost no more than $40 million CDN. Private sector corporations have also started delivering courses online. Ziff-Davis offers technical courses through ZDNet University. First Class Systems, a courseware development company in Fredericton, NB, also offers courses. Spectrum University is a non-profit group that supports Spectrum Virtual University, which offers free courses to students on the WWW.

The University of Phoenix, which has just opened a campus in Vancouver, is a private, for-profit university that started an online program in 1989. Students attend a virtual classroom, with one faculty member for every 10 to 15 students. Courses are six weeks long with weekly assignments, obliging students to visit their electronic classroom at least five days each week. The university designs the courses, then hires mostly freelance professors but provides no tenure. Online students currently account for less than 7% of the University of Phoenix's total student population, this despite the enormous amount of media attention its has received. Scholars.com, a Fredericton-based company started in 1996, delivers online Microsoft Certified Professional training. It now delivers courses to more than 1500 students at a time, all paying at least $1,000 per course. In 1997, the company was bought by CBT Systems and now employs more than 40 people in Fredericton and more than 15 in Phoenix, Arizona; a new office will open shortly in Australia. In addition, First Class Systems, JOT, Knowledge 3000, and other small courseware development/training companies are delivering online courses from NB.

A 1997 study by the University of Southern California found that only one in five companies made training available through computers. However, they expected to double the amount of computerbased training by the year 2000. The International Data Corporation estimates that interactive courseware is the fastest-growing training method, growing at an estimated 31 per cent. The market is expected to increase fivefold between 1996 and 2000, exceeding US $1.75 billion, or 15 per cent of total information technology (IT) training and education revenues. A more conservative estimate from American Society for Training and Development's State of the Industry report projects only 20 per cent growth by the year 2000. Senior training and technology executives from

Fortune 500 companies and major software companies interviewed in 1997 anticipated creating a learning intranet within their organisation, but more than 50 per cent of the intranet projects were still at the conceptual level.

The Canadian IT training and education services industry is estimated to be $635 million for 1996, a 17.5 per cent increase from 1995. The E-learning market represents 2 per cent, or $13 million, of the total market. By the year 2000, IDC Canada anticipates that this market share will rise to 22 per cent of the total, experiencing a compounded annual growth rate of 16 per cent. StatsCan estimated in 1987 that one third of companies provided formal training for their employees for a total of $1.4 billion annually. The Conference Board of Canada surveyed companies in 1990 and discovered a growth trend, with training expenditures of 444 companies reaching $315.9 million in 1989. In 1993, the Board found that 275 medium to large businesses had increased spending from an average of $659 per capita to $849 between 1992 and 1993.

The National Training Survey of more than 17,000 organisations in 1991 by the Canadian Labour Market and Productivity Centre found that 70 per cent of private sector respondents trained their employees, and gave a rough national estimate of CDN $1.35 billion for the Canadian market. A 1996 Quebec survey found that 63 per cent of Quebec companies trained employees on-the-job, and almost 30 per cent used outside consultants or private trainers. It also found that larger firms relied on internal training departments while smaller firms relied on outside suppliers. Despite the large amount of money being spent on training, Canada still appears to be lagging behind other countries on international measurements of training. The 1997 World Competitiveness Yearbook, published by the International Institute for Management Development, ranked Canada 17th on a scale of corporate training, behind Ireland, Belgium and Luxembourg. A large portion of E-learning delivered in Canada has been developed through US head offices and provided to Canadian subsidiaries.

The E-learning industry is still in its infancy. It was first introduced to the consumer market in late 1995 and is still seen as a complement to instructor-led classroom teaching. Market consolidation will not occur until the delivery format has reached a much higher level of market maturity and customer acceptance. As of 1997, a fully synchronous, real-time, online format of IT training using voice, data and video-conferencing was not available over the Internet/Intranet. Companies such as First Class Systems and DiscoverWare, who are Canadian-based, have found that their primary market is the US, not Canada. Firms such as Global Knowledge Network have developed training solutions and products within Canada and are focusing delivery on the Canadian, US and global markets.

New Brunswick companies with significant contracts in the online learning arena have focused on niche markets, e.g. Glacier's law enforcement training package, Ecom's involvement with the insurance industry and Pixel's training program for the Canadian Securities Institute. Some problem areas identified by Industry Canada that are hindering growth of the new media learning training sector include: the lack of a domestic marketing strategy aimed at industry, the need for a national association, lack of accreditation and quality standards, competition from Canadian subsidiaries that obtain training from their parent company, poorly-developed relationships with industry and financial institutions, limited partnering between public and private sector trainers, and a perception that public providers are unfair competition to the private sector. Nevertheless, Industry Canada's market assessment study of new media stresses that, "Canada has an enormous opportunity to seize world leadership in learning solutions . . . Canada can be known for knowledge and learning, just as the Swiss are known for banking and finance—perhaps not the biggest, but the best."

Educational Technology in Transnational Higher Education

The term 'Transnational education' can be defined as the education in which the learners are located in a country different from the one where the awarding institution is base. In the 1990s, demand in South East Asia was high, especially in Hong Kong, Singapore and Malaysia, and exporters, especially from Britain and Australia were eager to supply. The growth is set to continue, with the Global Alliance for Transnational Education estimating that demand for transnational higher education in Asian countries will rise to more than 480,000 students by 2020. Whether delivered through offshore branch campuses, twinning arrangements or international distance education, transnational education increasingly relies on information and communications technology to facilitate the routine crossing of borders by information, staff and educational materials.

The use of online learning in transnational education brings together, in an unfamiliar environment, students and educators whose experience of teaching and learning stems from very different cultural traditions. Educators who have taught international students in classrooms come to understand that students fro m different countries bring with them different experiences and expectations of teaching and learning.

A number of useful guides to teaching international students have been published in recent years, but so far there has been little discussion of cultural issues in online teaching. Some writers have pointed to the possibility of 'educational imperialism' in transnational education if transnational educators expect their students to simply adapt or conform to Western models of education.

Higher education has always involved the exporting of knowledge and techniques from educational 'centres' to the 'peripheries'. Now, with the advent of information and communication technologies, and the liberalization of trade in educational services, the speed and volume of the flow of ideas has intensified.

The rapid growth of technologically-supported transnational education has led to renewed concerns about cultural impacts. For example, Jacques Hallak, UNESCO Assistant Director-General of Education warned recently that 'I think the danger is that companies selling education outside their frontiers will attempt to impose the same standards everywhere, and this will dissociate education from the social, cultural and political origins of a country'. That is, the implicit social values of the exporting countries will inform curriculum, and the social and cultural context in which students live will be largely ignored. Indeed, since its emergence in the late 1980s, transnational higher education in South East Asia has commonly involved Western educators teaching offshore using educational approaches developed for local students with very little effort to tailor teaching for offshore students.

Educational technologies have increased the scale of transnational education by allowing institutions to more easily coordinate operations in different countries, however, there is no evidence that this has resulted in greater localisation of teaching approaches. Some writers on online education have argued that the opposite is the case. Jae-Eun Joo, for example, suggests that 'the Internet tends to reinforce the World Information Order, i.e. the flow of information from industrialised to developing countries, and fails to ensure mutual respect and the protection of the diversity of information, languages, and cultures' This tendency, Joo observes, is caused both by ethnocentrism on the part of educational exporters, and by the ease of adoption of electronically reproduced materials.

There is a strong temptation, he believes, for teachers and administrators in developing countries 'to simply copy or translate existing materials on the Internet, to save money and time, without considering their own social, cultural, historical, and educational contexts'. This tends to be a one-way flow of materials. Because of the power of Western mass media, people around the world are more receptive to online materials originating from Western countries than from other parts of the world, 'in the same way an Indian child can more easily enjoy a Disneyland movie than an American child can enjoy an Indian cartoon'.

More optimistic writers see new technologies as leading to new types of international relationships in knowledge production. While earlier forms of educational trade may have undermined local initiatives and perpetuated a cycle of dependency, the Internet facilitates, 'not so much an exporting as a reengineering of the educational paradigm to include people from many countries, studying materials designed for a multicultural audience, using technologies which facilitate cross-cultural communications'.

The technology of the Internet and the Web, he argues, 'is already breaking down traditional hierarchies and establishing a new kind of democracy about what constitutes knowledge'. What is clear is that while traditional hierarchies may be being broken down, they are being replaced by more fluid structures, which nonetheless form patterns of inclusion and exclusion on a global scale. Against this backdrop, there has been a growing discussion in exporting countries about how one should teach to diverse groups of students located in different countries. These issues have been particularly pertinent in Australia, because 12.5 per cent of students in tertiary education are foreign citizens and around a third of international students in tertiary education are located offshore.

Educational technologies can be used in ways that rigidly circumscribe students' options, or in ways that lead to greater flexibility for students and encourage selfdirected learning and student autonomy. In Australia, 'flexible learning' is often used as a euphemism for technologically-mediated learning, so great are the perceived links between technology and flexibility. 'Flexible learning' is an approach that attempts to provide students with greater choice about how, where, when they learn, and in practice this increasingly involves the use of educational technologies. The British Council's advice to students contemplating distance education courses highlights the new demands on students:

> The new electronic technologies used in distance learning can provide students with far greater involvement in the process of learning. These interactive technologies also allow students the exercise of far greater control over that process than is possible in many traditional learning environments. This means that students must take more responsibility for, and be more active in, their learning.

Such uses of interactive technologies can increase the autonomy of the learner, requiring them to choose the time, place and pace of study. More study is conducted in isolation and the extent of face-to-face contact with lecturers and classmates is often diminished in the shift from traditional forms of university teaching to technologically-mediated learning. At the same time, South East Asian international students are often characterised by Western lecturers as being less self-directed learners who defer more to the authority of the teacher and prefer more structured learning environments.

While educational technologies, and the flexibility they bring, may be welcomed by Australian students, these observations would suggest that students from South East Asian countries may not be so comfortable with such innovations.

In societies in where discipline and submission to authority is praised rather than individualism and freedom, teachers might feel too uncomfortable to take initiatives, to accept the scrutiny of peers, or to hand greater control to their students. Likewise, students accustomed to traditional methods may find it hard to adapt to active and innovating learning techniques.

There is a compelling argument, then, that flexible learning using educational technologies is not as appropriate in South East Asian countries as it is in more individualistic educational exporting countries. By expecting offshore learners to conform to Western expectations of student behaviour, multinational educators are engaging in a form of cultural imperialism, seeking to assimilate a diverse student body into an ethnocentrically defined norm.

Many have argued that teaching in transnational education should be tailored to the specific cultural context in which the students are located. Smith and Smith, for example, argued that, ..in those cases where a significant difference has been shown, it is prudent to consider adjusting teaching and support strategies to reflect those differences. Failure to take account at all of those differences runs the danger of being new colonialists who assume that the organisational, knowledge and belief structures that we develop in the English speaking West will transfer without adaptation to another culture.

While these warnings are very important, these writers tend to create a binary opposition between two opposed and internally homogenised cultural types – that of the importing country and that of the exporting country. By focusing on national-cultural differences in learning styles, critics of cultural imperialism treat cultures as unified static entities, rather than constantly evolving and fluid patterns of relations.

Transnational educators will point out that, while differences in teaching and learning may exist between exporting and importing countries, the differences are being reduced as common educational philosophies and techniques take hold around the world. Rather than being Western approaches, the educators would argue, the flexible and student-centred approaches that educators in all countries are introducing are based on universal principles of good teaching that transcend cultural differences irrespective of students' prior experience or expectations. However, we should not treat the rise of technology-based flexible learning in transnational education as simply the triumph of good teaching.

In South East Asia, educational commentators are increasingly promoting the use of educational technology as a way of enhancing the creativity and inventiveness of students. In Singapore and Malaysia, these personal qualities are seen as essential to future national economic development. In these countries there is a clear vision of an emergent form of educational delivery that is challenging existing educational traditions.

The Singaporean government's Masterplan for IT in Education sets out a strategy of using educational technology to encourage self-directed learning. Launching the policy, Prime Minister Goh Chok Tong explained that, 'We will use IT to encourage students to learn more independently, to learn actively'.

From the highest levels of government there is an explicit strategy of encouraging students 'to engage in more active and independent learning'. This policy has begun to have an effect on tertiary education in recent years, with Singapore's leading universities stating that they will encourage creativity and thinking skills in the curriculum and move away from a heavy reliance on written examinations as the sole form of assessment. The government is setting out to change the way students learn in order to meet the perceived workforce needs of a global information economy. These initiatives have much in common with policy shifts in the West that were widely described as a shift from Fordist to post-Fordist modes of educational delivery.

Unlike Singapore, which already has a well-developed higher education system, the primary concern of Malaysian higher education policy-makers and planners in the 1990s was to increase the participation rate, both by increasing enrolments in existing public universities (especially through distance learning) and by encouraging the growth of private higher educational institutions. The Malaysian government has expressed a desire to use the educational system to improve the skills of Malaysians, including their 'achievement motivation, their attitude towards excellence and to the fostering of the entrepreneurial spirit'. In practice, however, this has understandably taken second place to the expansion of student numbers.

While the government has been preoccupied with quantity, many educators have been focusing on questions of quality, and in particular, what they perceive to be a low level of creativity and independence among graduates. Senior administrators in the private higher education sector regularly expound on the links between IT and self-directed learning as part of their efforts to brand their own institutions as being innovative. Perhaps the clearest elaboration of these issues is provided on the Study Malaysia website, which is supported by the Malaysian government and both private higher education industry associations and contains comprehensive information on both public and private institutions.

Among its comprehensive overviews is a sole article on the future of higher education, entitled 'Shaping education for the future: the role of IT in institutions of higher learning'. This article sees technology playing a central role in transforming higher education: The education of this and next century must build a knowledge-based society where individuals are expected to be more creative, innovative and productive. The workplace of tomorrow will require employees with multiple skills, who are able to think creatively, to solve problems in novel situations.

In order to bring about such changes, the author explains, 'IT-supported learning must be exploratory and it must promote discovery, with students constantly engaged in finding, organising, analysing and applying information in creative and novel ways to solve problems'. In practice, he observes, this transformative potential of educational technology is rarely being realised. Existing patterns of teaching, learning and interacting are proving resilient, even as the medium of instruction changes:

The applications of IT in higher education are still based on the old models of teaching, mostly a case of reception-based learning migrating to a computer screen. Most of the times, students still read and memorise information. Video-conferencing and certain Web applications still tend to be used primarily for information transmission in a didactic style, no different from the classroom lecture model. Despite the resilience of more teacher-centred and rigidly structured approaches, as in Singapore, there is a widely held belief in Malaysia that educational technologies and flexible delivery can and should transform the relationship between learners and teachers.

While the Vietnamese government has not been so vocal about innovation and creativity in education, it has encouraged the growth of more flexible modes of delivery in higher education. In the early 1990s, enrolments in informal and flexibly-delivered courses (including distance education and part-time studies) in Vietnamese higher education institutions rose much faster than enrolments in formal courses (full-time on-campus courses). There are currently around 50,000 students enrolled in distance education at university level in Vietnam and this number is growing rapidly with increasing enrolments in transnational distance education programs.

The Singaporean and Malaysian governments and many educationists in these countries see educational technologies as a means to encourage greater self-direction and creativity on the part of students. Flexible learning is not seen as a foreign concept that threatens local educational traditions; nor is it seen as simply good teaching. The appeal of educational technologies is that they will require learners to be more pro- active and autonomous, and these personality traits are increasingly important in the 'knowledge economy'.

Technology is not as extensively used in Vietnamese higher education and, as a consequence, discussions concerning the implications of using educational technologies for teaching are not yet on the agenda. In light of this discussion of local policies for the introduction of educational technologies and the desired direction of change of educational leaders, we can see that educational exporters who seek to introduce similar approaches are not necessarily acting counter to the wishes of governments, but rather they act alongside local reformist educators as agents of change.

Learning Styles in Transnational Institutions

This section presents some brief case studies, which provide examples of the ways in which transnational institutions are using interactive technologies and how these affected student's learning styles in these institutions.

International Medical University: Located in Kuala Lumpur, the International Medical University (IMU) is a twinning institution aligned with several foreign medical schools. Students spend two and a half years studying at IMU and then two and a half years at an international university. Most students go on to complete their degrees in Australia, with smaller numbers going to the United States, Canada, and the UK. The course is designed to be consistent with the courses offered by its overseas partners. From 2000, IMU will be offering its own medical degree so students will be able to do their whole course in Malaysia.

In the mid 1990s, the university implemented a problem-based learning approach to medical education, as have most of the medical faculties at which their students will complete the second half of their medical degrees. At first, modules were presented each week on large display boards, including photographs, charts and text. However, each set of display boards took up a large amount of space and students complained that they could not get access to previous weeks' displays. In response, IMU established an online learning system to house these displays, offering students online access to study guides, lecturers' slide presentations, links to Web-based resources, self-assessments, announcements and discussion forums. The introduction of problem-based learning required students to dramatically change the way they learned.

After several years experience with problem-based learning, the university is finding now that the introduction of electronic delivery 'reinforces the need for them [students] to change their way of learning.' While most students are happy with electronic delivery, some complained about the corresponding reduction in the number of lectures. These students preferred lectures 'because the lecturer talks and you feel you're getting the information, whereas now *they* have to talk. The lecturer is just a facilitator, a guide.' IMU's experience reminds us that new technologies are being introduced into institutions in which there is often already an impetus towards studentcentred learning, illustrating a close connection between internationalisation, learning technologies and pedagogical innovation.

Monash University Malaysia: Monash University Malaysia has had a similar experience to IMU in many ways. An offshore campus like Monash University Malaysia is only made possible by telecommunications. E-mail, more than any other technology, is used extensively by administrators and lecturers to connect the university's campuses together.

New technologies allow the creation of global universities, in which administration and teaching can be organised across electronic networks that span the globe. Once the university is restructured as a technologically integrated multi-campus organisation, as many Australian universities now are, it is relatively easy to add new campuses as additional nodes to an existing network.

Lecturers felt that, compared to Australian students, Malaysian students expect more direction, closer supervision and have greater regard for lecturers. The university sets out to acculturate Malaysian students to Australian teaching and learning styles, for example by limiting lecturers' consultation times and providing extensive learning skills workshops to new students. Lecturers reported that in later years students become more confident as they come to understand what is required of them. The Australian character of teaching and learning was seen as an important feature of the campus's claim to be an Australian university campus in Malaysia, rather than one of the many Malaysian institutions teaching an Australian curriculum.

The most interesting feature of Monash University Malaysia for this study is its preference for traditional faceto- face teaching. Information technology is used extensively in administration and communications but in teaching and learning the campus has opted for a more traditional approach, even though Australian campuses of Monash are rapidly adopting technology in course delivery. Monash University Malaysia is able to charge higher fees than its competitors partly because it retains an emphasis on traditional forms of face-to-face delivery while other, less expensive providers, rely more on distance delivery techniques and part-time teaching staff. This is a response to perceived consumer preference for 'traditional' learning environments.

Many subjects are taught simultaneously on other Monash University campuses. In some cases, subjects that are taught by print-based distance education or online in Australia are taught face-to-face in classrooms at Monash University Malaysia. For example, the Bachelor of Communication degree is offered from Monash's Gippsland campus by distance mode in Australia but is taught face-to-face in Malaysia. Parents expect their students to have extensive face-to-face contact with lecturers so at Monash University Malaysia online materials are used as a resource rather than as a primary teaching method.

UNITAR: Universiti Tun Abdul Razak, better known as UNITAR, is a Malaysian private university which opened in 1999 as Malaysia's first 'virtual' university. It relies heavily on mediated instruction and plans to expand its network of distributed learning centres beyond

Malaysia's borders in the next few years. When the university was first proposed, the Malaysia Education Minister expressed concern about the lack of socialisation in remotelysupported distance education. In short, UNITAR was told, 'no socialisation, no education, no license, no operation', according to a senior administrator.

In response, the virtual university model was altered, requiring compulsory attendance at local study centres in all subjects. In the first semester, attendance is required for 22 hours per subject and in subsequent semesters students must attend eight hours of classes per subject. UNITAR has had to establish a network of local learning centres, some of which will be outside Malaysia, in which students can attend classes, interact with other students, sit exams and access computers and support staff. These are very similar to the learning centres of the established distance education providers in Malaysia, but with more reliance on educational technologies.

Due to the cost and unreliability of dial-up Internet connections in Malaysia, which were then prone to drop-outs and low bandwidth, UNITAR decided to distribute teaching materials to students on CD-ROMs. Students are required to go online to access the library, complete administrative tasks, participate in forums and tutorials. The CD-ROMs for the first year subjects are more tightly structured than those for later years, directing students through a linear sequence of materials and tasks. The CD-ROMs for first year subjects are clearly structured in a logical linear fashion. The CD-ROMs for later subjects are more 'resource-based', requiring students to use their own judgement more to make sense of the information provided and form connections for themselves. The later year subjects require students to be both highly motivated and possess the study skills required to manage their own learning.

UNITAR found that their students are generally technically competent and have dramatically reduced the amount of initial technical training their students receive. Instead, according to UNITAR, 'the issue is changing your mindset, being independent, managing your time.' To prepare students for independent study, the first CD students receive from UNITAR is 'Skills for Knowledge Workers'. This covers basic computer competence such as how to connect to the Internet, making use of word processors, Excel, Access and PowerPoint for their work in the university, but also time management, independent study skills and listening skills.

Asian Institute of Technology: The Asian Institute of Technology (AIT) is an international institution based in Bangkok. It was established over 40 years ago as the South East Asian Treaty Organisation Graduate School of Engineering to serve the educational needs of the South East Asian region and it continues to be funded by many governments and foundations. It now has staff from more than 25 countries and students from more than 40 countries.

AIT has two centres in Vietnam. The AIT Centre Vietnam, located in Hanoi, was established in 1993, as the institution's first branch outside Bangkok. It provides postgraduate education, short-term training courses, language training. Vietnamese students constitute the largest group of foreign students at AIT in Bangkok. The Hanoi centre was established to provide a lower-cost alternative for Vietnamese graduate students, enabling them to complete most of their degree in Vietnam. At the same time, the Swiss-AIT-Vietnam Management Development Programme has been established at the Ho Chi Minh City University of Technology. Jointly funded by the Swiss and Vietnamese governments, this centre delivers a graduate diploma programme in Management Development to Vietnamese business lecturers from local universities and working executives. It also provides management training and support to Vietnamese companies that are in the process of restructuring prior to privatization.

In the past, AIT's campus in Vietnam relied heavily on fax communications with Bangkok. Staff now use e-mail and the Web extensively to keep in touch with international colleagues and to remain informed about developments outside Vietnam. Students regularly use online resources and this differentiates them from the public education sector in Vietnam.

TMC Centre for Advanced Seminars: The TMC Centre for Advanced Seminars in Singapore offers its own short and diploma courses and acts as a local partner for distance education programs offered by Monash University, Deakin University, the University of Newcastle and the University of London. Since the currency crisis, the demand for foreign university courses delivered in Singapore has increased dramatically. While TMC does not providing any formal teaching, it does provides a range of other services to students enrolled in international distance education programs, including advertising and information sessions for prospective students, orientation programs, administrative support, face-to-face study group sessions, student support and counselling, local submission of assignments and library facilities.

Before the Internet, TMC students had fax and postal access to their overseas lecturers, and students were issued with a fax allowance for use of the TMC fax machine. Since 1995, TMC have provided students with access to Internet facilities so they can contact lecturers via e-mail, participate in discussion forums, conduct research and submit assignments online. Students are increasingly interacting with teaching staff from the foreign universities via online a-synchronous conference sessions, especially in computing and communications courses. But even with such online interaction, according to TMC administrators students still value local facilities and face-to-face academic support highly and there is little demand for courses taught online without such support.

Emergent Trends

There were a number of common themes in the experiences of these institutions. Firstly, these institutions' students expected to be provided with large volumes of information and expected that recall of this information would be assessed in examinations. This was usually described 'spoon-feeding', and was seen as a major challenge by those who sought to introduce more student-centred approaches.

Secondly, these institutions were consciously seeking to change students' behaviour by using educational technology to encourage self-directed learning. The objective was both to bring local practices into line with teaching and learning practices in the awarding university's home country, and to introduce what were seen as 'modern' approaches. Educators generally understood the difference as old versus new rather than local versus foreign. They perceived the foreign institutions as having more resources and therefore being more advanced, both technologically and pedagogically.

Thirdly, attempts at innovation have met with resistance from students, especially younger undergraduate students. All interviewees mentioned that students generally desired close supervision and direction from locally-available (as opposed to remote) teaching staff. Flexible approaches were more readily accepted by lateryear students and those in graduate programs. Students' reluctance to work independently and teachers' reluctance to relinquish control over learning were seen as major impediments to the introduction of educational technologies and more flexible modes of learning. In different ways, these pressures forced UNITAR to incorporate face-to-face teaching in what was initially planned as a purely distance education delivery model, and forced Monash University Malaysia to take note of its students' scepticism towards any forms of teaching that resembles distance education.

3

Higher Education and the Curriculum Development

Today, higher education is going through a maelstrom of change and this in turn is putting pressure on those who work in the system. In market terms, these are pressures to improve productivity. Widening access means that the character and needs of the student population are changing; there are increased numbers without any additional resources, leading to larger classes and increased assessment loads; there is pressure to provide more vocational courses that equip future employees with a wider, less 'academic' range of knowledge and skills.

In short, higher education is subject to economic imperatives defined by government and employers. Of course, it is essential to have a system that provides value for money. Generally the governments cannot afford to develop a mass higher education systemwithout reducing the unit of cost per student. But huge increases in student numbers are not easy to manage and all kinds of other linked changes are causing new problems, e.g. semesterisation which has doubled the assessment load by dividing the academic year into two independent parts; and modularisation which has done away with coherent course groups, making it often impossible to establish any depth of rapport between teacher and students, or between student and student. These things make up a higher education system which is stressful for those who work in it, and it is important to remember that this is the context in which ICT is being introduced.

The dream of policymakers and politicians is that ICT is the answer to the problem of how to create a mass higher education system that is affordable within the national budget. The hope is that ICT will deliver more costeffective teaching and learning. As a result, the introduction of ICT into higher education has been strongly politicised. There are huge expectations without due regard to the difficulties that are an inevitable part of any technological innovation in education. An example of this political euphoria was the announcement in 1996 that £33 million had been awarded by the Millennium Fund, to establish a multisite University of the Highlands and Islands, using ICT as a main medium of teaching. There is no doubt that this is a visionary idea, aimed at providing higher education in their home location to students in extreme rural areas, widely separated from their teachers by moors, mountains and lochs. It is a visionary idea, but it will also involve enormous complexity in establishing both the ICT networking and the changes in work practices essential for collaboration and sharing between many, many individuals in a large number of institutions.

In order to understand the impact upon staff of these changes in the context of higher education, it is useful to look at some of the typologies of institutional management that have emerged from research. For instance, as you read you may like to consider whether you are working in a bureaucratic or a collegial institution. To decide on the answer, you would need to consider factors such as the extent to which your institution is one in which decisions are made by a small management team and implemented by passing requirements down to more junior colleagues through a line management hierarchy.

Or the extent to which it is one in which decisions are made by committees that share power democratically among colleagues, through a process whereby colleagues meet in a forum for open and free debate and, through negotiation, reach a democratic decision. Of course, few if any will recognise the latter as being the way that their institution works. The socalled collegial organisational type is more likely to be one of 'restricted collegiality' , where certain professors exercise enormous power in these apparently democratic committee fora and lobbying prior to the meeting is crucially important. However, the patronage of an institution organised on the basis of 'restricted' or 'contrived' collegiality has certain advantages.

The impact on individuals of externally imposed change is mediated by institutional culture. The experience of the ICT innovation differs widely between one institution and another. One factor in this is that differing values of institutions create different kinds of power structures. For example, the ICT innovation creates career opportunities for the 'early adopters', but these opportunities tend to be much greater in bureaucratic organisations with line management structures, in which promotion is largely on the basis of administrative responsibility; and much more restricted in the old traditional universities where promotion is on the basis of excellence in research and scholarship.

Overlaying these traditional – and still prevalent – organisational types in higher education, the political debate over the last decade has moved higher education institutions more towards being kinds of enterprises. Both ideologically and in practical terms, there are many forces impelling universities towards an enterprise culture. Some are recruiting students from all over the world, and staff may be spending their time crossing the globe to teach parttime masters degree courses in different countries.

Some are recruiting many more mature students, often parttime, and are working closely with local business and industry. These changes in our system of higher education are important and exciting, but they imply a change in the culture. In particular, they do not fit easily with the pseudodemocracy of patronage and restricted collegiality.

There is a need for more rapid procedures for decisionmaking and for systems that can support the quick action stream of the entrepreneur. Almost all higher education institutions are changing their culture in line with the shifts in political ideology over the last twenty years. In trying to promote innovation it is important to be able to analyse this process of culture change in the organisations where we work. It helps to understand the fury that individuals often experience when they find themselves pushed by the imperatives of a different value system from the one that has underpinned their work over many years.

The critical component of organisational culture is its underpinning system of values, so that a change in culture equates with a change in values. In UK during 1996 a confidential report from the Higher Education Quality Council (HEQC), leaked to The Times Higher Education Supplement (THES), revealed a crisis among academics about the values of the system they were working within. According to the THES, the report said that research had found 'a considerable confusion over the nature and significance of UK first degrees'. Most academics consulted by HEQC 'seemed unclear whether a graduate today should be expected to possess the same general characteristics, specialist subject knowledge, or capacity for future development as fifteen years ago'. The report concluded that there was a need for institutions to be more explicit about what achievements are being judged, the distinctive character of particular degrees, and what is the minimum satisfactory level of performance or 'threshold' standard.

This crisis of confidence is an important part of the context for the ICT innovation in higher education. The uncertainty is by no means all bad. It provides an opportunity for redefining the nature of knowledge and breaking down the isolation of the traditional 'ivory tower' style university. Within the redefined university it is possible to give credit towards a degree not just for demonstrating conceptual 'academic' knowledge, but for experiential knowledge acquired in the workplace, for example for the generic competencies that are an essential characteristic of expertise in management. As a tool for teaching and learning, ICT has the potential to support the acquisition of these new kinds of knowledge. Within the redefined university .ICT has a part to play in redefining the nature of knowledge and radically changing the style of teaching.

An apparently innocuous change in technology may emerge as a serious threat to an organization because it would force it to transform its theory and structure. Technological, theoretical and social systems exist as aspects of one another; change in one provokes change in the others. And change in organizations has its impact on the person, because beliefs, values and the sense of self have their being in social systems. Schon's attack on bureaucracy and on the processes of 'dynamic conservatism' which make social systems 'self-reinforcing', reads like a rationale for the radical iconoclasm of British government policy in the 1980s. Indeed it is certain that the ideas he presented in his Reith lectures on the BBC, and later published in Beyond the Stable State, raised considerable interest and led to wideranging debate. There is also general agreement in the research literature that innovation goes through stages. According to Fullan's classic study, there are four stages:

- First the approach, when the innovation becomes known to potential participants leading to a period of negotiation, during which they decide whether or not to become involved.
- Then a period of adoption, in which participants begin to use the new resources and make a preliminary assessment of the opportunities they offer.
- Next the implementation stage, when the innovation is put into practice; at this stage, the innovation inevitably goes through a process of adaptation which may or may not subvert its original purpose.
- Finally, if the innovation has not been rejected during any of the previous stages, comes the stage of continuation or institutionalisation, in which the innovation becomes fully integrated with the routines of practice and achieves permanency, insofar as that is ever possible.

Fullan's research shows that many innovations fail to reach the stage of institutionalisation, and many are only partially implemented or are largely subverted to better suit the values and practices of those required to implement them. There is a pattern of passive resistance and incremental withering of the initiative. Fullan's main concern is therefore to look at the features which support innovation and enable it to overcome these barriers. For each stage he identifies likely problems and suggests strategies for tackling them, drawn from research evidence. He stresses the importance of the roles of all the different players and identifies the following characteristic features of successful innovation: staff development and participation, good relationships between teachers, support from the head, a clear timeline, good communications and an internal consultant to support teachers.

As an alternative to this six stage model another one was proposed by Somekh et al. According to this model

— Orientation is the stage when participants seek out information about the innovation.
— Preparation comes next when participants are getting ready to begin.
— Routine is the first stage of implementation when participants establish lowlevel, routine use.
— Refinement is the stage when participants seek to refine and improve their use of the innovation.
— Integration is the stage when participants take steps to integrate their use of the innovation fully into their practice.
— Creative Integration is the stage when participants seek more effective ways of using the innovation, going beyond what has been achieved by others.

This is a useful model when analysing the experience of individuals, particularly in explaining why an innovation can 'get stuck' at the stage of lowlevel routine use; in terms of using ICT for teaching and learning in higher education, this is minimalist use without achieving any change in the nature of teaching and learning. To go beyond this stage, participants need to do a lot of creative work refining their use, thinking it through, changing it, integrating it much more seriously into what they were doing before. What makes this stage both fascinating and difficult is that integration should change both sides of the equation; i.e. what was done before should be changed to integrate with the innovation, just as much as the innovation should be changed to integrate with what was being done before.

It is only at the stage of integration that the innovation ceases to be an addon. At the final stage of creative integration – which only a few will achieve – the innovation is being used in ways that have not previously been envisaged. It is this creative potential that makes the process of innovation so appealing to some people. It is common for people to experience a sense of panic in trying out new things, but some people do get a buzz out of the adventure of innovation, and providing support for those embarking upon the use of ICT innovation is partly about trying to enable them to experience a buzz rather than panic.

When ICT is introduced, what does that actually mean in terms of what it is like to be a teacher? Most people who teach have some kind of love of the job – a sense of personal meaning in what they do. Some of that will relate to their discipline, to what it is they are teaching, and what counts as knowledge in that discipline. Some of it will be what they have found useful and successful to do over the years. They may actually enjoy the way that they enter the lecture room and the way that they stand at the overhead projector. Probably they experience an intellectual payoff from preparing a lecture, a buzz from feeling that this one is going to go really well tomorrow. Probably they get a buzz from their relationships with students, and depend to a considerable extent on watching students' faces, perhaps on seeing if they can get a laugh, to provide confirmation of their own value as a teacher.

The move to ICT is very disruptive to a lot of these things. So, in asking people to adopt the use of technology in their teaching, we may be asking them to abandon a lot of what, over the years, has made teaching rewarding for them. Moreover, institutions are very territorial places. Individuals often feel a sense of ownership of the rooms where they teach. Using ICT may require them to go into rooms which are part of a more alien culture. There may be some potential loss for them in terms of their formal or informal status in the organisation. Very importantly, the introduction of ICT requires a high level of collaboration:

collaboration in course design, teaching in teams, joint development of resources and sharing of resources.

ICT is going to be used as an alternative to your input as a teacher, rather than perceiving yourself as having a creative role. ICT is not value neutral. Computers look as if they came out of the science or engineering laboratory, which they did, and for some people in disciplines like sociology, anthropology and English, that may be a not insignificant barrier. For them it may be very hard to feel good about using that kind of equipment in their teaching, and .working in a space whose alien feel may be reinforced by the title of 'laboratory'. The ICT innovation cuts across the established patterns of discourse that give members of each group a sense of meaning and identity, of belonging to a club. People instinctively feel anxious about working closely with people who use a different set of words.

The ICT innovation in higher education has the potential – some would say the obligation – to challenge existing pedagogical practice. If ICT is to be used effectively there are many decisions to be made.

— *Resources*. What should be the level of resources available for students? What would be costeffective now? Should every student be required to have a personal computer? Should every student have an Internet address? In some universities they already do, not in all. Should they all have unlimited access to the Internet? What would that cost? Who would pay for it? Can we really talk about effective use of ICT unless learners do have that kind of level of access?

— *Tasks*. What exactly are we doing with ICT? What is the nature of the learning task? Are we replacing lectures with some kind of interactive experience, or some creative experience, or some kind of information-seeking experience? If so, are those tasks really beneficial for learning, or is some of it time-consuming and not as efficient, perhaps, as the lecture, which in some senses is a very efficient way of 'one to many' teaching.

— *Teaching*. How does ICT change the nature of the teacher's role? In what ways can ICT bring new kinds of job satisfaction to teachers? How can we integrate interpersonal support for students with teaching methods that make use of ICT? What is the impact on teaching and learning if students have problems accessing the course website?

— *Course Organisation*. Should the organisation of teaching change to make better use of ICT? For example, should there be fewer lectures –more selfstudy - enlivened and extended lectures - tutorial support for selfstudy - occasional small group work?

— *Assessment*. Does ICT make it possible to change assessment practices radically, for example by an increase in machineread tests, more use of multiplechoice approaches, and more formative selftests in addition to summative assessment? How would changes of this kind be likely to affect the kind of knowledge that is tested?

Amongst a whole range of difficulties, two problems seemed particularly intractable because of the way in which they challenged institutional culture. The first related to course design.

Individual lecturers who were keen on using ICT in teaching were not going to be effective unless the whole structure of the course changed. Without a highlevel decision and agreement on collaborative action, it was inevitable that whatever ICT courseware was developed would be an optional extra that students could or could not use if they wanted to, in addition to the ongoing course. To introduce effective use of the kind of ICT resources becoming available necessitated radical change, of a kind that most of those trying to promote the ICT innovation were powerless to bring about. The second related to the fundamental purpose of assessment. Is the purpose of assessment to give feedback to students and thereby enrich their learning experience, or is assessment mainly for credentialing purposes, to sort students and categorise their level of success or failure?

Most of the work on the advantages of using ICT in assessment assumes the former, but the culture and traditions of universities are deeply rooted in the latter. There is considerable enthusiasm among academic staff for computer-assisted assessment, because of the increase in the assessment load that has resulted from the worsening staff-student ratio and semesterisation. But when it is assumed that the purpose of assessment is to categorise students' level of success and failure, the practical problems often appear insurmountable. Can you really have people sitting in a computer laboratory doing assessment on screen and ensure that they will not cheat? Can you really assess students while they have all those resources on their laptop, including access to the Internet? Again, they might cheat by just finding the references and reading them while they are doing the exam.

It is very difficult to see how there can be any radical change to the nature of learning while university – and national – culture makes these assumptions about assessment. However, it is at least helpful that the introduction of ICT is challenging this culture by introducing ways of making formative assessment a more integral part of learning. The outcomes will probably be a more balanced approach with some assessment for both purposes, but it is important for those introducing ICT to be aware of the distinction. So what can we say is successful use of ICT? To begin to grapple with this question we need to consider at least five different structural 'levels' of increasing complexity: students; individual lecturers; course teams and departments; the university as a whole; and alternative, 'virtual' higher education organisations. First there are the individual students. Is it sufficient for all students to have basic ICT tuition? A lot of universities now provide this and make some routine demands upon students to use ICT, for example to word process assignments.

If there is to be any major impact upon the learning opportunities of students, the next structural level, the course team or department, must be involved. This is the level at which it will be possible to plan changes to integrate ICT skills with module outcomes, and to begin to release resources to enable radical changes in teaching strategies. ICT can never be effective as an optional extra to existing pedagogical approaches; to be effective, ICT-related activities need to become an integral part of the planned delivery of modules by a department or team, requiring students to carry out ICT-related tasks as an obligatory part of their learning. This, in turn, has implications for the restructuring of universities.

Computer Conferencing in Higher Education

Computer conferencing is part of a software family known as 'groupware'. It allows groups of people to participate in a shared discussion by posting messages which are stored on a central host computer for others to retrieve and comment upon. There are five key attributes that distinguish computer conferencing as a unique tool for education. They are:

— many-to-many communication;

— place independence;

— time independence;
— text-based;
— computer-mediated interaction.

Related to these collective characteristics, researchers and theorists suggest computer conferencing presents a new paradigm , a new domain of education and a new learning environment that is distinct from other forms of distance education and face-to-face learning.

As a mediating tool, computer conferencing facilitates two-way interaction among participants, thus enabling a classroom situation to be simulated on-line. The virtual classroom has many explicit and implicit characteristics that distinguish it from its face-to-face counterpart and present new challenges for educators.

According to researchers and theorists in the field, computer conferencing does not represent a mere shift in venues; rather it introduces a new set of social dynamics, problems and opportunities for teachers and learners. Dramatic claims are made about its potential to break down traditional barriers of education, connecting students to resource-rich, collaborative and democratic environments. While such assertions may be promising to educators and students, they also represent a tendency within the literature to confuse the medium's technical potential with it as an approach to teaching and learning.

A number of scholars hail computer conferencing as a medium that offers equal opportunity for participation and thus challenges the traditional power relationships between teachers and students, shifting control from the teacher to a more democratic group orientation. Claims of this nature are generally based upon studies of response levels and distribution of turn-taking in computer conferences. For example, Harasim studied computer-conferenced seminars at New Jersey Institute of Technology, and found that teachers contributed proportionally fewer responses than students and far less than classroom-based instructors. She states: 'In a face-to-face class, an instructor might monopolize 60-80% of verbal interaction, while a computer-mediated communication instructor might only contribute 10-15%'.A study by Graddol at the Open University in the United Kingdom (UK) supports Harasim's findings about the relative horizontal distribution of responses in their courses which use CoSy computer conferencing software.

The potential of computer conferencing to promote high and equal levels of student participation is advantageous to teachers who favour group collaboration and student-centered discussions. However, research on this issue is young and several studies contradict egalitarian claims. Some of the most frequently asserted advantages of CMC are the flattening of hierarchies, the consequential expansion of participation, and the channeling of attention away from the messenger and onto the message. The interviewees had some sympathy with this point, but generally seemed to have adopted systems for reconstructing status.

The removal of physical and verbal cues may reduce initial social bias, but, As the conference progresses, participants attach certain characteristics to messages, and this leads to differences in the status of participants.

Active cliques of students within computer conferences tended to monopolize conversation and inhibit other members from joining in. In the conference transcripts they analyzed, 50% of the comments were made by 10% of the participants.

The group interaction made possible through computer conferencing has generated interest in this medium as a tool for active learning, collaboration and constructivist teaching.

Computer-mediated communication is particularly suited to collaborative learning because 'the medium facilitates information exchange and provides the shared space essential for group work'. In fact, the literature on computer conferencing is heavily biased toward such learning models.

The self-pacing made possible through asynchronous communication and the act of articulating one's thoughts in writing promoted thorough and well-formed responses on-line. The new technologies have contributed to a movement away from a traditional objectivist paradigm that views education as the transmission of information from teacher to student, to one that views knowledge as a personally constructed world view. The collaborative potential of computer-mediated communication makes it an ideal tool for constructivist teaching. Distance educators can and should take advantage of this potential and encourage students to make their own meanings through collaboration with others.

Notable researchers on computer conferencing assert that the asynchronous group interaction of the medium demands a shift in the teacher's role from information presenter to facilitator of discussion Unlike traditional classroom activity, in which the teacher directs the instruction, leads the lessons, prompts responses, and paces the class, on-line group learning is student centered and requires a different role for the teacher, of facilitator rather than lecturer. The teacher plans the activities but then follows the flow of the conversation, offering guidance as needed rather than strictly adhering to the preplanned agenda or syllabus.

The rhetoric tends to simplify complex and varied teaching and learning models prevalent in classrooms today (physical and virtual) into two polarized camps: traditional, didactic, teacher-centered instruction that supposedly dominates face-to-face classrooms versus active, collaborative, student-centered learning environments possible through computer conferencing. While this rhetoric may help to dramatize the authors' points, it does little to help understand the complex pedagogical issues involved and factors related to or influenced by the medium. Teachers who favor student interaction and group discussion in their classrooms often have an easier time adapting to the on-line environment.

Rapid exchange of written communication creates a unique form of expression. The juxtaposition of personal exposure which results through on-line participation and the relative anonymity of faceless contact creates a 'new social space' that has its own set of dynamics. People are able to manage the presentation of their identity in more deliberate ways, taking time and editing messages to convey a certain tone. Thus, the on-line personality, Feenberg contends, is profoundly modified through self-conscious editing. Reflective thinking is a positive outcome of text-based interaction cited by researchers.

Written communication is a 'meta-cognitive skill' that gives occasion 'to make explicit to oneself the aspects of an activity that are usually tacit'. That is, the act of writing forces one to articulate, with enough clarity to be understood by others, personal thoughts and in so doing, helps the writer to examine their own reasoning process. Computer conference software stores all contributions in a database for participants to retrieve and review at their convenience. The transcript, as an evolving artifact of the online discussion, is a significant resource for learning. Students reported increased aattentiveness to written contributions over verbal exchanges in face-to-face classrooms and found the transcript offered complete notes that were impractical to track in a live discussion.

Text-based communication lends the opportunity for students to improve their writing skills. However, in a study of factors related to students' 'readiness' for computer conferencing, The medium 'presupposes the ability to read, write and type well'. Instead of presenting an opportunity for equal and unbiased participation, the narrow bandwidth of written communication may present a formidable barrier for weaker writers. Another potentially negative aspect related to text-only communication is the 'information overload' that results from the volume of text that accumulates as the discussion progresses. Students also perceive a loss of personal contact and clarity of message due to the lack of physical presence, voice intonation, gesture and other tacit cues

The traditional academic emphasis of evaluation on written work may cause participants to be overly selfconscious about the quality of their online messages and inhibit spontaneous expression.

The research on computer conferencing is relatively new to mainstream educational literature. The issues addressed in this narrow yet growing body are widespread and frequently illdefined. There is a tendency within the literature to confuse the potential of computer conferencing as a medium and a tool of education with it as an approach to teaching and learning. The problem of confounding medium and method becomes even more confusing when the discussion of computermediated communication is tied to a particular educational paradigm.

Authors occasionally point to teaching strategies and student input as salient factors in determining the extent to which the potential of the medium to promote collaboration was actualized. However, most lose sight of these factors in their conclusion, favoring dramatic claims about the medium's inherent promise for progressive education.

Despite the medium's inherent support of a learnercentered environment, there is still a possibility that old patterns of teaching and learning will predominate. Tutors who were meant to be facilitators and resource people, available to be consulted when needed, might end up, with the complicity of their students, reproducing the social role of the classroom teacher as authority figure. This goes against the potential of [computermediated communication] for promoting the educational use of 'many-to-many' communication because it puts the teacher at center stage. Is it not possible that computer conferencing, like other classroom tools, is simply at the service of its users and therefore dependent upon the educational approaches employed? Similar questions surround claims about the egalitarian nature of the medium and the shifts in teaching roles that are proposed.

Many features of computer conferencing promoted in the literature – interactivity, collaboration, reflection, and self-direction are not inherent in the medium, instead this medium can be passive, didactic, competitive, spontaneous, and other-directed. Student participation, course design and instructional style are some of the salient factors that impact whether these elements emerge. The promise of computer conferencing for increased reflection, collaboration and intellectual amplification are largely dependent on the individuals who meet in these 'electronic classrooms'.

ICT Tools: Challenges in Classrooms

With the widespread use of information and communication technologies (ICT), there is understandable interest in the impact of ICT on teaching and learning. Although it is often claimed that computer technologies and the Internet have the potential to change both teaching and learning, teachers have been subjected to public pressures to use new technologies before they, and we, have a clear understanding of their impact on classroom practices and student learning.

Schools and classrooms are being equipped without adequate research or attention to the professional preparation of teachers. The belief that classrooms should be equipped with technology is predicated on the belief that technology can improve the rate, quality, amount, and effectiveness of learning. Although attractive, this belief must be tested with sound research. It is thus critical that the available research be assembled, reviewed, and critiqued as a prelude to pinpointing areas of future research and policy development.

Many studies show that preschoolers are "learning optimists" who rate their own abilities highly, underestimate task difficulty, and hold positive expectations of success. During middle childhood, children begin to distinguish ability, effort, and external factors in explaining their performance. How they attribute success and failure on tasks influences the likelihood of developing an intrinsic motivation to persist at challenging tasks and the development of effective metacognitive skills. This in turn influences performance on academic tasks.

Attitudes: Research supports conventional wisdom indicating that students who are positively disposed toward tasks or subject matter are likely to learn more and learn more easily. For this reason, student attitudes toward computer use could have an impact on their learning. Only one finding in the research on attitudes is clear: Children who are exposed to computers have a more positive attitude towards computers than those who are not.

Positive attitudes towards technologies allow for their productive use throughout life. Another finding is also relatively clear: Despite years of initiatives to engender positive attitudes among women toward ICTs and improve their efficacy in using them, men and boys still have a higher computer self-efficacy and more positive attitudes towards computers than girls and women. This discrepancy remains despite the reported use of computers in school rising to a non-gender differentiated level. It seems that simple exposure to computers does not guarantee positive attitudes towards them, or at least the positive attitudes are being mitigated in girls and women.

The gender discrepancy is being reduced, but much more slowly than predicted. Gender differences have several implications. On a very basic level, it has been argued that the software most commonly used does not appeal to girls as much as boys, and should therefore be structured differently. On a social level, differences in attitudes have ramifications for school performance and achievement, especially in the context of group work. This topic will be discussed more fully in the section devoted to achievement below.

Attributions: Positive attributions of academic success fuel a sense of mastery and are part of a positive cycle of learning that is associated with academic success. In this cycle, successes are attributed to ability and internalized while failures are discounted and attributed to situational factors beyond the control of the learner. In contrast, negative attributions of academic performance can give rise to learned helplessness, which is associated with poorer school performance. In this cycle, successes are discounted and attributed to luck while failures are internalized as indicators of low ability, leading to an overall sense of helplessness and failure. Students with learned helplessness perform less well on academic tasks than students who attribute their success to their own abilities.

Attributions to ability versus luck are also related to gender differences, making the area an important one for research. Despite the vast body of research on this topic in general, there is a paucity of work investigating how these cycles are manifested in relation to computer technologies. We could find only two studies on this topic. The first demonstrated that attributions to ability and task difficulty had a more significant effect on performance than attributions to luck and effort on computer tasks. The second study investigated the effect of gender on children's reactions to success and failure on computerized tasks. It found that boys were more likely to attribute failure on the tasks to unstable and external causes than were girls. In contrast, girls were more likely to attribute success on the tasks to unstable and external causes .

Achievement orientation: There have been a number of recent large analyses investigating whether access to a computer or use of a computer in instruction improves academic achievement. An analysis conducted by Statistics Canada using data from Ontario's Education Quality and Accountability Office's province-wide tests. These data were gathered in 1997 from 115 000 third graders in Ontario's English-speaking schools. While other factors such as smaller class sizes were found to be related to higher academic achievement, this study found no relationship between the presence of a computer in the classroom and the achievement of third grade students. In the United States, similar work has been done looking at the results of National Assessment of Education Progress (NAEP) tests. These tests, administered nationally every two years in mathematics and reading alternately, assess the effect of a number of variables, including computer use, on academic achievement.

The most recent analysis available used the scores on the reading test for students in grades four and eight. The analysis revealed that students who used computers in the classroom at least once each week do not perform better on the NAEP reading test than do those who use computers less than once a week. This was true even accounting for the comfort and training with computers that teachers reported: The analysis was restricted to teachers who reported that they were moderately well prepared to use computers for instructional purposes.

There are many examples of innovative programs combining access to technology with instruction designed to complement the new technological resources. Woodrow and colleagues have longitudinal evidence of the effectiveness of technology-enhanced instruction in a secondary science environment. In particular, they report on the experiences of high school students in a multimedia environment in Physics and Science classrooms. They have a substantial amount of data collected through interviews and questionnaires that indicate that the students enjoy working in the multimedia environment and believe that they are learning specific knowledge and general learning skills in a way that would not be supported by traditional instruction

Positive relations between computer use and achievement as a function of exposure to computer assisted instruction have been reported by Renaud, who looked at science performance of seventh grade low achievers. Similarly, van Daal et al. reported dramatic increases in reading and spelling performance of kindergarten students who were exposed to a computer-based reading and spelling program over those not exposed to a computerized program. In addition, one very well controlled study found a clear, positive relationship between the use of hypermedia instruction and achievement in engineering courses. There is thus some empirical support for a positive effect of technologies on student performance.

There has been a long-standing argument that the use of computers for instructional purposes increases motivation in children. Children without access to a computer at home will find it more motivating to go to classes where they have the opportunity to use a computer. Although intuitively reasonable, they offer no experimental support for this statement. Children using computers were highly motivated to complete their assignments and demonstrated high levels of curiosity, achievement orientation, and personal ownership of the project.

The use of technology in Israeli classrooms in high school increases pupils' self-efficacy and motivation to study and succeed. These motivational effects are also extendable to therapeutic settings. Similar results have been found with eighth and ninth grade science students. Unfortunately, none of these projects had a control group of students that did not use computers. One study that did have a control group showed no significant effects of computer work in task achievement of seventh and eighth graders, but the students did report valuing the computerized task more than the non-computerized control task. Other work refutes this argument, however.

Group work with the use of a computer does not by itself increase learning or satisfaction, but rather aspects of social facilitation and the collaboration process underlie many of these results. Third grade pupils working in groups on computer tasks have higher levels of interaction and, unlike other tasks, most of these interactions were concerned with solving the problem. When asked, children in her study reported that the limited time they had on the computer required them to focus on the task at hand, thus concentrating their efforts and encouraging on-task interactions.

There are few studies on how computer systems and learning environments are designed, constructed, and maintained. Stuve reports on a three year descriptive case study in which he explored the role of technology in the classroom after it had been installed, that is, how it was used by both the teachers and the children over several years. He found that specific features of the classroom environment, for example the location of the printer in relation to the class and the quality of the computers, had important impacts on how projects were structured and how learning activities were maintained. He argues that the realisation of technological innovation is socially constructed, with a complex interaction among students, teachers, and the physical and social environments supporting the technologies. This is the only study we could find that investigated this issue. Although it is a well-documented study, its descriptive nature does not permit hypothesis testing. It is imperative that more rigorous experimental research be done on this area. The design of the learning environment also includes the ratio of computers-to-students, affecting the size of learning groups that can be formed.

The nature of hardware and software affects both its use by and its impact on the learner. The design of hardware and software must take into account both motor and cognitive skill differences between children and adults. Low-level design details such as number of mouses and type of mouse had significant effects on children's performance and motivation.

There is as yet very little comprehensive or rigorous research investigating the software design and the effects of design features on student learning and performance. Although the role of visual presentation in information processing is well understood, increasingly sophisticated auditory presentations require further investigation. His preliminary findings suggest a role for both auditorally and visually complex programs and interactions. The use of multiple windows in complex tasks helps fourth grade students complete their work better than the use of single window presentations.

Gender plays a significant part in the effectiveness of the design interface for kindergarten children. They found that boys preferred the use of navigational buttons when searching for assistance whereas girls preferred to ask for help. In addition, girls preferred scenes that changed slowly, incorporated text into the game, and were colourful with an emphasis on reds and yellows. Boys preferred scenes that changed quickly and emphasised blues and greens.

The software programs used in schools receive very poor evaluations, despite a clear understanding that instructional materials are more effective if their development has been informed by research. Metacognitive knowledge includes knowledge about the self, the task, and strategies for learning. Memory and general problem solving skills also play a role in the effective use of metacognitive resources. The development and implementation of successful metacognitive skills can significantly influence learning and scholastic performance. Group work is seen as one of the major places where computer use can add to traditional instructional practices. The participation that is required when children are grouped around a computer, as opposed to working in isolation at individual computers, can have a positive effect on performance

Peer based interaction at the computer allows for exploration of the relationships between cognitive, metacognitive, and social processes. In particular, co-operative learning on computers is argued to facilitate peer interaction and have implications for motivation, self-esteem, and social behaviours. The extent of group effectiveness, at least in the 9-12 age group, is determined by several crucial factors, including the degree of autonomy developed by students, type of negotiation within a group, and the extent to which pupils appropriate the task.

The task assigned has been shown to dictate whether more or less autonomy is desirable. For ninth graders in a physics classroom, too much autonomy diminishes learning about the data themselves. High levels of autonomy on difficult synthesis tasks (reading) were detrimental to the performance of the fifth graders they studied; even though more structured help was available through the computer program, the children chose not to use it to the detriment of their learning.

Student choice as to whether or not to use available structure can, at this age, result in diminished performance. Younger students, such as the five and six year olds perform better when there are adults mediating the learning and providing structure. With older students, however, greater autonomy can be positive.

In terms of the benefits of computer use, who is doing the work seems to be just as important as what work is assigned. The importance of the pupil-teacher interaction is crucial in determining the composition of groups to include the diverse personality and work types that encourage the best group performance.

Training children in social skills is a better determinant of computer-based problem solving abilities than either gender or group composition. Memory strategies such as rehearsal become more effective over time and lead to better retention of information. One of the major technological attempts to encourage the use of rehearsal strategies in learning, and thus better retention of information, has been the use of computer-assisted instruction (CAI).

There is a general argument that using computers makes pupils better problem solvers and autonomous learners by encouraging the development of independent thinking skills beginning as young as preschool

Elementary students require more and more cognitive control over their artistic creativity as they develop, and thus programs should be devised that allow them this control while at the same time encouraging their artistic expression. The largest volume of research on the impact of technology in the content areas has been conducted on mathematics instruction. Mathematics instruction also has the longest history of using technology for instructional purposes and boasts several impressive systems and programs for the instruction of mathematics and mathematical concepts.

Student attitudes toward computers and computer related technologies improve as a consequence of exposure to them. The use of ICTs for group work can be beneficial if teachers are able to take into account the complex interplay among the age of the students, the kind of task, and the amount of independence allowed. An aspect of the educational setting that should not be overlooked is the age of the students, as the effect of computers on different age groups can be radically different.

Multicultural Curriculum

Multicultural education will be as successful as commitment to it by school administrators. Regardless of the level of commitment programs initiated under the guise of multiculturalism must receive reinforcement from administrators who are accountable for the success of established multicultural initiatives. A key factor in any proposed multicultural initiative is curriculum development. A multicultural curriculum should be considered for several reasons: (a) provides alternative points of view relative to information already taught in most educational systems; (b) provides ethnic minorities with a sense of being inclusive in history, science etc.; and, (c) decreases stereotypes, prejudice, bigotry, and racism.

Educational institutions have been dictated too long by attitudes, values, beliefs, and value systems of one race and class of people. At its most fundamental level, multicultural education represents an orientation to schooling and the teaching-learning process that is grounded in the democratic ideals of justice and equality. Justice and equality have always been the focus of schools, but there is a substantial body of historical and contemporary evidence which demonstrates that the schooling experiences of most students of color, as well as many white students from economically poor and politically disempowered backgrounds, are inferior to those provided to white students from middle class, politically dominant backgrounds.

Due to this disparity, proponents of multicultural education call for a studied restructuring of many of the long-standing policies and conventions of public schooling. There are five critical dimensions of multicultural education: content integration, knowledge construction, prejudice reduction, equity pedagogy, and empowering school culture and social structure.

i) *Content integration*: The goal of content integration is to expand the curriculum by incorporating contributions of diverse cultures into traditional disciplines of study. Arguably, this dimension is easily realized through technology. For instance, teachers at all levels have used the World Wide Web to extend the available learning resources. Electronic mail and multimedia technologies promote communication and interactions between diverse groups with the purpose of helping students learn more about content they study in subject areas as social studies, science, psychology, and even foreign language. Many educators who acknowledge potential benefits of a merger between technology and multicultural education call for updating the physical infrastructures of schools. In schools where such updates (i.e., re-wiring) have occurred, teachers are making widespread use of the internet and other computer-based technology. The knowledge and skills students acquire in these schools typically are being reinforced by computer availability and internet access in their homes. This reality contrasts sharply with that of students from poor/working class backgrounds who attend schools where the notion of re-wiring for internet access may seem superfluous in light of the absence of basic resources. Nor are these students likely to have internet access at home.

ii) *Knowledge construction*: Knowledge construction dimension promotes critical literacy by examining the manners in which scholars and scientists contribute to their respective fields of study. Knowledge construction builds upon content integration by making explicit the worldviews and perspectives that inform knowledge claims. Similarly, it expands the legitimate sources of knowledge by helping learners recognize that their own experiences both within and beyond school are viable foundations for acquiring knowledge and skills. Teacher educators are being called upon to use technology to promote and reinforce the knowledge construction process. Part of acquiring facility in knowledge construction is understanding phenomenon from the perspectives of others. To this end, teacher educators are making use of Internet technology to promote more critical engagement with subject matter.

iii) *Prejudice reduction*: Prejudice reduction is about eliminating all forms of bigotry. Also, it involves promoting healthy personal identity devoid of the tendency or need to denigrate those who differ from self. Multimedia presentations and distance learning technologies are being used to establish learning exchanges between students of diverse cultural backgrounds and thereby reduce prejudice and stereotyping. Likewise, technology is being used to promote positive self-concept and foster positive relationships between students from diverse backgrounds in geographically diverse areas. Such efforts have included videoconferences, computer conferences, interactions on the Web, and e-pals. Technologies used with middle grade students have included interactive compressed video and use of two-way televised communication systems via telephone lines. Teacher education students are using distance learning technology, multimedia, and e-mail to engage in cross-cultural and diverse regional interactions with other prospective teachers.

iv) *Equity pedagogy*: Equity pedagogy is about equalizing opportunities to learn. It involves incorporating various strategies and techniques that attend to learning styles and intelligence types. Writers interested in the nascent relationship between technology and multicultural education are discussing the urgency of using technology to address the various ways in which learners from diverse backgrounds best acquire school knowledge and skills. Nevertheless, it is difficult to discern whether current efforts to merge technology and multicultural education are addressing this fourth dimension directly. Indeed, some writers are concerned that technology may inadvertently privilege certain ways of processing information while it devalues others. An important issue for many contemporary educators, particularly in the university setting, is whether internet technology is in any way superior to face-to-face instruction. It would appear that one advantage internet technology holds over face-to-face classroom format is in its ability to provide educators and students wide access to a cross-cultural professional and learning community. This can be accommodated through e-mail, bulletin boards, and chatroom sites.

v) Empowering school culture and social structure: Multicultural education proponents contend that in order to provide high quality experiences for all students, many traditional aspects of schools will need to be reconfigured. This is referred to as empowering school culture and social structures. Its ultimate purpose is to change the taken-for-granted policies and practices of schools that, while useful to some students, have greatly diminished the schooling experience for many others.

Role of Internet Technologies

With online technologies, discourse communities are expanded to encompass interactions and collaborative exchange projects among peers from diversified cultural backgrounds. The expanded communities open opportunities for learners to interact with multiple perspectives that challenge their existing knowledge constructions and impose cognitive conflicts requiring negotiation.

With the new online tools and their potential to enrich learning experiences beyond the capabilities of a traditional setting come new challenges for educators and educational researchers. There seems to be a link between the technologies and authentic learning and collaborative learning in general; between technologies and student-centred, constructivist practices; and discussions in the literature examine those capabilities. However, educators are aware of the void in the literature of empirical reports testing the related hypotheses. Thus, there is an urgency to develop and implement research designs that accommodate the nuances of learning atypical of nontechnology, teacher-directed environments, as well as to explore alternative instructional paradigms that optimise the potential benefits of online technologies for learning.

The internet is the world most powerful computer network connecting personal computers, sophisticated mainframes, and high speed supercomputers around the globe. Because a myriad of computers and programmes are part of the internet, incompatibility problems can result because information is created using different computers and software.

In 1989, a group of scientists at the European Laboratory for Particle Physics (CERN) in Geneva, Switzerland began developing an internet tool that would link information produced by all of the CERN researchers. The tool provided a way to link textual information on different computers and created by different scientists. The object was to overcome issues of incompatibility and utilise a new way of linking made possible by computers, called "hypertext". Rather than presenting information in a linear or hierarchical fashion, hypertext permits information to be linked in a web-like structure. Nodes of information can be linked to other nodes of information in multiple ways. As a result, users can dynamically criss-cross the information web using pieces in the order most convenient to them.

The CERN project resulted in an innovative front-end to the internet, now referred to as the World-Wide Web

(WWW). The web provides users with a uniform and convenient means of accessing the vast resources of the internet. In 1993, the National Centre for Supercomputing Applications (NCSA) at the University of Illinois pushed the CERN scientists' idea further by creating a software tool called Mosaic. Mosaic is an easy to use graphical user interface that permits text, graphics, sound and video to be hyperlinked. Mosaic was the first of the internet tools that are now referred to as "web browsers". Other well-known browsers include Netscape and Microsoft's internet explorer.

Web browsers permit users to connect to the internet and facilitate accessing information located on another remote computer. The web browser links to the remote computer just long enough so that the information you need can be sent to your computer for you to view. Documents created to be viewed by a browser are formatted using Hypertext Markup Language (HTML). HTML solves incompatibility problems by using standardised tags which indicate such things as whether a piece of text should be plain, bold, italic, or linked to another piece of text. Pages of information on a computer formatted with HTML and accessible to someone with a web browser, are referred to as 'home pages' or 'web pages'.

The web have made the internet a more user-friendly environment. The ability to integrate graphics, text, and sound into a single tool means that novice users do not have to struggle with such a steep learning curve. In addition, organisations and individuals can create home pages independently and link to other home pages on their own computers or to pages created by others on different computer systems. The web can be used by the distance educator to build a classroom home page. The home page can cover information about the class including the syllabus, exercises, literature references, and instructor's biography. The instructor can also provide links to information on the web that would be useful to students in the class. Other links can access library catalogues or each student's individual home page. In addition, the home page can link students to a discussion list or listserv that set up for student communication. It is also a relatively simple matter to use the homepage to create forms that students can fill out and that will end up being sent to you as an e-mail message.

The web allows more opportunites of interaction. The interaction itself is categorised within a learning context with the purpose of task/instructional completion or social relationship building, with a mixture of both types of interaction being common. Interactions should involve complex activity by learners to include engaging and reflecting, annotating, questioning, answering, pacing, elaborating, discussing, inquiring, problem-solving, linking, constructing, analysing, evaluating, and synthesising. The levels of interactivity include: (i) interaction between participants and learning materials, (ii) interaction between participants and instructors/ experts, (iii) interaction among participants, and (iv) management/feedback communications, Although content and social interaction are interwoven into highly interactive web-based courses, each will be discussed independently to further explain the role of both forms of interaction in a web-based course.

Content interaction is based on the theory of learning that is most appropriate to achieve educational outcomes within the course itself. In many web-based courses, multiple layers of learning outcomes exist, thus suggesting that multiple strategies may be incorporated into the course. Some courses may include an intensive case study, while maintaining a weekly schedule of online lectures and discussion sessions. Other courses may adhere more loosely to a semester-long simulation with its outcome being an explanation of findings and events. It is difficult to prescribe one best fit for content interaction, given the wide range of possibilities available on the World Wide Web.

It is important, however, to ground the design of the learning environment in solid theory and pedagogy, as distance learning has been criticised for having very little, if any, theoretical context. Hannafin, Land, and Oliver discuss grounded design as a context for dealing with the range of design decisions that best facilitate learning outcomes. Grounded design is defined as the systematic implementation of processes and procedures that are rooted in established theory and research in human learning. Social interaction is a key element in online learning. Given that the nature of online learning is anytime anywhere, the potential for isolation and frustration exist. The social interaction of the course must, at least initially, be designed into the course.

Through collaboration and communication, the opportunity for learning more about peers and connecting with them in non-task specific conversation is more likely to occur. Although social interaction may have very little to do with a course, it is still valued as the primary vehicle for student communications in a web-based learning environment. Non-task/content specific social interaction may include conversation in a chat room, inquiries about used textbook purchases, or questions about using a new version of a piece of software. When collaborative teams of students work toward project completion, there is still the need for relationship building in the learning community. Relationship building is a necessary component of collaboration and communication and the perceptions of the efficacy of this type of social interaction can impact the learning outcomes of the course.

By the very nature of social interaction, learners are directly able to foster content interaction.The overuse or misuse of interaction strategies can lead to boredom, overload, and frustration. It lessens the likelihood that students will be able to surmise what is important, and once again, frustration may occur when students perceive interaction as online busywork. The more interactive the web-based course becomes, the more complex it is to use. For novice distance learners, complexity may very well lead to more frustration and isolation. Future web-based tools hopefully will promote collaboration and interaction online in a much easier-to-use format.

For now, designers of web-based courses should weigh the frequency and the quality of interactions required that best facilitate the learning outcomes to be achieved, where frequency does not always equal quality. The attributes of web-based instruction should be filtered through the philosophy and pedagogy that is presumed appropriate for the course, preferably adhering to the grounded design approach suggested by Hannafin. Oftentimes, lists of strategies and tactics are provided as design suggestions for web-based courses. When suggested out of context, it is difficult to surmise how the online experience may be structured.

For example, in a list that suggests threaded discussions be used, there is still little detail as to how they are to be used within the learning experience itself. In a more behaviourist notion, threaded discussion may be used to elicit responses to given questions. In a situated learning environment, threaded discussions may be used to discuss influences on the environment with a scientist in an attempt to determine why native plants are not surviving. Instructional content is the central component of a web-based course, as this is where new knowledge, skills, and abilities are presented. Whether student's learn declarative knowledge or participate in a large-scale simulation, the way in which knowledge is shared sets the stage for all interactivity within the web-based course.

When given a choice, instructors many times will select land design instructional methods and techniques that are consistent with their theoretical and philosophical views. Instruction is presented either through an instructor-centred approach or through a more student-centred approach. There are times when one style of instruction is better than the other.

When the outcomes of instruction are to analyse, synthesise, or evaluate, or when ill-defined authentic problems are the focus, a more student-centred approach would best facilitate the learning outcomes. An instructor-centred approach would work well for instruction that is procedural, declarative, or well-defined in role and definition. Much of what exists online as web-based courses appears to have a strong instructor-centred influence. In much of the instruction, information is presented, examples are provided, practice exists, and in many cases, feedback is available through mentors and instructors. Student-centred learning is appropriate for outcomes of instruction that are focused on analysis, synthesis, and evaluation.

Student-centred learning provides interactive, complementary activities that enable individuals to address unique learning interests and needs, study multiple levels of complexity, and deeper, understanding. Using open-ended strategies for learning, such as situated, learning, learners will actively construct meaning to determine how to proceed. This student-centred approach fosters a greater responsibility for learning and requires students to be more self-regulated in their approaches to learning. In some cases, scaffolding is provided that will facilitate self-regulation, thus providing strategies that students can use to create unique approaches to complex problems.

Collaborative online learning environments is an obvious strategy for promoting interactivity. Many of the same factors that exist for campus-based students in collaborative groups parallel collaboration on the web. Topics such as group size, group role definition, group assignment and shared grading all are issues as well on the web. A collaborative group's members should be committed to the "group goal" and to maximising each other's learning. Johnson and Johnson suggest very strongly that groups do not become collaborative just because someone assigns them together as a group. An effective collaborative group requires positive interdependence, group and individual accountability, promotive interaction, and interpersonal skill.

Quality can be obtained through highly interactive courses. Occasionally, however, a strong collaboration component in the course may hinder some students' participation. If, for whatever reason, some students are unable to participate in collaborative, group building exercises, those students may be left to communicate with only the instructor or mentor. Many students complain about getting too much information online, not being able to follow concurrent threads in a threaded discussion, and not being about to keep up with multiple conversations occurring in chat sessions. Despite some of the negative student comments, much can be said about conversation and e-discussion. Written communication seems to be more reflective, as students have more time to compose their thoughts and articulate in the manner intended online.

Monitoring is essential for survival in a web-based environ-ment, even more so than in a traditional environment. This element of web-based design is not included, yet it is essential that work independently and can self regulate their own learning. Many cognitive strategies can be embedded within a web-based course, along with tips and ideas for time management and independent learning. Performance support can be defined as an electronic system that provides integrated access to information, advice, learning experiences, and tools to help someone perform a task with the minimum of support by other people.

Supporting performance for the technical and even motivational components of the course is important and must be considered when a web-based course is designed and presented. In addition to supporting entire programmes at a distance, performance support can also provide in course assistance. Peer-to-peer interactive communication is another type of multi-way interaction between individual learners and the faculty member and commonly between learners and the learning group. This features is most often implemented with text chat; more sophisticated communication options are implemented with voice communications. May allow selective interaction between learners and/or instructor, but control of the conversation is shared equally among all participants.

Web based delivery is attempting to address all three Learning Formats, with varying degrees of maturity and success. Successful distance education programmes seek to combine all three forms of learning in programmes of study. Development of web-based courses can be very demanding, and often quite different from developing other kinds of media. Most self pace web based training includes the following features:

i) *Copiers*: Outline and overview to tell learners what the learning is about, what the learning goals are, how long it will take and what instructors expect of them.

ii) *Body content*: Must read area where you put your introduction and explanations, procedures and instructions. But remember, most users don't like to read a lot of copy on the screen so keep it short, simple and to the point

iii) *Demonstration or practice*: Demo, practice the lesson or simulate an environment, where possible.

iii) *A self checking quiz*: It gives trainees immediate answers and scores is part of the value added of WBT.

iv) *Help desk.* Provide an e-mail address or phone number on your WBT pages so learners know where to get help.

Online learning provides access to a potentially vast new student population. For students, the attractions are convenience and flexibility. Students can schedule schooling around their everyday lives without being constrained by the rigidity of regular class hours and the necessity of being in a physical classroom. Faculty members, on the other hand, are apt to feel concern and anxiety about engaging in this most-talked-about but never-experienced online teaching. Integrating unfamiliar technology into one's instructional strategies can be stressful at first. Even good instructors who have experience using the internet for social and/or professional reasons can suffer from unexpected barriers to successful implementation, such as technology problems, student dropout, work overload, and overwhelming amounts of administrative housekeeping.

One of the top requirements for the success of distance education is the availability of quality faculty support. Post-secondary institutions commonly employ faculty development specialists to assist faculty members in their online course development. The number of these positions is growing at a fast pace. Developing an online course is a complicated and time-consuming process, with many new and unique elements for instructors. Without the help of support services, developing and implementing successful online course can be an uphill battle. The demands that developing and teaching online courses pose to instructors are unique and novel. The faculty development specialists must accommodate the increased support needs of faculty. Instructors are likely to approach the project with a fair amount of anxiety, which is justifiable.

In order to make the development process efficient and faculty-friendly, faculty development specialists must keep in mind the aspects of the course development process that facilitate success. The goal of many online courses is the creation of a learning community, one where students and the instructor collaboratively share responsibility for the creation of joint knowledge as they jointly share responsibility in addressing learning tasks. Students who thrive in this environment tend to be more introverted in face-to-face situations, those who reflect deeply, are self-directed in their learning and are intrinsically motivated. Learners need to see the value of such learning properties engendered by this environment as collaboration, constructivism, interactivity, reflection, self-direction, individualisation, and experiential learning.

In the web-based course, a number of new communication elements confront the learner and must be addressed: asynchronicity, multiple conversations, interactivity, information overload, and pacing. Other online characteristics, such as social norms, instructor relationship, student role, and the academic atmosphere, are largely carried over from other school experiences. Students take these factors into consideration in developing learning approaches to work effectively online. Some are directly related to the technology, such as means of processing online information, deciding when and how to contribute, expressing oneself through written communication, dealing with multiple conversations and a deluge of messages, and determining interactivity. Other learning strategies come from prior study patterns in school and work settings: setting goals, individualising assignments, managing time, establishing attitudes, and seeking and using feedback.

Beyond just providing technical support, virtual institutions are using their help desks to route urgent administrative or academic requests to the appropriate office for timely attention. Redesigning a course for web-based delivery can be quite involved, requiring a steep learning curve, especially where there is limited institutional support for this activity. When a regular teacher decides to accommodate some distance students as well as the classroom ones, she or he finds there is twice as much work if taught like two different sections of the course. Course developers and instructors are often part-time, adjunct faculty and may be doing this in addition to their other full-time jobs. To attend to all of the web conference areas can be demanding, especially when there are 15 to 25 students enrolled in a course. Some educators claim that the time involved in delivering an online course can be up to three times as much as a face-to-face one, but this need not be the case it teachers and students budget their online time. Due to the emphasis placed on student participation, teachers need to shift roles to facilitating and managing peer-learning, instead of lecturing or inserting themselves as often into the discussion as they might in the classroom.

There are institutions who have adopted an independent study model of web-based education that demands more investment in up-front course development, but can accommodate greater numbers of students without continual faculty involvement during delivery. For example, Brigham Young University's Independent Study programme allows students to start their courses on any date with a year to complete; they also provide automatic grading of web-based, multiple-choice assignments with immediate feedback.

These courses are supplemented by related websites, multimedia resources on CD-ROM, and have optional online discussions with peers. The institutional dimensions of academic student support are similar to those faced by lower-tech delivery systems, but the college or university offering web-based courses needs to mount these services online.

The provision of a web-based programme was a chief reason distance students chose the institution, and it is the means by which students interact in their courses. They expect that other communications with the campus about academic and administrative matters will be online as well. These fuller academic supports go beyond single-course interaction, and therefore require programmatic responses like: online counselling for educational adjustments and advising for degree planning; assessment for prior learning; student discussion areas; online career centres; and access to academic resources via the internet to support their degree programme study. Students who lacked these environmental supports attributed their failure to external factors such as insufficient time, distractions, and circumstances that arose over which they had little control.

Readiness is the major component of successful online learning. Readiness includes personal factors such as a compatible learning style, proficient computer skills, an interest in the content of the course, mastery of prerequisites, and good reading, writing, and keyboard skills. It also include, such environmental factors as having a quiet, roomy study area, a social network of family friends, and work associates that value the student's educational pursuits, a lifestyle with existence within it for distance study, and technical/institutional assistance in place for obstacles that might arise. Institutions are obliged to present realistic and accurate information about course demands, but their marketing efforts sometimes overshadow this voice.

Effective counselling as the primary means of accomplishing this. This role, assumed by full-time counsellors, tutors and support staff means being supportive, encouraging, and pastoral to some extent. Such counselling sets forth realistic expectations about online study demands for working adult students who have been away from college and/or never juggled their education with other roles they must play. The counsellor suggests, needs to let students know that it is those who take direct responsibility and control of their college experience that prove to be most successful. This counselling can also address the readiness factors listed above and assist students with time management, organising their situation for a successful educational role and activities, and garnishing support from spouse, children, and their employer.

For many years distance programmes have accepted most standard forms of prior learning credit as it related to the student's degree programme, such as accredited college transcripts, CLEP test scores, and ACE, PONSI, and DANTES recommended credit equivalents. However, individualised credit by evaluation (CBE) was restricted to in-person settings. No longer will this be the case, however. SUNY-ESC's Centre for Distance Learning has begun individualised CBE in common areas, done at a distance through e-mail, the phone, and mail and such an web-based environment is being designed. Other virtual supports are social in nature, such as announcement areas, student bulletin boards, and topical conversation areas; these integrate students with their peers, create an online Community of scholars, and create institutional affiliation. The British Open University (BOU) Students' Association maintains several hundred such conferences covering the gamut of topics to bring together its student body. It operates a bulletin board for events and activities of student interest. A majority of adult distance students pursue further education for career advancement or change. These individuals are returning to college as necessity learners—where education is essential for them to keep or obtain a job—or as rainy day planners—where education provides a safety net to give them options if opportunities come up or something goes awry in their current position. Therefore, an important student service on the virtual college site would be a career centre. Such a centre could have such features as information about jobs and employment; career testing and counselling; networking about jobs with other students, university personnel, and alumni; as well as links to online job search services.

4

Impact of Globalisation

Globalisation is a "tricky term for some, it connotes free flow of ideas, capital, people and goods around the world. For others, it implies the hegemony of the capitalist system, the domination of rich nations and corporations and the loss of national identity. It would thus appear that globalisation is not an unmixed blessing. It may promote "growth through increased technology and knowledge transfers in developing countries but it could also be sometime a source of instability.

The changes to which higher education all over the globe increasingly is exposed, are complex and varied, even contradictory, and the comprehensive concept of globalisation are far from clear and well defined. Nevertheless, the concept of globalisation indicates that the various changes are somehow interrelated and creating new forms of interdependencies between actors, institutions and states. For the sake of this chapter , we stress the following tendencies within the overall force of globalisation:

— *the rise of the 'network' society*, driven by technological innovation and the increasing strategic importance of information, and symbolised by the expansion of the Internet;

— *the restructuring of the economic world system*, with the transformation to a post-industrial knowledge economy in the core, the emergence of newly industrialised nations, and the growth of new forms of dependency in the developing world; the rapid integration of the world economy with increasingly liberalised trade and commerce, resulting in new opportunities but also in relocation of production;

— *the political reshaping of the post-Cold World War order*, with strategic shifts in power balances and the emergence of new regions challenging the hegemony of the 20th Century superpowers, but also with increasing global insecurity and an endless list of regional and local conflicts;

— *the growing real but also virtual mobility* of people, capital and knowledge, possible because of new transport facilities, the development of the Internet and an increasingly integrated world community, but also provoked by the will among the hopeless to escape poverty, new mass migrations and refugees escaping war and insecurity;

— *the erosion of the nation-state* and its capacity to master the economic and political transformations, together with the weakness of the international community and its organisations, widening the gap between economic activity and socio-political regulation, and leading to unbound global capitalism but also to new international forms of crime;

— *the very complex cultural developments*, with on the one hand aspects of homogenisation such as an increasing cultural exchange and multicultural reality, but also the worldwide hegemony of the English language and the spread of commercial culture, and on the other hand elements of cultural differentiation and segregation such as fundamentalisms of various kinds (including new nationalisms), regressive tendencies, intolerance and a general feeling of loss of identity.

These forces and tendencies are not the only ones which define the social environment in which higher education has to operate at the start of the 21st century; reference has to be made as well to the demographic challenges, the spread of aids, endemic poverty or religious conflicts, just to name a few. Globalisation also means that institutions and even states no longer can give their own answers to all these challenges, but that they also have become interdependent in their policy-making processes.

Globalisation and Issues in Higher Education

Education, as a service industry, is part of globalisation process under the umbrella of General Agreement on Trade in Services (GATS). There is, however, distinct possibility that this might force countries with quite different academic needs and resources to conform to structures inevitably designed to service the interest of the most powerful academic systems and corporate educational providers breeding inequality and dependence. Globalisation can lead to unregulated and poor quality higher education, with the world wide marketing of fraudulent degrees or other so-called higher education credentials. While these are obvious problems, globalisation can also have advantages, particularly for India, which has a large educational system and infrastructure and diverse human capabilities.

Given the array of theoretical and epistemological perspective presented in the general social science literature on 'globalisation', it is difficult to assess not only the nature and dimensions of globalisation, but also what it might mean to the field of education. Very few educational researchers or theorists have attempted to make connections between the economic, political and cultural dimensions of globalisation and the policies and practices of education.

It appears as though the phenomenon of globalisation will mean many different things for education. Most certainly, in the near future, "it will mean a more competitive and deregulated educational system modelled after free market but with more pressure on it to assure that the next generation of workers are prepared for some amorphous 'job market of 21st century' It will also mean... "that educational system will increasingly provide the sites of struggle over the meaning and power of national identity and a national culture. And finally, schools will no doubt also be the sites of various counter-hegemonic movements and pedagogies"

Globalisation, though a recent phenomenon, is a reality, which cannot be wished away. It is, however, difficult to measure its long-term effect on the course of socio-economic development in various countries. In fact, because of the large disparities in the economic position of the countries inhabiting the globe, it would be imprudent to arrive at any standardised formula of assessing the effects. Each country is an entity in itself and requires to be studied differently. It is however necessary to stress that a thoughtless and unimaginative entry into the globalised market would not be in the best interests of the countries, particularly those, which are striving to grapple with the problems of slow economic and social development.

The impact of the various trends and challenges related to globalisation on higher education institutions and policies is profound, but also diverse, depending on the specific location in the global arena. There is a danger of generalisation and oversimplification when dealing with globalisation; diversity has to be recognised but also to a certain extent promoted. Nevertheless, an attempt can be made to define some general tendencies in higher education that in one way or another relate to globalisation:

Globalisation and Knowledge Society

Globalisation and the transition to a knowledge society seem to create new and tremendously important demands and exigencies towards universities as knowledge-centres. Scientific research and development of technologies are crucial activities in a knowledge and information driven society and will become even more important in the future. Not only in the core countries of the developed world, but increasingly also in other parts of the globe will research and development activities become the motor of economic growth and social development. Because there is a move away from the traditional scientific research paradigm and towards more 'Mode 2' oriented research, and because of the fact that also outside the fields of natural sciences research becomes strategically important for corporations and governments, the role and importance of science and technology will continue to grow. Since long, scientific research is intrinsically internationally oriented, but the internationalisation of research has accelerated strongly during the last years.

International communication (publishing, conferences, electronic networking) within the scientific community and quality norms for scientific personnel benchmarked to international standards have to be developed by universities that aspire the quality label of research universities. As a side effect of the globalisation of research and development, the academic profession itself becomes more mobile and an highly competitive international market of researchers is emerging, with organised migration of researchers and brain drain as one of the consequences. The new role of universities as 'knowledge centres' stretches out to other functions than science and research however. Universities are called upon to take up responsibilities in society and culture at large, to act as mediators in conflicts, to deepen democracy, to dynamise cultures, to function as centres for critical debate and ethical conscience. The high demands placed upon universities worldwide create tensions in institutions, and at the same time stimulate other organisations to engage also in those kinds of activities, sometimes with the idea in mind that traditional universities will not be able to meet those new demands.

Increasing Demand for Higher Education

Many observers expect an increase in the demand for higher education worldwide. In the developed world the knowledge society will ask for even more highly qualified knowledge workers. Economic development, modernisation and demographic pressure will fuel the demand for higher education also in other parts of the world, only limited by the inability of the poor to finance the cost of higher learning. Local institutions nor governments will have enough resources to deal with this massification of demand in many countries, leaving an unmet demand in the upper and middle classes of many countries in the ex-Soviet Union and the southern hemisphere to international and virtual providers.

The demand for higher education will not only grow quantitatively but will also become more diverse. Despite some decline in their value as credentials on the labour market in the developed world, traditional qualifications (degrees and diplomas) will remain the most important product of higher education institutions, but they will be supplemented by specialised programmes, vocational and competency-oriented training and modular courses adapted to a new lifelong learning demand, even if higher education institutions are not the main providers in these fields in many countries. In other parts of the world however, credentialism still is on the rise, sometimes leading to a kind of 'paper chase', fuelled by the (sometimes overrated) expectation that degrees and diplomas are the gateway to economic prosperity and social security by promising a job in the public sector.

New communication technologies and the Internet provide new opportunities for a more flexible delivery of higher education, thereby creating a new demand in some countries and meeting demand in others where traditional institutions are incapable to do so. All together, these developments underpin the assertion that higher education will become one of the booming markets in the years to come. This expansion and massification will not be matched by a proportional rise in public expenditure, leading to an increase in private and commercial provision and creating huge problems of access and equity.

Regulatory Issues

Internationalisation and globalisation lead to an erosion of the national regulatory and policy frameworks in which universities are embedded. Most modern higher education institutions are product of national developments and policies and are fully integrated in national educational systems. In an increasingly international environment—marked by a globalised and liberalised marketplace, globalising professions, mobility of skilled labour, an international arena of scientific research and academic personnel, and international competition between universities and between universities and other institutions and companies –, the national character of policy frameworks creates more and more tensions. Institutions already acknowledge this and are developing partnerships, consortia and networks to strengthen their position in the global arena.

Mobility programmes, such as ERASMUS/ SOCRATES or UMAP, and schemes such as the European credit transfer system have tried to stimulate internationalisation in higher education with full respect to the various national policy frameworks. Globalisation challenges this more or less voluntaristic policy and asks for more thorough international harmonisation of policy frameworks, higher education structures, degree systems and even curricula.

The process started with the Bologna-Declaration in Europe is a clear example of this, but in the context of free-trade agreements, like for example NAFTA or MERCOSUR, similar tendencies of international harmonisation of higher education systems exist also in other parts of the world. In the longer run this eventually will lead to the generalisation of the bachelor/master-degree structure, the hegemony of English as the lingua franca in higher education and scientific research, the development of compatible credit transfer and accumulation systems to recognise, transport and validate teaching and learning experiences, the international recognition of degrees and diplomas, a negotiated consensus on core knowledge and competencies and their place in curricula, especially in specific professional fields, etc.

Like in other social fields, globalisation will create resistance and counter tendencies in the field of higher education, asking for the recognition of the importance of the national language, the specific degree architecture, the cultural embeddedness of curricula, etc. Such tendencies are not always to be seen as retrograde or counter-productive to globalisation. Globalisation in higher education does not necessarily imply international standardisation and uniformity, but asks for policies balancing the global and the local.

To a large extent resistance to globalisation in higher education is also motivated by a rejection of the marketisation perceived to be inherent in globalisation and a defence of a 'public good' approach to higher education. However, many make the error to identify a 'public good' perspective towards higher education with an exclusively national policy framework. An international regulatory framework is needed to transcend the eroded national policy contexts and to some extent to steer the global integration of the higher education systems. Without such a framework the globalisation of higher education will be unrestrained and wild, generating a lot of resistance and protest.

Higher Education Market

One of the most visible manifestations of globalisation is the emerging 'borderless' higher education market. The huge increase in the worldwide demand in higher education, the budgetary and capacity problems of many nations to meet this demand, and the opportunities created by new communication technologies and the Internet, shape an environment in which new, mostly for-profit providers successfully can expand the supply of educational services. Universities from North America, Europe and Australia take initiatives to reach out their educational provision to this international higher education market, by active recruitment of international, fee-paying students to the home institution, by establishing branch campuses or franchising and twinning agreements with local institutions, or via distance education and e-learning and other transnational activities. The international demand for higher education has also invited new providers from outside the higher education sector to enter the scene.

The 'business of borderless education comprises various forms and developments; among which also combinations are possible, such as new for-profit private universities, corporate 'universities' media companies delivering educational programmes, professional associations becoming directly active in higher education, and companies with high training needs establishing their own training facilities. Many of these new providers extensively use the Internet as delivery channel; in some cases they develop into real 'cyber-universities' with a very limited physical presence. Drifting away from the old academic culture of traditional universities – and sometimes even openly questioning it –, and blurring the distinctions between academic, research-driven education and vocational training, they defy the age-old identity of universities.

In some niches, such as business administration studies, their substantial growth poses a direct threat to the market position of existing traditional universities, although in many other sectors of mass delivery of initial higher education degrees their capacity to compete with the publicly funded institutions is very limited.

However, in some countries, mainly in Eastern Europe, the former Soviet Union and the developing world, their presence even on this level is substantial, due to insufficient domestic public supply and the growth of demand in middle classes willing to pay for higher education. Although there are also less reputable initiatives and real 'diploma mills', the reaction of national governments and traditional universities in some countries to these new providers is sometimes exaggerated. To some extent their development even enriches the higher education sector, awakes innovation also in the old institutions and challenges productively the academic tradition. Still, important issues of access and equity on the one hand and quality on the other are raised by the global rise of private, for-profit higher education.

Commodification of Education

To begin it is helpful to distinguish between the rise of the market, 'with its insidious consumer-based appropriations of freedom and choice' and its impact on education, and globalisation. They are wrapped up—one with another—but it has been possible to talk of the marketisation of education without having to refer to delocalisation and the activities of multinationals. Now, that is increasingly difficult.

As we know, commercial concerns look constantly for new markets and areas of activity. In the last quarter of the twentieth century, and particularly in those states where neo-liberal economic policies dominated, there was strong pressure to 'roll-back' state regulation, and to transform non-market and 'social' spheres such as public health and education services into arenas of commercial activity. According to Colin Leys, such a transformation—the making of a market—entailed the meeting of four requirements:

- The reconfiguration of the goods and services in question so that they can be priced and sold.
- The inducing of people to want to buy them.
- The transformation of the workforce from one working for collective aims with a service ethic to one working to produce profits for owners of capital and subject to market discipline.
- The underwriting of the risks to capital by the state.

What we have here is a process of commodification—and the development of attempts to standardise 'products' and to find economies of scale. The expansion of higher education in Britain and Northern Ireland during this period, for instance, involved a the restructuring of courses and programmes so that they could be marketed. This included marketing new courses such as MBAs, modulisation, and the increased use of part-time and distance learning programmes. The introduction of student loans and course fees has raised, significantly, the direct cost placed upon students—and helped to change people's orientation to higher education away from that of participants towards being consumers.

The massive increase in university enrollment was, however, less a consequence of government policy, than the impact of changing perceptions of the labour market. The surge in student numbers occurred because it became clear to large numbers of people that *not* having a degree disadvantaged them in the labour market.

At a certain point in what had been a steady, slow expansion, large numbers of people started to feel they really had better get a degree, because not doing so would be such a bad move. The first wave set off another and so on.

There has also been a transformation of the labour force in higher education—and a growing orientation to profit generation. Salary levels have decreased significant relative to other key groupings; increased bureaucratisation and pressures on universities to reduce costs have reduced the time for 'scholarship and disinterested learning' and the doubling in the numbers of students per lecturer has led to a progressive decline in the quality of teaching and the satisfaction it gives to learners and teachers. Similar pressures can be found at work in other areas of education.

We have also seen some very significant movements towards corporatisation in schooling and non-formal education. In the 1980s and early 1990s this was initially carried forward by the rise of managerialism in many 'western' education systems. Those in authority were encouraged and trained to see themselves as managers, and to reframe the problems of education as exercises in delivering the right outcomes. The language and disposition of management also quickly moved into the classroom via initiatives such as the national curriculum. There has also been the wholesale strengthening of the market in many education systems.

Schools have to compete for students in order to sustain and extend their funding. This, in turn, has meant that they have had to market their activities and to develop their own 'brands'. They have had to sell 'the learning experience' and the particular qualities of their institution. To do this complex processes have to be reduced to easily identified packages; philosophies to sound bites; and students and their parents become 'consumers'. As Stewart demonstrated some time ago there is a fundamental problem with the way that such business models have been applied to educational and welfare agencies.

The real danger is that unthinking adoption of the private sector model prevents the development of an approach to management in the public services in general or to the social services in particular based on their distinctive purposes, conditions and tasks. The result has been a drive towards to the achievement of specified outcomes and the adoption of standardised teaching models. The emphasis is less on community and equity, and rather more on individual advancement and the need to satisfy investors and influential consumers. Education has come to resemble a private, rather than public, good.

As might be expected, such marketisation and commodification has led to a significant privatisation of education in a number of countries. In the United States, for example, schooling, higher education and training have been seen as lucrative markets to be in. Giroux reports that the for-profit education market represented around $600 billion in revenue for corporate interests. Over 1000 state schools have been contracted out to private companies.

In Britain education management, 'looks like it is about to become big business'. Educational Action zones have had significant corporate involvement. The Lambeth Zone is run by Shell, for example, not the local education authority. In Southwark, the education service has been contracted out to Haskins, and Kings Manor School, Guildford became the first state school to have its administration has been handed to a private company

Seeking to turn education into a commodity, framing it in market terms, and encouraging the entry of commercial concerns could be seen as simply an expression of neo-liberal politics in a particular state or area. However, we need to understand the nature of the forces that have pushed governments into adopting such policies—and it is here that we can see the process of globalisation directly at work.

Globalisation has impacted upon the nature of the agencies that 'school' children, young people and adults. The question we are facing now is, To what extent is the educational endeavor affected by processes of globalisation that are threatening the autonomy of national educational systems and the sovereignty of the nation-state as the ultimate ruler in democratic societies? At the same time, how is globalisation changing the fundamental conditions of an educational system premised on fitting into a community, a community characterised by proximity and familiarity?

At first glance it would seem that national governments still have considerable freedom to intervene in education systems. Government, for example, has significantly increased the scale of central direction and intervention through the use of national curriculum requirements, special initiatives and other, institutional means. However, as soon as we examine the nature of this expansion of intervention we can see that the overriding concern is with economic growth and international competitiveness—and that the efforts of politicians have been deeply flawed and their record dismal.

While there is some direct intervention in the governance of national educational systems by trans-national agencies such as the IMF and World Bank, the impact of globalisation is most felt through the extent to which politics everywhere are now essentially market-driven. 'It is not just that governments can no longer "manage" their national economies', he comments, 'to survive in office they must increasingly "manage" national politics in such a ways as to adapt them to the pressures of trans-national market forces'.

De-localisation and Changing Technologies

As well as conditioning the political context, globalisation has found expression in some very direct ways—via , for example, the de-localisation of schooling. Since the 1980s, there has been a degree of 'parental choice; within state schooling. It has been possible to choose which schools to apply to at both primary and secondary levels. While much primary school application is local, a significant proportion of secondary school application is not. This has both severed the link between locality and schooling and undermined the idea of community schooling.

A further degree of delocalisation has occurred as a result of scares around child protection and truancy. While schools might be local, access to the neighbourhood and of neighbours to the school has been restricted. The most visible signs are the security gates and fences that are part of the perimeter of schooling. Such measures inevitably strengthen the idea that the school is somehow separate from the community where it is located—and this is further intensified by the regime of testing and centralised curriculum construction that has been the hallmark of the education system since the early 1980s. There has been significantly less room for more local community-oriented explorations and student projects. As we have seen, the main forces framing the centralised curriculum are economic and directly linked to globalisation.

To these developments must be added changes in educational technology—especially the use of the internet and other computer forms, and the growth of distance learning. At one level these can be seen as an instrument of localisation. They allow people to study at home or at work. However, they usually involve highly individualised forms of learning and may not lead to any additional interaction with neighbours or with local shops, agencies and groups. They also allow people from very different parts of the world to engage in the same programme—and student contact can be across great physical distance.

The term adult learning has been substituted for adult education in many policy and academic discussions in recognition of these sorts of shifts and more recently there has been a major growth in attention to notions of lifelong learning. The shift may, as Courtney suggests, reflect a growing interest in learning, 'however unorganised, episodic or experiential', beyond the classroom.

There has been a fundamental shift in the behaviour of 'ordinary citizens', 'who increasingly regard the day-to-day practice of adult learning as routine, perhaps so routine that they give it little explicit attention'

Economic, social and cultural changes mean that many now live in 'knowledge' or 'informational societies' that have strong individualising tendencies and a requirement for permanent learning reflexivity. As a result, Field goes on to suggest, many adults now take part in organised learning throughout their lifespan; that the post-school system is populated by adults as well as by young people; and that 'non-formal' learning permeates daily life and is valued.

Typical of the last of these has been a substantial increase in activities such as short residential courses, study tours, fitness centres, sports clubs, heritage centres, self-help therapy manuals, management gurus, electronic networks and self-instructional videos. In these latter examples we can see an important aspect of the growing trans-national corporate presence in education and learning—and the extent to which profits are dependent on people continuing and extending their self-directed learning projects and activities.

Higher Education and Consumerism

There are many ways of making money from formal education, 'but the most widespread is the use of the school as an advertising medium'. The attraction is obvious—schools represent a captive market. Through the use of teaching packs, sponsored videos, advertisements on school computer screen savers and the like, large companies are able to bring their brand directly into the classroom. In so doing they are looking to gain a certain legitimacy as well as the raising general brand awareness. Schools also have the distinct advantage for corporates of organising their students along key demographics such as age and supposed academic ability—so it is possible to target advertising and marketing. The shortfall of funding for key aspects of schooling such as computing, sport and recreational and eating facilities: fast-food, athletic gear and computing companies have stepped in.

Many teachers and their managers remain 'deeply ambivalent' about the movement of commerce and advertising into schools. There is a belief that children need at least one 'commercial-free zone' Students in many northern counties are, generally, 'intense consumers'. They are prepared to and/or want to 'spend large amounts of money on brand names and fashionable and popular items'. However, while many may be critical of certain aspects of consumer culture, they are far less likely to be critical of consumption itself.

As educational systems become more marketised, colleges, schools and non-formal education agencies seeks to build relationships based more on viewing learners as customers rather than participants The main role of the teacher-turned-classroom manager is to legitimate through mandated subject matter and educational practices a market-based conception of the learner as simply a consumer of information. The result of this incursion by commerce, and the widespread seeping of managerialism, market-thinking and consumerism into the orientation of educators is a basic inability within many schooling systems and agencies of informal education to address critically questions around globalisation, branding and consumption.

Higher Education and WTO

Higher education is increasingly seen as a commercial product to be bought and sold like any other commodity. Higher education commercialisation has now reached the global marketplace. The World Trade Organisation (WTO) is considering a series of proposals to include higher education as one of its concerns, ensuring that the import and export of higher education be subject to the complex rules and legal arrangements of the WTO protocols and free of most restrictions. In the United States, the National Committee for International Trade in Education and a group of mainly for-profit education providers are supporting this initiative. The established higher education community, including the American Council on Education, is not involved in this undertaking.

The WTO initiative poses a severe threat to the traditional ideals of the university, as well as to the national and even institutional control of education, and therefore needs careful scrutiny. We are in the midst of a true revolution in higher education, a revolution that has the potential to profoundly change our basic understanding of the role of the university. The implications are immense and as yet little discussed or understood. It is especially alarming, but not surprising, that the U.S. Department of Commerce's Office of Service Industries is behind the effort to commercialise higher education in the United States and worldwide.

Higher education institutions everywhere are subject to global trends—massification and all of its implications, the impact of the new communications technologies, accountability of academic institutions to government, an increasingly international and mobile academic profession, global research networks, and other phenomena.

Many of these developments link academic institutions and systems globally. The use of English as the lingua franca for scientific communication and for teaching, especially when combined with the Internet, makes communication easier and quicker. The advent of multinational higher education institutions makes it possible to disseminate new curricular and other innovations quickly and to meet the immediate needs of students and the national economies of countries that lack adequate providers of higher education.

For centuries, universities were seen as institutions that provided education in the learned professions and scientific disciplines. Universities, as independent and sometimes critical institutions, preserved and interpreted, and sometimes expanded, the history and culture of society. In the 19th century, research was added to the responsibilities of the universities, followed a little later by service to society. Academic institutions were, in the main, sponsored by the state or the church. Even privately sponsored institutions were defined by the service mission. Higher education was seen as a "public good," as something that provided a valuable contribution to society and was therefore worthy of support.

Universities were places for learning, research, and service to society through the application of knowledge. Academe was afforded a significant degree of insulation from the pressures of society—academic freedom—precisely because it was serving the broader good of society. Professors were often given permanent appointments—tenure—to guarantee them academic freedom in the classroom and laboratory to teach and do research without fear of sanctions from society.

Today, trends such as the rise of the Internet and the globalisation of knowledge have the potential for creating severe problems for academic institutions and systems in smaller or poorer nations. In a world divided into centers and peripheries, the centers grow stronger and more dominant and the peripheries become increasingly marginalised. Inequalities grow more pronounced. There is little leeway for academic systems or individual universities to independently develop in the increasingly competitive and fast moving global higher education scene dominated by the world-class universities in the industrialised countries. The traditional academic center becomes ever stronger and more dominant–mainly in the English-speaking countries of the North (the United States, the United Kingdom, Canada) and in Australia, and in the larger countries of the European Union.

The norms, values, language, scientific innovations, and knowledge products of countries in the center crowd out other ideas and practices. These countries are home not only to the dominant universities and research facilities but also to the multinational corporations so powerful in the new global knowledge system. Information technology companies such as Microsoft and IBM, biotechnology and pharmaceutical firms (Merck or Biogen), multinational publishers like Elsevier or Bertelsmann, among others, dominate the new international commerce in knowledge, knowledge-based products, and information technology. Smaller and poorer countries have little autonomy or competitive potential in the globalised world. Globalisation in higher education exacerbates dramatic inequalities among the world's universities.

With the growing commercialisation of higher education, the values of the marketplace have intruded onto the campus. One of the main factors is the change in society's attitude toward higher education—which is now seen as a "private good" benefiting those who study or do research. In this view, it seems justified that the users should pay for this service as they would for any other service. The provision of knowledge becomes just another commercial transaction. The main provider of public funds, the state, is increasingly unwilling or unable to provide the resources needed for an expanding higher education sector.

Universities and other post-secondary institutions are expected to generate more of their funding. They have had to think more like businesses and less like educational institutions. In this context a logical development is the privatisation of public universities—the selling of knowledge products, partnering with corporations, as well as increases in student fees. The proliferation of private academic institutions of all kinds, especially in the for-profit sector, is another by-product of commercialisation. Education companies, some of which call themselves universities, sell skills and training, awarding degrees or certificates to customers (students). Research is seen as a fungible product rather than an inquiry conducted to advance the frontiers of science.

In these changed circumstances, it is not surprising that those motivated by commerce, in government and in the private sector, would concern themselves with ensuring that "knowledge products" are freely traded in the international marketplace. If these interest groups have their way, higher education in all of its manifestations will be subject to free trade discipline just like bananas or airliners.

The rules of the WTO, and its related General Agreement on Trade and Services (GATS), it must be remembered, are legally binding. There is a danger that regulations relating to higher education will be included in an international agreement "under the radar" and without much analysis. When something becomes part of the WTO regime requirements and regulations, it is subject to complex arrangements. The implications for higher education are immense, not only because of a new set of international regulations but because the university will be defined in an entirely new way: the overriding goal of GATS and the WTO is to guarantee market access to educational products and institutions of all kinds.

The trade in higher education is, of course, more difficult to codify than bananas. But efforts are now under way to do precisely this—to create a regime of guidelines and regulations to institute free trade in higher education. The WTO would help to guarantee that academic institutions or other education providers could set up branches in any country, export degree programmes, award degrees and certificates with minimal restriction, invest in overseas educational institutions, employ instructors for their foreign ventures, set up educational and training programmes through distance technologies without controls, and so on.

Educational products of all kinds would be freely exported from one country to another. Copyright, patent, and licensing regulations, already part of international treaties, would be further reinforced. It would become very difficult to regulate the trade in academic institutions, programmes, degrees, or products across international borders. Those wishing to engage in such imports and exports would have recourse to international tribunals and legal action. At present the jurisdiction over higher education is entirely in the hands of national authorities.

The questions raised by this initiative relate to the very idea of higher education and to the future of academe especially in the developing nations and in smaller countries. How would countries, or individual universities, maintain their academic independence in a world in which they had minimal practical and legal control over the import or export of higher education? How would accreditation or quality control be carried out? Would there be a distinction made between public or private nonprofit higher education—the "gold standard" for centuries—and the new and aggressive for-profit sector? Would wealthy profit-driven multinationals force other higher education institutions out of business? Would a full-time professoriate with claims to academic freedom survive? One thing is very clear—once the universities are part of the WTO jurisdiction, autonomy would be severely compromised and advanced education and research would become just another product subject to international treaties and bureaucratic regulations.

The greatest negative impact of WTO control over higher education would occur in the developing countries. These countries have the greatest need for academic institutions that can contribute to national development, produce research relevant to local needs, and participate in the strengthening of civil society. Once universities in developing countries are subject to an international academic marketplace regulated by the WTO, they would be swamped by overseas institutions and programmes intent on earning a profit but not in contributing to national development. It is not clear that accrediting and quality control mechanisms that now exist in many countries would be permitted, at least as they relate to transnational educational providers.

Every country needs to maintain essential control over its academic institutions. At the same time, individual universities need an adequate degree of autonomy and academic freedom if they are to flourish. For centuries, traditional universities have performed a central function in society. While that function has changed over time, it has not disappeared. The challenge of the new initiatives and globalisation generally is one of the most serious since the medieval universities faced the rise of nationalism and the Protestant Reformation in the 16th century. For almost a millennium, universities have defined themselves as institutions with a core educational mission and a common understanding of the values of academe. For much of this period, universities were understood not only as institutions that provided education in practical fields of knowledge but as central cultural institutions in society. In the 19th century, science and research were added to the academic mission. Universities were recognised as special institutions by society precisely because their goals went beyond everyday commerce. Now, all of this is under threat.

The academic community itself is in considerable part responsible for the changes. Some universities have all too willingly allowed themselves to be caught up in commercial activities and to compromise their traditional roles. The establishment of "for-profit" subsidiaries by such renowned institutions as New York University and Columbia University is symbolic of these compromises. Monash University, a well-known Australian institution, is establishing profit making branches overseas. The University of Chicago's business school has opened branches in Spain and Singapore. Universities in China devote much of their attention to providing profit-making consulting and setting up technology companies. Many universities have gone "on-line" to sell their courses and degrees to customers in all parts of the world.

If universities are to survive as intellectual institutions, they must pay close attention to their core responsibilities of teaching, learning, and research. Maintaining loyalty to traditional academic values will not be easy, but the costs of growing commercialisation are much greater.

Governments and other public authorities need to give the universities the support they need to fulfil their mission. Constantly squeezing the budget, demanding ever greater accountability, and insisting that the university fundamentally change its goals does not in the long run serve the public interest. The public must also respect the underlying values of higher education.

The developing countries have special academic needs that must be protected, and any WTO-style treaty would inevitably harm the emerging academic systems of the developing countries. Third World universities are now involved in many international relationships, but these arrangements are based on national needs and allow choice among programmes and partners.

The proposed WTO initiatives bring all of the pressures now being felt by universities worldwide into sharp focus. If higher education worldwide were subject to the strictures of the WTO, academe would be significantly altered. The idea that the university serves a broad public good would be weakened, and the universities would be subject to all of the commercial pressures of the marketplace—a marketplace enforced by international treaties and legal requirements. The goal of having the university contribute to national development and the strengthening of civil society in developing countries would be impossible to fulfil. Universities are indeed special institutions with a long history and a societal mission that deserve support. Subjecting academe to the rigours of a WTO-enforced marketplace would destroy one of the most valuable institutions in any society.

PRIVATISATION

Privatisation suggests a movement away from public financing and toward private financing. For higher education, the term includes a range of activities taking place on campus. Generally, in the name of financial necessity, colleges and universities cut services, undertake aggressive outsourcing, reduce the number of regular tenured teaching slots, and increase tuition. This takes place against a background of state-defined accountability standards as legislators take a more assertive role in setting education goals. Privatisation includes more centralised decision making, declining acceptance of academic norms, loss of faculty autonomy, and developing private funding sources.

The trend toward privatisation has been associated with an historical shift in the population served by higher education. Traditionally, colleges and universities were understood as experiences for an elite few, but, increasingly, they have become a normal part of the educational experience of larger and more diverse student populations. This evolution from elite to mass accessibility has resulted in higher education more closely resembling a public utility than an experience reserved for privileged elites.

The shift to higher education as public service has resulted in legislators treating it like any other public utility: they demand the most effective service at the most affordable price. The language used to define "effective" and "affordable" derives from a business model for generating value, where value is linked directly to short-term monetary gain. This redefines the traditional understanding of higher education's value, where value is linked directly to the long-term welfare of communities made up of informed citizens actively participating in the democratic process.

Privatisation increases the pressure on traditional higher education institutions to operate more efficiently, to pursue goals set by outside interests, and to market more aggressively. While such efforts can help an institution financially, they can also weaken collegial, knowledge-driven academic culture through the adoption of management practices more typical of business culture. Practices such as contracting out services and restructuring workforces represent market-driven attempts to control payroll, diversify and stabilise revenue, and shift costs to consumers.

Colleges and universities use outside vendors to provide a wide range of services. Most colleges indicate they are considering outsourcing even more services. The top five reasons colleges cite for contracting outside vendors include financial, quality improvement, equipment, human resources and staffing solutions, and safety/liability measures. Restructuring the workforce and controlling payroll. Most new full-time faculty positions in higher education are not tenureeligible.

Shared governance is a system in which those affected by the decisions participate in the decision making. In colleges, shared governance includes governing boards, administration, and faculty, with the participation of staff and students. This approach recognises the contributions and requirements of all members in a group consensus process. The results of this approach may include empowerment, equal partnership, and a vested interest in successful outcomes. This is at the heart of the academic tradition and supports the faculty's role in shaping institutional policies and programmes. Erosion of faculty participation in decision making is one possible result of restructuring the higher education *workforce.*

Diversifying revenue streams and stabilising income. In the past, education was place bound. With few exceptions, students had to come to campus to take classes, and colleges could count on maintaining the market because of the huge development costs necessary to build a new campus. That geographic protection is challenged by the maturation of computer technology and the Internet, making it possible to deliver college courses anywhere at any time.

More typically, technology supports a hybrid model of web-enhanced education that allows a college or university to rent a classroom, hire some part-time faculty members, and deliver a canned class at a very low price to whomever enrols. These colleges centralise library holdings, student records, student aid processes, and other administrative functions on a web-based system. The price of entry into a new higher education community is negligible.

The portable college can offer courses and programmes with a large potential enrolment, targeting students who otherwise might attend traditional colleges in the region. Many, but not all, such colleges are operated as for profit enterprises. They receive no funding from states, but utilise student aid packages to attract students. While portable colleges will not replace traditional colleges, they will and do compete for students among place-bound colleges. This new class of institution adds to the market pressures on traditional higher education institutions.

Contract training and other entrepreneurial efforts represent additional strategies, not only for diversifying revenue streams but also for stabilising income. These efforts include counteracting unpredictable state support by shifting the focus of institutions away from the core educational mission toward efforts at revenue enhancement. Again, the priority of economic objectives displaces the academy's traditional goals. The effect of shifting attention toward other revenue sources is to take time and attention away from the core functions of the institution.

Shifting costs to consumers. We are reallocating public funding for higher education away from support to institutions and toward individual student aid. The admissions office, business office, and student aid office have grown in importance on every campus, and business concepts and their expression—such as market share, efficient pricing, and the student as customer have crept into the enrolment conversation. Loans have increased as an overall share of the student aid package, which can serve to make students acutely aware of the need for immediate employment upon graduation to pay them back. Because it can affect students' institutional choices—as well as their decisions about whether to pursue a liberal arts education—this dynamic amplifies the increasingly market-driven character of higher education.

Forces spreading privatisation

The first force that is spurring the spread of privatisation in higher education is the rise of an information-based economy. Now the sources of wealth come from knowledge and communication instead of natural resources and physical labour, which once characterised the United States as an industrial society. This is a global rather than a national economy. The New Economy puts a premium on intellectual capital and the people who produce it. This means that the demand for higher education is expanding dramatically. Education is needed throughout a lifetime, and the marketplace for that education is international. This growth makes education appealing to the private sector.

Second, the demographics of higher education have changed substantially. Students above age 25, women, working adults, and part-time attenders accounted for most of the enrolment growth in the 1980s and 1990s. Less than a fifth of today's college students meet the traditional stereotype of attending school full time. For the new majority of students, higher education is not as central to their lives as it was for previous generations of students. Research shows they want a very different relationship with their college than students have historically had. They are looking for just four things: convenience, service, quality, and low cost. They are unwilling to pay for activities and services they do not use. What they are asking for is a stripped-down version of higher education minus the plethora of electives and student activities. They are prime candidates for adult-oriented, for-profit institutions, such as the University of Phoenix, which offer limited majors, few electives, and instruction by part-time faculty at convenient hours for students with great customer service in nearby locations in the suburbs and the business districts of our cities. They are also excellent candidates for for-profit or not-for-profit distance learning programmes that are available in their homes or at their offices at any hour.

Changes in the demographics of traditional students will also affect the future of higher education. The number of 18-year-olds is growing at the rate of more than 1 percent per year. However, the growth is occurring disproportionately in the South and the West. In addition, an increasing proportion of high school graduates are now attending college—currently 65 percent, compared with 42 percent in 1970. The result is a tidal wave of new enrolments coming to higher education and varying dramatically by state.

Third, higher education is being subjected to greater criticism than in the past on issues varying from low productivity and high cost to the quality of leadership and the inadequacy of technology use. This is an invitation to a private sector that rightly or wrongly sees higher education as the next health care industry.

A fourth force is the advent of new technologies, the nation's love affair with the Internet, and the growth of enormous capital for investment. Higher education is an appealing investment for the private sector. Not only is it perceived as troubled and slow to change, but it also generates an enormous amount of cash and its market is increasing and growing global. "Customers," better known as students, make long-term purchases lasting two to four or even more years, thereby providing a very dependable cash flow and revenue stream. Enrolment in higher education is also counter-cyclical, which is very unusual in a business.

College and university enrollments, translated as dollars, grow when the economy is bad because people are more likely to go to college when they cannot find work and to drop out at a greater rate when there are more jobs. On top of all of this, states and the federal government subsidise the higher education industry through their financial aid programmes. It's a terrific package. The results have been impressive. Venture capital firms with an interest in education are increasing substantially. Many major investment houses are developing higher education practices.

The convergence of knowledge organisations is a fifth force. Television and cable networks, publishers, symphony orchestras, public libraries, universities, and museums, among others, are all starting to engage in the very same activities. Each of these organisations is in the content business, whether that content is packaged as books, television shows, concerts, exhibits, or courses. What each is now attempting to do is to expand the audience for its content and the number and kinds of venues for distributing that content.

Finally, public trust in government has declined in recent years. The result is declining confidence in the non-profit sector and rising confidence in the for-profit sector.

Challenges of Privatisation

The twenty-first century has brought with it profound challenges to the nature, values, and control of higher educations. Societal expectations and public resources for higher education are undergoing fundamental shifts. Changes both within and outside the academy are altering its character – its students, faculty, governance, curriculum, functions, and very place in society. Crisis and change in higher education "have been the rule, not the exception." Nevertheless, current changes are transforming higher education to an extent perhaps greater than since the end of World War II. A common thread runs through these issues: challenges to the content of colleges' and universities' "social contract." These challenges are apparent in ongoing conflicts over public and private benefits of higher education, equity and merit, undergraduate and graduate education, "basic" and commercially oriented research, or institutional autonomy and public control.

States today have become "minority partners" in the colleges and universities that typically bear their names. On average, states now supply only a little over one-third of public colleges' revenues. Yet because these funds generally pay most basic instructional costs, such as faculty and staff salaries, state support remains critical to public institutions. Over the next decade, a combination of acute state revenue constraints, competing demands for state resources, and ongoing changes in public attitudes toward higher education will likely result in continued shrinking and unpredictable state support for higher education. Although many private colleges are also facing serious budget difficulties due to rising costs, market limits on tuition increases, reduced private giving, and declining endowment income, public institutions, which generally have less ability to tap private sources, will be hit harder.

Shrinking State Funding

Because higher education is the largest discretionary item in states' budgets, state funding for higher education tends to rise when the economy and resulting state revenues are good and to drop during recessions. Even during boom times, funding may be less than it appears once inflation and rising enrolments are taken into account. During the economic recession of the early 1990s, states cut higher education appropriations by amounts unequalled in constant dollars since at least

World War II, despite enrolment growth. In the late 1990s, state funding per student finally began returning to pre-1990 levels – only to be cut almost immediately during the recession early in the new century. .

Long-term prospects for state higher education funding are not favourable. Many experts believe that states' revenue problems will persist even after the economy improves because state tax systems are obsolete – for example, a growing percentage of economic activity is in non-taxed services and Internet sales – and because voter-imposed limits have made raising revenues more difficult. At the same time, an estimated 40-50 percent of state expenditures is locked up in mandated programme costs. These mandated costs are expected to increase, which already consumes about 20 percent of state budgets, as the rising numbers of the elderly require more health services. Also, state actions taken during economic boom times, such as tax cuts or implementation of popular new programmes, are hard to eliminate when the economy weakens.

In this environment of restricted revenues and mandated expenditures, higher education funding is a tempting target to cut, not only because it is discretionary but also because colleges, unlike many other state programmes, can tap other revenue sources, and because a growing proportion of the public believes that students should pay more of their college costs. Unpredictable state funding is equally problematic.

Unexpected cuts made during the academic year, after faculty have been hired, programmes put in place, and student fees set, leave institutions with difficult choices. Declining capital dollars for funding to construct, renovate, and maintain classroom or research buildings and campus infrastructure may be as big a constraint on institutions' ability to accommodate enrolment growth, recruit faculty, and conduct research as are state appropriations for operating expenses.

As institutions seek to offset declining state dollars, public colleges and universities are becoming increasingly "privatised." While the declining proportion of state funding at some institutions is due in part to success in obtaining more extramural grants and private donations as well as growth in auxiliary enterprises, nationally two-thirds of the change reflects the substitution of tuition and fee income in place of state support.

Many public institutions are themselves pursuing privatisation as a means to raise revenues or reallocate scarce state dollars. Some institutions are requiring that certain academic programmes, especially high-demand, high-return professional programmes like law or business, become fully or nearly fully funded by clients (students), business, or other private sources. Many law and business schools became fully self-supporting by 2004, and many other public research universities have been exploring similar moves; most already charged business, law, and medical students much higher fees than those charged other students.

Even teacher or school administrator training programmes have been privatised in some cases. While institution often want to use the state dollars "saved" for programmes less able to charge high fees, the result in some cases may be a further decrease in state funds. Institutions are pursuing other strategies as well. Many are expanding self-supporting part-time degree programmes geared to working professionals.

Community colleges and other institutions are expanding contract education programmes with specific businesses or industries. Both public and private universities have adopted commercial technology transfer and other for-profit collaborations with industry. Colleges and universities are "outsourcing" many institutional functions to private vendors or other education institutions, including operation of residential dorms, employment training, and even academic functions such as remedial education and beginning language instruction. University hospitals have formed partnerships with both nonprofit and for-profit health organisations. Other institutions have established shared-use facilities with private enterprise.

Consequences of state funding declines

State funding declines and resulting institutional strategies raise the following questions:

Access, success, and diversity

How will further tuition increases affect student access to and success in higher education? Unless sufficient need-based financial aid is provided, low-income students and historically under-represented ethnic groups may be excluded. Even if students and their parents are able and willing to pay higher tuition, some institutions and state policy makers facing fiscal pressures are preparing to cap or even reduce enrolments, despite growing enrolment demands.

Impacts on faculty

Over the next decade, many new faculty will be needed, both to replace the large numbers of expected retirements and to teach the growing numbers of students. How will conflicting forces of budget constraints and the need for new faculty affect how many faculty will be hired and for what types of positions? Although student/faculty ratios could rise—indeed, many faculty positions were eliminated during the recession of the early 2000s, primarily by not replacing tenured faculty and not renewing contracts for non-tenure-track faculty—new faculty will nevertheless be needed. In this environment, both public and private institutions may hire an increasing proportion of faculty who are ineligible for tenure, generally at lower salaries than tenure-track faculty.

Programme reallocations

In a more market-driven environment, will institutions respond by shifting programme resources toward fields that promise tuition-paying students high-paying jobs or that bring in more external research grants? To date, the impact of budget cuts on programmes appears largely unplanned. In some cases, disproportionate numbers of faculty positions in certain fields have been left vacant, leaving an imbalance between faculty expertise and institutional needs.

In terminating non-tenuretrack faculty, institutions have indirectly made decisions to reduce or eliminate programmes such as remedial education, beginning language courses, and teacher education, which often depend heavily upon non-tenure-track faculty. Repetitive across-the-board cuts have gradually weakened once viable programmes until they become obvious candidates for termination. However, as fiscal constraints continue, more institutions are intentionally reducing, consolidating, or eliminating specific programmes. State policy makers have at times been the driving force behind programme reallocations.

Over the next decade, humanities and social science programmes may be at risk if institutions implement budget systems that require departments to generate income equal to their costs. Or to generate revenues, these departments may increase both enrolments and teaching loads and reduce teaching costs by using more adjunct faculty. If so, this would exacerbate the difference, especially within universities, between a relatively low teaching-load and highly research-oriented science and engineering sector and a relatively high teaching-load and less research-oriented humanities and social sciences sector. If institutions are to prevent such imbalances from growing, they may need to consider reallocating scarce dollars to support important areas unlikely to be sustained by extramural dollars or high tuition. Where programmes are being eliminated, students should be given adequate resources or alternatives to complete their degrees.

Conflicting pressures on governance and control

Within the institution, budget constraints may lead to both greater centralisation and greater decentralisation of authority. Slaughter concluded that retrenchment "generally undermined faculty participation in governance and faculty authority over the direction of the curriculum." At the same time, institutional decisions to require academic units, especially professional schools like business and law, to become self-supporting through tuition revenues or private gifts and contracts tend to shift control from central administration to more autonomous units and to diminish adherence to institution-wide missions. At the state level, many states are demanding greater and more detailed accountability of diminishing state revenues, for example, over faculty workload, even as other states are considering reducing controls in exchange for reduced state appropriations.

Impacts on the higher education system as a whole

Will declining state funding, along with government or market limits on tuition, widen the gaps between the "haves" and the "have-nots" in the higher education system overall – between faculty and student resources at most public institutions and those at well-endowed private institutions, between elite and less elite institutions within the public sector, between tenuretrack and non-tenure-track faculty, or between science and non-science fields? The answer in many cases appears to be "yes."

Over the past decade, the gaps have grown between public and private institutions on a number of measures generally considered quality indicators, such as faculty salaries and student/faculty ratio, leading to questions about whether public institutions can retain past levels of instructional and research quality. This problem may be particularly severe at public two-year or four-year comprehensive institutions, which have fewer opportunities to offset declining state dollars with federal grants or private gifts. Another issue is the distribution of students among institutions. If tuition at public institutions continues to rise, will enrolments shift from public to private higher education or from four-year to less expensive two-year institutions?

In recent years some small shifts in these directions occurred. However, enrolment shifts to public two-year colleges assume that two-year colleges will have the resources to enrol more students and that students can afford their rising fees. If insufficient resources force institutions and students to make choices, non-traditional students, including returning adults and those whose initial preparation precludes admission at other institutions, may well be shut out of traditionally open-door community colleges.

Commercialisation

In the past 25 years, significant changes in the nature of scientific research have occurred. These include the development of fields and techniques not even imagined a quarter century ago, growing university/industry collaboration in the commercial marketing of research discoveries, increased targeting of federal research funding for specific projects, more political involvement in funding – and in prohibiting funding – of research in politically charged areas, and a movement toward "big science" projects involving hundreds of researchers and billions of dollars.

Between 1980 and 2000, industry funding for university research and development (R&D) in science and engineering grew much more rapidly than any other funding source, nearly doubling as a percentage of total university research dollars, from four to almost eight percent. Although this is a small percentage of total dollars, industry support plays a much larger role in certain fields, such as biotechnology and civil engineering. During the 1990s, pharmaceutical funding for university biomedical research shot up. At a time when there are concerns that the growing national deficit together with increased expenditures for federal defence and security may lead to reduced federal research funding, researchers may seek industrial sponsorship much more aggressively.

University/industry partnerships, where researchers in both sectors are jointly involved in research activities, have also grown dramatically over the past two decades. This trend reflects the increasing permeability of boundaries between the two sectors, as universities engage in more commercial marketing and as more new Ph.D.'s take jobs in industry but maintain ties with their former faculty advisers. One indicator of this is the growth in the number of university-based research centres with close ties to industry, which increased nearly two and one-half times between 1980 and 1990. Another indicator is the increasing proportion of articles co-authored by academic and industry researchers in fields such as engineering, as well as physics and clinical medicine. Federal and state agencies have further stimulated these partnerships by linking research funding to industry participation; as a result, even public funding takes on characteristics of industry sponsorship.

University/industry collaboration can provide additional sources of support for university research, access to a broader range of talent, and more rapid development and transfer of useful products like vaccines. However, such collaboration is also subject to potential problems. These include hindering the flow of research information and of graduate students' degree completion when industrial sponsors require researchers to delay release of potentially marketable results; suppressing undesirable results; and skewing research agendas toward corporate interests. Nor are these impacts limited to the hard sciences and engineering.

High-profile cases where corporations have provided millions of dollars to universities in return for prior review of and right to delay presentation or publication of results or for influence in setting the research agenda have raised concerns about bias and inhibition of research, as well as the use of universities' credibility to legitimise industry goals.

A still more problematic trend is the growing involvement of university researchers and of universities themselves in the commercial marketing of scientific and technological discoveries. During the 1980s, leading university researchers established or became associated with for-profit biotechnology and other "high-tech" companies based on their federally funded university research. Many universities have established for-profit technology-transfer units designed to speed the flow of scientific discoveries and products to the private sector and bring dollars to the institution. They have also encouraged spin-off companies based on faculty research and have acquired equity in the spin-off firms they generated. Universities have moved aggressively into securing commercial patents, especially in drug and other biomedical areas, as well as negotiating royalty and licensing arrangements with private companies.

Between 1993 and 2002, the number of patents issued to academic institutions increased almost two and one-half times, although two-thirds of these went to just 13 universities or university systems. These trends reflect the confluence of two developments: a growing eagerness of universities to exploit the economic potential of research activities conducted under their auspices and the readiness of entrepreneurs and companies to recognise and invest in the market potential of this research.

Many of these efforts suffered a setback when the high-tech "bubble" burst in the economic recession at the start of the twenty-first century. Nevertheless, despite strong faculty opposition in some cases as well as the limited success of these initiatives at most universities, they are likely to grow, especially during a period of limited state and federal funding, because they promise universities increased revenues.

Like industry sponsorship, commercial marketing of university research also poses threats to the research system, among them the possibility that it will create conflicts of interest for individuals and institutions, restrict the flow of information, increase the university's fragmentation into entrepreneurial fiefdoms, and shift power to non-academic personnel who typically control for-profit enterprises within the university. Critics also charge that commercialisation may further shift research priorities toward more marketable areas in science and technology fields, distort traditional academic missions, and replace science dedicated to the public good with the "privatisation of knowledge."

Changing Approaches to Higher Education

The governance and coordination of higher education differs enormously by public versus private control, type of institution, and state, and it differs within each of these categories as well. Historically, most higher education institutions had their own governing boards, although their powers and those of different campus constituencies varied widely. While most institutions and almost all private ones still have individual campus governing boards, most students and faculty now study and teach in institutions that are part of multi-campus systems, a few with hundreds of thousands of students. In addition, all but a handful of states have a statewide coordinating or governing board with some degree of authority or responsibility for all public post-secondary institutions in the state and sometimes for the state's private institutions as well. During the 1980s and 1990s, significant and sometimes unpredicted shifts in the powers and structures of governance or coordination at each of these levels – campus, multi-campus, and statewide – occurred. Political and budgetary forces make it likely that additional changes will occur in the next decade.

At the campus level, the past two decades have seen contrary movements toward more centralisation and more decentralisation of authority. College and university presidents and other top administrators have gained more authority to deal with budget pressures and external demands for accountability, and continuing pressures make it likely that this trend will continue. Simultaneously, a number of institutions have decentralised substantial control to individual schools and departments as a means to centre accountability in the units directly responsible for instruction and research, and more institutions are exploring this option. Some units, especially professional schools, have in effect been spun off from the larger university

Decentralisation and "responsibility-centered budgeting," which rewards entrepreneurship and priority setting, are creating new approaches intended to increase flexibility at lower institutional levels and, in some cases, enable resource reallocation to other institutional functions or units. These approaches, however, also raise questions as to whether university-wide missions and values will be maintained and whether departments that typically have not had the slack that comes with large amounts of external funding will retain their priority. Shared governance between trustees, administration, and faculty is another ongoing campus governance issue. At some institutions, particularly elite universities with long histories of faculty influence, shared governance remains strong. At these institutions, except in extraordinary cases, faculty in departments and through academic senate committees retain authority to make faculty hiring and promotion decisions, select graduate students, determine the curriculum, and with administration set the broad outlines for campus priorities and directions. However, some scholars argue that at many institutions faculty have become "managed professionals." Moreover, shared governance may be undermined in the future as the percentage of faculty who are not permanent increases.

Governance and structures of multi-campus systems are in considerable flux. As with campus governance, there are conflicting trends, and generalisations are difficult because the functions, powers, and integration of these systems vary substantially. In some cases they are loose collections of very different types of institutions. In other cases they are a set of relatively similar campuses with common admissions and faculty promotion standards, under a relatively strong system-wide board and administration. During budget crises, system-wide administrations have often been cut more extensively than those on the campuses.

Depending on their powers and traditions, system-wide governing boards and administrations have the potential to exercise broad leverage over their campuses through budget and programme review powers. Systems may act as buffers against political intervention or as channels for it. On the one hand, system boards and administrations may reduce campus autonomy and flexibility if they impose inappropriately standardised priorities or expectations. Systems also increase bureaucratisation and make shared governance more difficult to achieve. On the other hand, system-wide leaders can bring to bear broader perspectives on the overall educational needs of the campuses and the state. System leadership—boards, administrators and system-wide faculty committees—may be especially important in matters that have relatively weak campus constituencies but are important to the system or to the state, such as undergraduate general education, teacher education, or improvement of school education. They may also ensure that a last surviving programme in a particular field is not eliminated through uncoordinated actions by individual institutions. Especially during tight budget periods or under political pressure, system administrations may provide incentives for intercampus collaborations that individual campuses are unable to mount—for example, for programmes in less studied languages. How well these collaborations survive when budgets improve is uncertain, however. Moreover, where a system office does not exercise adequate quality control, other more political actors, such as the state's executive branch, may step into the vacuum.

5

Higher Education and the Pedagogy

School curriculum can now incorporate methods of reaching children of different learning styles as well as allowing students to convey their ideas in a context that suits their needs. Whether it is a spreadsheet, a web page or a multimedia presentation, it is creating meaning for and by individual students.

With the use of proper assessment such as electronic portfolios, learning logs, and teacher student interviews, both teacher and students are able to let learning happen in new and innovative ways. It no longer depends on the test scores, but the process of asking the right questions, contacting the right sites or people, and putting it all together in a comprehensive display of learning. It is very easy for students to take information off the Internet and call it their own.

Students are learning when technology is a tool and when it is a distraction. As a teacher, it is readily accessible to see how learning is taking place. It eliminates the focus of learning how to use computers and shifts the concentration to how to utilize computers as a tool to express a higher level of learning. There is no better way to provide professional development for teachers as they begin to see the potential of collaborative projects. It allows teacher to step out of the forefront and guide students in using technology critically to become life long learners.

Many teachers who are not familiar with technology have a fear of using the Internet as a teaching tool. With the accessibility of comprehensive online projects already prepared, complete with mentor support and step by step lesson plans, teachers will be more inclined to take the risk, as will the students. If the project is multifaceted, so is the outcome. Teachers can work closely with students and other educators to reach educational goals and standards. Teachers will then be inclined and encouraged to incorporate online projects into the curriculum.

With the numerous sites that match teachers up and mentor them through the process, there is little room for apprehension. A technology aware teacher can be paired with another teacher to complete a collaborative project together. Teachers can work as mentors to each other exposing new teachers to the wonders of learning with the Internet. Eventually teachers develop the confidence to create their own online projects to further the individual needs of each student. This is especially helpful in customizing the education for students with special needs.

With proper use of rubrics, assessment, learning logs, electronic portfolios, teachers can successfully manage and guide students to a higher level of learning. The Internet has been a crucial part of school curriculum and online projects have allowed teachers the structure and security to take the risks necessary to allow students to flourish in this online learning environment.

The Internet and collaborative online projects are changing education, assessment, professional development and our overall global connectivity. Online collaboration only opens the doors and minds of all involved the students, teachers and community. It is a shift in traditional teaching, but one that finally **allows** students and teachers to step out of the textbooks and connect with real lives and situations.

In many parts of the world, technology education is a subject area in transition. This has, and continues to be the case in countries such as America, the United Kingdom and Australia. Curriculum reform in technology education seeks to modify the workshop-based industrial arts tendency to focus on industrial hand and machine skills to a focus more concerned with critical and creative higher-order thinking skills.

These types of technology subjects are designed to respond to societal changes, such as those evident in many of the world's current post-industrial technological societies. The traditional pedagogy of workshop-type industrial arts subjects was, and in many cases still is, "show and follow", and it has been used to good effect in the building of student competencies, particularly industrial skills.

However, technology education's evolution is transforming the subject from one that requires students to imitate teacher-prescribed industrial hand and machine skills to one that is argued to be unique in the school curriculum. Technology education is evolving to become a subject that is concerned with an individual student's ability to solve real world problems by integrating specifically relevant knowledge of materials, technological processes, and systems.

Technology education students are encouraged to reflect on and modify their thinking through their involvement with some form of technological design-type process. For example, the National Curriculum for Design and Technology in the United Kingdom places importance on each student's ability to combine both the practical (hand skills) and theoretical (thinking skills) during their individual and group technological problemsolving activities by stating that students are expected to:

..learn to think and intervene creatively to improve quality of life. The subject calls for pupils to become autonomous and creative problem solvers, as individuals and members of a team. They must look for needs, wants and opportunities and respond to them by developing a range of ideas and making products and systems. They combine practical skills with an understanding of aesthetics, social and environmental issues, function and industrial practices. As they do so, they reflect on and evaluate present and past design and technology, its uses and effects. Through design and technology, all pupils can become discriminating and informed users of products, and become innovators.

The International Technology Education Association (ITEA) emphasizes the requirement for students to become technologically literate. All American states that promotes the development of technological literacy in students. One of the principles that guided the formation of these standards is the requirement for students to participate in "active and experiential learning".

The Technology for all Americans document states that:

> The technological design process involves the application of knowledge to new situations or goals, resulting in the development of new knowledge. Technological design requires an understanding of the use of resources and engages a variety• of mental strategies, such as problem solving, visual imagery, and reasoning. Developing these mental abilities and strategies so that they can be applied to problems is a significant aspect of technological literacy. These abilities can be developed in students through experiences in designing, modeling, testing, troubleshooting, observing, analyzing, and investigating.

The recent changes in technology syllabi (Australia), curriculum documents (United Kingdom), and standards statements (America) are requiring that teachers and students acknowledge and embrace a restructuring of the balance of instructional power. The technology learning environment is currently undergoing a transformation from one that incorporates predominately teacher centered teaching and learning strategies to one more oriented to student centered learning.

For example, the current Industrial Technology and Design Subject Area Syllabus (IT&D) in Queensland, Australia has been formulated in response to the Technology Key Learning Area Syllabus and emphasizes the requirement for teaching strategies that facilitate particular types of student- (learner) centered learning activities.

For both teachers and students in technology education, the traditional norms or expectations associated with teaching and learning are now changing. Students are expected to become more autonomous toward their learning, and teachers are expected to facilitate this type of student learning activity. However, an apparent paradox exists within the subject's transition, and this may serve to hinder the change of focus from teacher- to student-centered learning.

The paradox for both teachers and students is the necessity for teachers to demonstrate for students the safe and proper use of a range of hand, machine, and computer skills, as well as model for students a range of technological problem-solving skills. These types of skills provide students with the opportunity and facility to fulfill the various requirements of the technological design process, regardless of learning environment type.

For example, students participating in CAD lessons initially require some form of teacher exposition of the necessary skills to facilitate their competent use of the CAD program. Once known and understood, this knowledge serves to support student-initiated design and problem-solving activities within the same CAD learning environment. Similarly, more traditional workshop environments support students' procedural abilities, in terms of hand and machine skills, until students are adept at applying these previously acquired skills during their technological design activities.

Therefore, technology education as a subject area has not necessarily devalued the traditional hand and machine skills of workshop industrial arts-type subjects, but rather it has revalued these skills in conjunction with cognitive problem-solving skills to have particular significance within the technological design process.

For both teachers and students of technology education, the prescribed need to continue with teaching strategies that are associated with the norms of industrial arts-type subjects, creates tensions. These tensions occur as a result of changes in technology syllabus focus (i.e., from industrial skills to thinking skills) and the subsequent pressures these changes impose upon teachers and students with regard to the redistribution of learner and teacher pedagogic control.

It is not suggested that the skills-based curriculum constructed from the industrial arts syllabi of the recent past totally disassociated students from using thinking skills. However, it is argued that traditional industrial arts programs focused more on skills-based instruction, and that the current expectation is for technology education to focus instead on a student's technological problem-solving abilities using cognitive, hand, machine, and other skills provided by teachers or acquired by students directly for this purpose.

The need to develop both hand skills and problem-solving abilities requires technology teachers to walk a pedagogic tightrope. On the one hand, teachers need to develop in students a degree of manual dexterity in the use of materials and processes, using both hand and machine tools. These skills have been traditionally taught by a teacher-centered "show and follow" strategy, the most familiar and comfortable strategy for industrial arts teachers.

On the other hand, technology teachers need to facilitate with students the autonomous development of their own cognitive and metacognitive strategies when solving technological problems. These are created through their involvement with the technological design process. It is argued that these types of learning environments require a teacher-facilitated studentcentered pedagogy.

It is the balance teachers create between teacher-centered and studentcentered pedagogies within their technology classrooms that influences how students perceive the learning situation, and ultimately how and what they learn in technology education. Bell says that the issue of balance between student-managed (centered) learning activities and teacher-directed (centered) learning activities by stating that:

Learning is a dynamic process, and the location of the balance between teacherdirected and student-managed activities can likewise be expected to be always dynamic. The emergence of personal ownership of learning is the hallmark of a true student, and shifting the balance to foster the growth of such independence is perhaps the key challenge within teaching at this level. It is a challenge which must be approached sensitively as teachers recognise and respond to the needs of the individual. While the balance between teacher-directed and student-managed learning may not be critical, the direction in which it is moving for each individual certainly is. Learning partnerships develop as the strategies intermingle and the distinction between formal roles becomes blurred. In such partnership-centred learning the balance is found.

The concept of partnership-centered learning provides a more optimal teaching and learning strategy for providing the required dynamic balance between teacher exposition and student autonomy in technology classrooms. That is, as the technology learning situation dictates, teachers must adjust their teaching strategies from learner- to teacher-centered (e.g., from student autonomy to teacher exposition).

It is the continually adjusting learning partnership created between teachers and students that helps to facilitate the desired higher-order thinking outcomes of students (e.g., critical and creative thinking, problem solving, and decision making), which are said to be encouraged by the technological design process.

Cognitive Holding Power Concept

Aspects of cognitive theory in the form of Cognitive Holding Power were used to examine the relationship between students' use of procedural knowledge and the task environment in various technology classrooms. The Cognitive Holding Power (CHP) concept is defined as the press exerted by an educational learning environment, which causes students to utilize certain levels of procedural knowledge.

The press refers to the learning environments' influence on positive or negative goal attainment and is activated by the types of tasks with which students engage during their learning activities. Two factors that are interpreted as being most influential in terms of CHP are the teacher and the subject matter. The CHP concept is significant because it interprets a learning environment's influence on students' use of different levels of procedural knowledge.

Stevenson and McKavanagh interpret procedural knowledge in terms of hierarchies or orders. First order procedural knowledge is defined as knowledge of how to perform specific skills, much the same as the industrial skills that students in traditional industrial arts-type technology learning environments would be expected to perform. Second order procedural knowledge is defined as knowledge of how to apply problem-solving skills that assist with the application of previously acquired first order skills and conceptual knowledge to new and unusual situations. Second order procedural knowledge would be expected to be evident during students' technological problem-solving activities (higher-order thinking) in design process-based technology education classrooms. Third order procedural knowledge is defined as knowledge whereby judgments can be made as to the appropriateness of all other levels of knowledge in specific circumstances.

Of particular significance for technology education is the ability of the CHP construct to differentiate between learning environments that press for either first order procedural knowledge, learning environments that have first order cognitive holding power (FOCHP); or learning environments that press for second order procedural knowledge, learning environments that have second order cognitive holding power (SOCHP).

An instrument has been developed, validated, and found reliable in assessing learning environments relative to students' perceptions of the press for different levels of procedural knowledge. The Cognitive Holding Power Questionnaire (CHPQ) requires students to respond to 30 questions that relate to the amount of control students perceive they or their teachers have over their learning activities. Each question in the CHPQ requires students to respond to a five-tiered Likert scale, ranging from almost never to very often.

In Australia, each school's Head of Technology Education Department (HOD) rated his own department's teaching orientation as being either designbased, manual arts-based, or a combination of the two. In many Queensland high schools, the subject title "manual arts education" is used to define an industry-related subject area that in other parts of the world would be best recognized and defined as "industrial arts education."

The rating process was conducted in consultation with the researcher and therefore enabled good consistency of description among schools as to the characteristics that constituted a design, industrial arts, or a combined technology learning environment. Fundamental to how HODs described their school's approach, was the extent to which students contributed to their own learning within a design process curriculum.

These teachers (HODs), by their own volition, saw the difference between industrial arts and technology education as being one of student-centered learning (design/tech ed.) versus teacher-centered learning (industrial arts). The modification of the CHPQ was restricted to the changing of the questionnaire's title to the Technology Environment Response Form (TERF).

The student responses to the modified version of the CHPQ were tabulated and recorded using the Statistical Package for the Social Sciences. Means and standard deviations of student responses regarding FOCHP and SOCHP were analyzed with reference to school teaching orientation, year level, and gender. A study found that students interpreted an increased press for SOCHP relative to the extent of design-based teaching orientation in their technology learning environment.

That is, technology subjects with a design-oriented teaching strategy exhibited a superior mean result for SOCHP to that of both industrial arts and the combined categories. However, the mean results for FOCHP were consistent across all three teaching orientations. Results for SOCHP and gender and year level in design-based learning environments reinforce the previous mean results found for SOCHP and design-based teaching orientation. That is, students in design-based technology learning environments relative to age and gender perceive a higher press for SOCHP than do other forms of teaching orientation.

The cognitive activities of technology students in different types of technology learning environments indicate that students do experience an increased and significant, yet unsubstantial, press for secondorder procedures (higher-order thinking, e.g., technological problem-solving) in design-based technology classrooms. Results also indicate that students are equally pressed for first-order procedures (skill development) throughout all forms of the technology learning environment, regardless of that environment's design component.

This empirical research evidence regarding students' perceptions of their own learning activities provides support for the argument that design-based technology teachers are currently grappling with the need for some form of balance between teacher support (FOCHP) and student autonomy (SOCHP). It appears that students do perceive significant control over their learning in design-based classrooms.

The norms of current technology curriculum practice, which are rooted in teacher demonstration and exposition, continue to exist as a possible result of technology education's craft traditions. These norms may be causing design-based teachers to balance their instruction in the direction of teacher control.

Some study suggest that teachers do recognize the need to mix pedagogies in order to balance their curriculum. However, the changing emphasis within all forms of technology curriculum documentation from industrial skill development to cognitive skill development, dictates that the balance between teacher-centered and student-centered learning should now favor the direction of the latter.

It appears that design-based technology education teachers are currently adopting a more learner-centered approach to curriculum delivery, but are doing so while still maintaining a certain level of student perceivable control over what, how, and when students learn. These technology teachers may be placing more importance on the making (doing) phase of the design process in preference to (but not excluding) the thinking and planning stages.

Now in the subject's evolving history, it appears that students perceive the balance between teaching strategies as being only marginally weighted toward the more student-centered strategies of the design process. The lecture and demonstration strategies of industrial arts education still appear to have considerable influence concerning how students perceive control over their learning.

The historical roots of technology education in industrial arts education may be one factor that skews students' expectations toward learning in design-based technology classrooms in the direction of the traditional lecture and demonstration, teacher-centered approach. The possible consequence of students' expecting to learn in design-based classrooms through more traditional teacher-centered methods might be that teachers choose to teach to student expectations.

Teachers may feel that they are violating the currently accepted norms (lecture and demonstration) of learning and teaching in technology education by adopting more student-centered, problem-solving type pedagogies. In a study of creativity development and the design approach to learning in technology education, the perceptions teachers and students hold of each other have an effect on creative endeavors and thus on student higher-order thinking. Students do not feel that teachers model the processes involved in creative activity and are therefore not considered competent in this area.

In other words, instructional methods change from teacher-centered to student-centered learning, as the teacher deems appropriate. That technology teachers who adopt this type of instructional tactic are predisposing students to the safety inherent in the instructional norms of industrial arts, rather than to the potential risks associated with the more independent types of student learning activity found potentially within the technological design process.

In short, Curriculum reform for technology education teachers requires that they create with students a learning partnership, and that this partnership should promote learner autonomy. If students are to perceive a substantial level of control over their own learning, this partnership must favor student-initiated learning activity.

The inherent value of the concept of partnership-centered learning for technology education lies not so much in its yearning for pedagogic balance, but in the idea that traditional teaching and learning roles become blurred and that in the process, the direction of change (i.e., from teacher-centered to studentcentered) becomes of more importance for the individual student than the overall extent of any change.

Holistic Technology Education

A school that adopts a curriculum, that aims for a holistic understanding of technology, does so because it produces a better educated person than a curriculum which does not. Increasingly, more is asked of technology educators to be holistic in the understanding conveyed to learners of technology itself in order to make better informed technical and design decisions in a wider range of applied settings.

The ability of the learner to naturally consider social and environmental factors, for example, when seeking solutions is seen by some State education systems in Australia as fundamental to a genuine education in technology. In philosophy, the holist position asserts that to understand the particular one must understand its relation to the whole and that only through reflection of one's sensation based applications can genuine knowledge be critically affirmed.

The combined apparently independent paths of the State and the Holist positions set a compelling scene not only for the socio-economic necessity for holistic technology education in the curriculum but also for Technology's status as a key curriculum agent in the knowledge formation process of educated individuals.

The notions of holistic education are in themselves not new. However, what is relatively new in Australia is that expressions such as "holistic solutions" are entering new draft Design and Technology secondary school syllabi. There is a need to understand technology itself holistically in order to teach it with greater knowledge structure for learners. Redressing foundations for understanding technology itself is overdue in our rapidly changing societies and economies.

In addition to new school systems requiring students

to learn technology holistically, there are emerging signs that such understanding is also becoming a vocational attribute expected of employees. A desired capability is for employees to naturally be disposed to include social and environmental decision factors in their contribution to enterprise and production.

Holistic Understanding and Knowledge of Technology

There can be many approaches to understanding the technology phenomenon. A schema gives teachers a framework to evaluate just how holistic a lesson or curriculum is and can help a teacher decide what educational tasks to include and how to construct the educational context and experience that will foster holistic understanding in technology and design.

The premise that holistic technology education is a necessary, rather than desirable, outcome of schooling. The classical holist position in education may be illustrated as follows:

— To know things is to know things in relation;

— To know a part is to know how it connects with the whole.

In the process of codification, different impressions of the same object or process are utilized so that interrelations might be recognized. It is the total vision which we call knowledge.

Many teachers would argue that they already teach technology holistically. Phenomenology of technology and knowledge development allows a teacher to use a basic principles approach to formulate a universal schema or cognitive framework. With basic principles, a teacher can indeed determine what to include in lessons and evaluations to ensure reasonable holistic coverage of any technical education.

Surprisingly, that technology education and practice are not only a how-to experience, but significantly a know-why experience. The latter is fundamental to the human act of creating new knowledge itself, not just using knowledge. Know-why capability is important for principles development. It fosters the reason why for things in many settings, accommodating both the benefit of situational learning while also enabling learning transfer or innovation to occur.

Holistic education in technology enables transfer of understanding to novel lifelong encounters, a quality lacking in much of how-to training in technology particulars. Curricula and pedagogy that normally segregate knowing and doing raise substantial educational concern and have so for many years. For Dewey,

A divided world, a world whose parts and aspects do not hang together, is at once a sign and a cause of a divided personality. When the splitting up reaches a certain point we call the person insane. A fully integrated personality, on the other hand, exists only when successive experiences are integrated with one another. It can be built up only as a world of related objects is constructed.

Dewey was quite strong on this issue. We need to show how things are interconnected as necessary interdependencies to give the technology or technique meaning to students. This highlights the importance of holistic education. A segregated education for Dewey was not an education:

On the intellectual side, the separation of 'mind' from direct occupation with things throws emphasis on things at the expense of relations or connections...[Education] must find universal and not specialised application.

Dewey's work clearly opens one of the differences

between technology education and technical training. the latter being geared to vocational, specialized short-term task skills; the former, lifelong human capability. Our interest is in technology education that shows us the basic principles for teaching technology holistically: the interconnectedness or dependencies of technologies.

Praxis in Technology Education

The road from dialectics to praxis is an interesting one for technology educationists because it addresses twists and turns (even head flips) from knowing as an essentially theoretical (idealistic) process to a social-material (surprisingly design- and technology-like) process. Hegel, a German idealist philosopher was an idealist because for him, thought does not merely correspond to reality; it produces reality: our thoughts are our reality and so all knowledge can be formulated through pure reason.

"Dialectic" was Hegel's name for the pattern that logical thought must follow. Broadly, he argued that conscious thought proceeds by way of contradictions. Its process is by triads, where each triad consists of thesis, antithesis, and synthesis. The concept of "sharp" is not adequately understood without reference to an alternative "blunt." Both the thesis concept of sharp and the antithesis concept of blunt define each other and therefore require each other.

Each concept as related, as mutually defining, is their synthesis. At this moment a new level of reasoned understanding is achieved. Put another way, a person starts with a proposition, the thesis; this is consciousness as "understanding" and proves to be inadequate by itself. The person's mind must therefore generate its alternative, the antithesis. However, this on its own also proves inadequate.

The resolution of the opposites, therefore, requires

that they be combined into a synthesis. This is the level of conscious thought, or reasoned understanding. From here, the whole triadic process may be repeated, the synthesis leading to a new thesis, and so on. The essence of Hegel's dialectics is "the grasping of opposites in their unity", a significant first step in building our basic principles for holistic technology education.

Important to Hegel's philosophy of dialectics is that "knowing" for him begins, proceeds, and ends at the level of ideas. For him, matter is a product of mind, rather than mind being the highest product of matter. All our knowledge comes from pure theoretical reasoning. Feuerbach is important because his view of knowing and understanding introduced material objects as a necessary, not merely desirable, condition for knowledge. This revelation further builds our basic principles for holistic technology education. Experiences from the environment outside the mind are now significant.

Marx was regarded by some as more of a social theorist, interested mainly in economics and history than in any particular philosophical doctrine. Essentially Marx, too, inverts Hegel's idealism. He extracted and supported Hegel's notion of dialectics, but rejected his idealist approach. He supported Feuerbach's inversion of Hegel, but differed from his concept of materialism in terms of the central notion of human practice, specifically the social dimension of practice.

Marx rejected Feuerbach's relation between subject and object in which the subject is passive and contemplative, restricting himself to receiving or reflecting reality. Here, knowledge was simply the result of the actions of objects in the external world and their effects upon the sense organs.

Marx, therefore, identified the strengths and weaknesses of Hegel's idealism in dialectics and

Feuerbach's passivity in materialism. Marx attempted to resolve the problems of idealism and materialism in his system of historical materialism, the central concept of which focuses on the practical interaction, which must occur between a person and his/her material and social environment.

In parallel with Hegel's dialectics, the synthesis of people and their environment, via practical human socially contextualized activity, meant that a new level of awareness was achieved. It is significant to divert slightly at this point to bring in a key notion that centres the importance of technology learning to a society. Technology is not the slave of science nor the neutral tools in designing. Rather, technology is one of their full and equally rich symbionts and plays an active role in knowledge formation!

Marx departed from Hegel and Feuerbach by the importance he places on actual human labor or practice. He adopted a dialectic methodology in that he contrasts and identifies the inadequacy of "pure" idealism and "pure" materialism; he synthesized the two at the new level of historical materialism. This introduces the importance of time. The applied setting is subject to evolutionary influences.

Both theory and practice in the applied setting are resolved best, according to Marx, via human material practice in social and historical context. Marx's thesis of historical materialism is essentially the foundation of praxis. Praxis and technical activity concern the effect of instruments and tools in the human transformation experience. Praxis, so far has been concerned with practical human activity and the interaction of mind and matter, or human and environment.

Ihde acknowledged that technologies need to be understood in context and in purpose of application. That is, different kinds of technologies and tools transform our knowledge differently. Also, the same tools and technologies placed in different "world" settings transform our knowledge differently, including the same tools/technologies in different social and/or material environment settings, that is, different world settings.

This is significant because it raises the necessity for understanding that both choice and design of tools and choice and design of world settings alter our knowledge. Technologies are context sensitive- a key notion in technology choice, transfer, and innovation diffusion. Designs of tools and environments are socially and environmentally interdependent.

To present technology teaching and learning as value- and context-neutral is to misinform the learner. The ability of the learner to naturally consider social and environmental factors when seeking solutions to design and technical challenges is fundamental to a genuine education in technology. Human, tool, and environment in an applied setting are the minimum elements of any technological activity.

Each element is a resource and constraint, and each require the other to define their value in the applied setting. The elements are interdependent. Technology cannot be reduced to less than these general elements and as such, technology is their product. We therefore may need to understand and teach these elements and their dependent relationship explicitly.

What develops as important in lhde's work is the notion that praxis, though necessarily producing artifacts from the human-environment interaction, must increasingly include artifacts as a mediator in the interaction. To teach any technical process, to evaluate technologies, or to make design decisions that ignore this interdependent schema of human, artifact/tool, and environment is indeed not an education in technology.

The basic principles of holistic technology education now appear to have structure, a structure articulated elsewhere as technacy education. When teachers instinctively claim that they include social (human) factors, technical (tool) factors, and environmental (material) factors in their lessons for specific applied settings, they indeed have good reason to believe their pedagogy is heading toward being holistic.

However, this coverage cannot be delivered in a general way. It is important to present the interconnections in explicit detail highlighting necessary and specific dependencies that make sense. A key requirement is to set learning experiences and assessment tasks for each lesson and unit of work that not only address highly specific links that define the elements in relation to each other, but also their total effect as a design and technology solution in the applied setting. In a very real sense, technology is the product of the schema interacting to satisfy a need or an aspiration.

Teachers who seek justification for deciding what may constitute the minimums of holistic solutions in design and technology may refer to the schema proposed here. A holistic understanding of technology develops through structured or enabling-learning experiences that make explicit, in detail, the interconnectedness of human, tool, and environmental factors, where these three factors mutually require and define each other and act as both resources and constraints in the applied setting.

The schema gains strength through historical examination of the nature or phenomenon of technological activity where not only are all three factors defined by each other, but design and technology experiences, if taught holistically, as interconnected, are a condition to new knowledge creation. Technology education is not merely a know-how, but necessarily must be understood and presented in the curriculum to learners as a know-why subject.

**Effective Educational Practices

Distance Learning

Distance Learning is becoming a major issue in education and in strategic planning for regional development. To the college administrator it is a possible source of an entirely new model for deploying resources for students. For businesses it is both a way of changing the traditional methods used to teach skills and a possible new source of profitability. For multinational organizations like the United Nations Development Programme (UNDP) or the World Bank, Distance Learning may have the potential to deliver the precious resource of knowledge to some of the most destitute countries of the earth, while at the same time stimulating the growth of fledgling telcom infrastructures.

Distance Learning is a significant topic in Information and Communications Technology (ICT) discussions because it is both a medium and a metaphor. As a medium, it promises to deliver knowledge to the poorest countries and as a metaphor it connotes the harnessing of many ICT capabilities in a noble cause what Alfred Bork calls "a new learning paradigm." For those who view education as the most important priority for the world's poorest countries, Distance Learning is perhaps the most significant method for accomplishing a miraculous, leapfrogging transformation. Even in the continent of Africa, which, by any standard, is among the world's poorest regions in ICT and especially Internet deployment, there are scores of significant attempts to implement Distance Learning. The Japan International Cooperation

Agency (JICA), a significant donor in developing countries, sponsored Distance Learning in Africa last year and found an abundance of Distance Learning programmes being initiated and managed, even in some of the world's most destitute countries. These programmes use all the technologies that are normally associated with Distance Learning: correspondence courses, radio, television, telephone, Internet, telecenters, CDROM and satellite broadcasting.

Despite the proliferation of Distance Learning applications worldwide, there has been a problem in comparing results of technology-assisted instruction with traditional methods, even in the most developed countries. The Institute for Higher Education Policy, supported by the American Federation of Teachers and the National Education Association, examined Distance Learning in the United States and concluded, "there is a paucity of true, original research dedicated to explaining or predicting related to distance learning." This finding seems improbable since there have been thousands of studies comparing Distance Learning with "traditional" teaching. Yet most of these studies have been found to be flawed statistically, either not controlling for extraneous variables, or use subjects that are not randomly selected, not controlling for reactive effects, etc.

The literature on Distance Learning implementation in developing countries, like that in the United States, is characterized by a paucity of data about assessment and cost. Even the great multilateral organizations, like the World Bank and UNDP, seem reluctant to do economic outcomes measurements that could guide effective implementation. From the perspective there are two very simple dimensions that can and should be used in developing policy level decisions about Distance Learning investment. The first is total programme cost. Programme cost includes all the materials, technology, advising, infrastructure, rent, travel, software and hardware, etc., that must be paid by an organization or donor to achieve the desired result.

Several viable cost models exist to facilitate this computation. The second variable is yield—the aggregate result or outcome that was obtained for the investment. Yield can be measured in graduation rates, new approaches developed for further improvement, job success after training, etc. Romania developed a four-step approach for measuring the yield of technology courses using a traditional model widely employed by large global businesses. The methodologies exist but organizations seem unwilling to employ them.

Five Distance Learning approaches are positioned on an x-y graph. The ideal case is an approach that has low cost and high yield, the upper left segment of the graph. The least valuable case is in the lower right part, where high costs are accompanied by low effectiveness. Correspondence courses are positioned on the graph as being the best mix of cost and yield. This form of Distance Learning has been used since mid 1800's and is still highly effective in poor countries. Despite the difficulties of postal systems and the delays in lesson transmission, correspondence courses are widely employed. In the middle of the cost/ yield continuum are the combination of correspondence with TV as well as with and radio and Internet/ CDROM. Each of these has its own strengths and weaknesses.

Radio is the dominant electronic communications device in the world, but is sometimes cumbersome to use in distance education without adequate recording systems. TV is also popular but not as available as radio. Most African countries, for example, have several hundred radio receivers per 1000 inhabitants but less than a third of that for TV. CD-ROM has the advantage of combining the best of WWW and audio, but the disadvantage of requiring computer skills and culture. The yield of virtual universities in developing countries is relatively low, compared with the cost. Virtual universities are expensive, require good bandwidth, and need an ICT infrastructure that is daunting, even for a developing nation.

While this method is ideal from a theoretical perspective, it is not likely to deliver results proportionate to its cost for a decade or more. The most successful private virtual university in the US, University of Phoenix, has market-driven entrance requirements; i.e., students must be over 21 and have a job. Africa has approximately one-fifth of one percent of the world's Internet host sites. Many of the poorest countries of Asia show Africa-like numbers, too, since over half the Asia totals are due to one country: Japan. (China is emerging rapidly-with over 20 million Internet users.) Even in the regions where bandwidth and host site numbers are exceptional, as in the US, Britain, Finland and Netherlands, the kinds of user services needed for synchronous or asynchronous Internet availability around the clock are still not adequate to provide broadband service to a large population. So even the Inter-net-rich countries do not have sufficient broadband service. Courses, to some Internet-based courses, and ultimately to completely virtual universities. An example can be found in the experience of China in leveraging the potential benefits of Distance Learning.

The evolution of culture, infrastructure, technology, content and deployment has led to extremely rapid developments. The diffusion of the Internet in China in business and government has been closely linked to the rise of Distance Learning at Chinese universities. China has experienced two generations of technology-assisted Distance Learning. The first is broadcast/TV-based

Distance Learning, which has led to China having the largest education network in the world. This network consists of the Central Radio and TV University (CCRTV), forty-four Provincial TV Universities (PTVU's) and thousands of branch schools and study centers. Over one hundred million Chinese are currently receiving training or further education through special television channels, and as of 1997, more than two million Chinese had received university diplomas from these TV universities.

Since less than one in ten graduating high school students has a chance to enter college, there is increased demand from that population to matriculate through technology-based means if the campus-based curriculum is not offered. Another large demand comes from students who are already matriculated, including those in colleges, high schools and primary schools. Millions need help with tutorials, focused learning in a specific area of specialization or the opportunity to take a course not offered at their school or region. A recent studies of China's Internet Development found that country-wide there were 22.5 million people online, 69 percent of whom used dial-up connections. About 60 percent of these users were between 18 and 30 years of age. Of six main Internet Service Providers in China, one, CERNET, has been designated as the primary provider for the academic community and is offering links in the 500 kilobits-per-second range.

China approach as an exemplar. Distance Learning is destined to become a major contributor in the implementation of new models of teaching, worldwide. The Chinese experience may be highly valuable as a pointer toward the ideal approach. China has made effective, sequential use of all the predecessor Distance Learning methodologies, from correspondence courses to radio, TV, CDROM, Internet and World Wide Web and is poised to leverage that experience into a significant use of virtual universities. This suggests several points that may be appropriate for developing countries that are not as successful so far as China has been. Move slowly up the technology curve. The example of virtual universities trying to succeed in Africa in spite of the severely limited Internet technology infrastructure is a reminder that the predecessor Distance Learning technologies need to be mastered and ramped up before attempting to leap to higher technology levels Invest more in people than in technology. In developing countries the budget allocations often are tilted toward equipment, infrastructure and content. A higher overall yield is possible if the major investment is in facilitating users to become fully indoctrinated and conversant with the ICT milieu, thereby assuring the highest return on technology investments.

Place strategy before structure. Often the acquisition of a technology comes before the rational process of planning for its use. A maxim taught in business schools is that the structural decisions, like buying teleconferencing facilities, should be preceded by a strategic agenda, which can result in more rational and efficient use of any technology. Such a process would probably deter the early implementation of a virtual university in a poor country until there had been much more careful migration up the technology curve.

E-Learning

There is no doubt that the use of e-Learning is increasing in both the educational and corporate sectors. Most recent data from one of the top learning management system providers (WebCT) indicates that it is working with nearly 2,500 institutions in 81 countries (although by far the majority are in the USA, Canada, UK and Australia). These vary from fully online institutions such as the University of Phoenix to traditional universities including the October 2002 alliance between Stanford, Princeton, Yale and Oxford to provide courses for their alumni to the OpenCourseWare Initiative launched by MIT in April 2001. There have been many success stories related to online education and some failures.

The cost implications for universities vary considerably on the scale and on the quality of the course content. One source indicated that a fully Virtual University for 2,000 students costs in the order of US$15 million (personnel, computers, location). An individual course costs between US$50,000 to US$500,000 for advanced systems. For instance, one traditional university estimated that extension courses cost from US$10,000 to 20,000 after an initial infrastructure investment of US$500,000. For the corporate sector, Forrester, an independent research firm that helps companies assess the effect of technology change on their operations, interviewed training managers at 40 Global 2500 companies and found that all but one of them already had online initiatives in place. Around 500 training directors clearly shows the new priorities:

— Sixty percent had an e-Learning initiative.

— Eight-six percent had a priority of converting current instructor-led sessions to learning.

— Eighty percent will set up or expand knowledge-management programmes.

IBM saved US $200 million in 1999, providing five times the learning at one-third the cost of their previous methods. Using a blend of Web-based (80 percent) and classroom (20 percent) instruction, training costs by 35 percent while improving consistency and scalability.

Many other success stories exist. However, it is also true that some firms that have spent large amounts of money on new e-Learning efforts have not received the desired economic advantages.

While some studies show greater benefits in favour of face-to-face delivery, research results consistently demonstrate superior benefits of e-Learning in general. In addition to higher performance results, there are other immediate benefits to students such as increased time on task, higher levels of motivation, and reduced test anxiety for many learners. While the majority of the 49 studies they examined no significant difference between e-Learning and traditional classroom education, nearly 30 percent of the studies that e-Learning programmes had positive outcomes based on student preference, improved grades, higher cost effectiveness, and a higher percentage of homework completion. It is not hard to find learner enthusiasm for e-Learning.

The majority of 1,002 students who responded to an e-college.com survey said they chose the online format because of the flexibility and convenience of the programme. More and more data is being gathered on how trainees feel about the use of e-Learning technologies. For example, the following results were obtained from an ASTD-Masie Center study involving the experiences of more than 700 e-Learners:

- — Eighty-seven percent preferred to take digital courses during work hours
- — Fifty-two percent preferred e-Learning in a workplace office area
- — Eighty-four percent would take a similar e-course if offered again

— Thirty-eight percent said they generally preferred e-Learning to classroom training.

E-Learning offers an alternative for capacity development that is cost effective, convenient and effective. It presents the possibility of bringing educational alternatives to regions and learners that otherwise would not have access to them locally. It also fosters the creation of a worldwide network of trainers, practitioners and experts in the field, in this case of environment and human development. Essentially, universities would continue as research centres and degree-granting bodies, but a student's education would be more fluid in time and place.

Direct Teaching

Many studies show that direct teaching can be effective in promoting student learning. The process emphasizes systematic sequencing of lessons, a presentation of new content and skills, guided student practice, the use of feedback and independent practice by students. The traits of teachers employing effective direct instruction include clarity, task orientation, enthusiasm and flexibility. Effective direct teachers also clearly organize their presentations and occasionally use student ideas.

The use of direct teaching can be traced to the turn of the last century; it is what many citizens and parents expect to see in classrooms. Done well, it can yield consistent and substantial results. Wholeclass teaching of diverse groups may mean that lessons are too advanced for slower students and too repetitive for the quick. In the last decade or two, moreover, theorists have tried to transfer more control of lesson planning and completion to students themselves so that they 'learn to learn', as several subsequent practices exemplify. Six phased functions of direct teaching work well:

1. Daily review, homework check and, if necessary, reteaching;
2. Presentation of new content and skills in small steps;
3. Guided student practice with close teacher monitoring;
4. Corrective feedback and instructional reinforcement;
5. Independent practice in work at the desk and in home-work with a high (more than 90%) success rate; and
6. Weekly and monthly reviews.

When teachers explain how new ideas in the current lesson relate to ideas in previous lessons and other prior learning, students can connect the old with the new, which helps them to better remember and understand. Similarly, alerting them to the .learning of key-points allows them to concentrate on the most crucial parts of the lessons.

Advance organizers help students focus on key ideas by enabling them to anticipate which points are important to learn. Understanding the sequence or continuity of subject-matter development, moreover, can be motivating. If students simply learn one isolated idea after another, the subject-matter may appear arbitrary. Given a 'mental road map' of what they have accomplished, where they are presently, and where they are going can avoid unpleasant surprises and help them to set realistic goals. Similar effects can be accomplished by goal-setting, overviewing and pretesting before lessons that sensitize students to important points and questions that they will encounter in textbooks and will be presented by teachers.

It may also be useful to show how what is being learned solves problems that exist in the world outside school and that students are likely to meet in life. For example, human biology that features nutrition and its implications for food choices is likely to be more interesting than abstract biology. Teachers and textbooks can sometimes make effective use of graphic advance organizers. Maps, timetables, flow charts depicting the sequence of activities, and other such devices may be worth hundreds of words.

In the 1980s, cognitive studies on teaching sought ways to encourage self-monitoring, self-teaching or 'meta-cognition' to foster achievement and independence. Skills are important, but the learner's monitoring and management of his or her own learning have primacy This approach transfers part of the direct teaching functions of planning, allocating time and review to learners. Being aware of what goes on in one's mind during learning is a critical first step to effective independent learning. Some students have been found to lack this self-awareness and must be taught the skills necessary to monitor and regulate their own learning. Many studies have demonstrated that positive effects can accrue from developed skills.

Students with a repertoire of learning strategies can measure their own progress towards explicit goals. When students use these strategies to strengthen their opportunities for learning, they simultaneously increase their skills of self-awareness, personal control and positive self-evaluation. Three possible phases of teaching about learning strategies include:

1. Modelling, in which the teacher exhibits the desired behaviour;
2. Guided practice, in which students perform with help from the teacher; and
3. Application, during which students act independently of the teacher.

As an example, a successful programme of 'reciprocal teaching' fosters reading comprehension by having students take turns in leading dialogues on pertinent features of texts.

Tutoring

Tutoring gears learning to student needs. It yields particularly large effects in mathematics-perhaps because of the subject's well-defined sequence and organization. If students fall behind in a fast-paced mathematics class, they may never catch up unless their particular problems are identified and remedied. This individualized assessment and follow-up process is the virtue of tutoring and other means of adaptive instruction.

Peer tutoring (tutoring of slower or younger students by more advanced students) appears to work nearly as well as teacher tutoring; with sustained student practice it might be equal to teacher tutoring in some cases. Significantly, peer tutoring promotes effective learning in tutors as well as tutees. The need to organize one's thoughts in order to impart them intelligibly to others, the need to become conscious of the value of time, and the need to learn managerial and social skills are probably the main reasons for benefits to the tutor.

Even slower-learning students and those with disabilities can be in the position of teaching to others if they are given the extra time and practice that may be required to master a skill. This can give them a positive experience and increase their feelings of self-esteem. The success of two other practices in this booklet the teaching of learning strategies and co-operative learning-is attributable to instructional features similar to those of tutoring.

Mastery Learning

More than fifty studies show that careful sequencing, monitoring and control of the learning process raise the learning rate. Pretesting helps determine what should be studied; this allows the teacher to avoid assigning material that has already been mastered or for which the student does not yet have the prerequisite skills. Ensuring that students achieve mastery of initial steps in the sequence helps ensure that they will make satisfactory progress in subsequent, more advanced steps. Frequent assessment of progress informs teachers and students when additional time and corrective remedies are needed. Mastery learning appears to work best when the subject-matter is well organised.

Because of its emphasis on outcomes and careful monitoring of progress, mastery learning can save learners' time. It allows more time and remediation for students who need it. It also enables faster learners to skip material they already know. Since mastery learning suits instruction to the needs of each student, it can work better than giving the whole class the same lesson at the same time. Such whole-class teaching may be too hard for some learners and too easy for others.

Mastery learning programmes require special

planning, materials and procedures. Teachers must be prepared to identify the components of instruction, develop assessment strategies so that individual students are appropriately placed in the instructional continuum, and provide reinforcement and corrective feedback-while continuously engaging students in lessons.

Co-operative Learning

Learning proceeds more effectively than usual when exchanges among teachers and learners are frequent and specifically directed towards students' problems and interests. In whole-class instruction, only one person can speak at a time, and shy or slow-learning students may be reluctant to speak at all. When students work in groups of two to four, however, each group member can participate extensively, individual problems are more likely to become clear and to be remedied (sometimes with the teacher's assistance), and learning can accelerate.

With justification, co-operative learning has become widespread. Not only can it increase academic achievement, but also it has other virtues. By working in small groups, students learn teamwork, how to give and receive criticism, and how to plan, monitor and evaluate their individual and joint activities with others. It appears that modern workplaces increasingly require such partial delegation of authority, group management and co-operative skills. Like modern managers, teachers may need to become more like facilitators, consultants and evaluators, rather than supervisors. Nonetheless, researchers do not recommend that co-operative learning take up the whole school day; the use of a variety of procedures, rather than co-opera-tive learning alone, is considered to be most productive.

In addition, co-operative learning means more than merely assigning students to small groups. Teachers must also carefully design and prepare for the small-group setting. Students need instruction in skills necessary to operate successfully in small groups. Decisions must be made about the use of individual or group accountability. Care must be taken in establishing the mix of strengths and needs represented by students in the groups. Attention to these details will increase the likelihood that the co-operative groups will produce increased learning.

Adaptive Education

Adaptive instruction is an integrated diagnostic-prescriptive process that combines several of the preceding practices-tutoring, mastery and co-operative learning, and instruction in learning strategies into a classroom management system to tailor instruction to individual and small-group needs. The achievement effects of adaptive programmes have been demonstrated. The broader effects of adaptive instruction are probably underestimated, since it aims at diverse ends that are difficult to measure, including student autonomy, intrinsic motivation, teacher and student choice and parental involvement.

Adaptive education requires implementation steps executed by a master teacher, including planning, time allocation, task delegation to aides and students, and quality control. Unlike most other practices, it is a comprehensive programme for the whole school day, rather than a single method that requires simple integration into one subject or into a single teacher's repertoire. Its focus on the individual student requires that barriers to learning are first diagnosed and then a plan developed to address those needs.

A student with special needs or experiencing academic difficulties becomes the shared responsibility of a team of teachers and specialists. Such an approach to education calls for teachers to develop a broad spectrum of teaching approaches, along with knowledge of when to use each of them most productively, and to co-ordinate their efforts with those of other professionals providing support to a student. Time and opportunity to do this are crucial for implementation of adaptive education.

Skilful professional management is required to integrate all aspects of the programme. For example, curricular co-ordination means more than a plan for the teaching of subject-matter skills and knowledge across grade levels as it applies to all students. Instead, it encompasses the relationship of that curriculum to the abilities and needs of each student. Consequently, central-office staff, principals and teachers need more than usual training to install and maintain adaptive programmes. As goals for school become more clear and uniform, it should be increasingly possible to develop and employ systemic approaches, such as adaptive education.

Academic and Social -Emotional Learning

In every society, students will inherit social roles now occupied by adults. Our education systems have the job of preparing students for this eventual responsibility. Therefore, around the world, people want to improve education. Some want to strengthen basic academic skills; others want to focus on critical thinking. Some want to promote citizenship or character; others want to protect students against the dangers of drugs, violence and alcohol. Some want parents to play a larger role; others feel the entire community should be involved. There are some areas of growing consensus. As indicated by numerous polls of parents and community leaders, clear what want students to know and to be able to do, and this defines what want schools to teach. We want young people to:

— Be fully literate, able to benefit from and make use of the power of written and spoken language, in various forms;

— Understand mathematics and science at levels that will prepare them for the world of the future and strengthen their ability to think critically, carefully and creatively;

— Be good problem-solvers;

— Take responsibility for their personal health and well-being;

— Develop effective social relationships such as learning how to work in a group and how to understand and relate to others from different cultures and backgrounds;

— Be caring individuals with concern and respect for others;

— Understand how their society works and be prepared to take on the roles that are necessary for future progress;

— Develop good character and make sound moral decisions.

All of these are aspects of what some refer to as the education of the whole child. Educating the whole child is not a new idea. It is rooted in the writings and teachings of many ancient cultures. Yet, achieving the kind of balance that encourages all students to learn, work and contribute to their fullest potential has been a continuing challenge as our world has grown more complex and our communities more fragmented. All of these can be expressed in the single term, social-emotional learning, and it is this form of education, when added to academic learning, that provides educators with the possibility of capturing the balance students need.

While some may disagree about what is most important, educators, parents, business leaders and those who make social policy share the same set of concerns. Schools must become better at guiding students toward becoming literate, responsible, non-violent, drug-free and caring adults. The challenge of raising literate, responsible, non-violent, drug-free and caring students is familiar to parents, policy makers, administrators and teachers. Experience and research show that each element of this challenge can be enhanced by thoughtful, sustained and systematic attention to the social and emotional skills of students. Indeed, schools worldwide must give students intellectual and practical tools they can bring to their classrooms, families and communities.

Social-emotional learning provides many of these tools. It is a way of teaching and organizing classrooms and schools that help students learn a set of skills needed to manage life tasks successfully, such as learning, forming relationships, communicating effectively, being sensitive to others' needs and getting along with others. When schools implement high-quality social-emotional learning programmes effectively, the academic achievement of students increases, incidences of problem behaviours decrease, and the relationships that surround each child are improved. Social-emotional learning is sometimes called 'the missing piece', because it represents a part of education that links academic knowledge with a specific set of skills important to success in schools, families, communities, workplaces and life in general. As recent world events have taught, there is a danger to each of us-locally and globally-when students grow up with knowledge but without social-emotional skills and a strong moral compass. Hence, a combination of academic and social-emotional learning is the true standard for effective education in the world today and for the foreseeable future. Effective, lasting academic and social-emotional learning is built upon caring relationships and warm but challenging classroom and school environments.

Lasting social-emotional learning, sound character and academic success are founded on classrooms and schools that are not threatening to students and challenge them to learn more, but do so in ways that do not discourage them. Also, these schools are places where students feel cared about, welcomed, valued and seen as more than just learners—they are seen as resources.

— Greet all students by name when they enter the school or classroom.

— Begin and/or end the school day with brief periods of time for students to reflect on what they have learned recently and what they might want to learn next.

— Create rules in the classroom that recognize positive behav-iour, such as co-operation, caring, helping, encouragement and support. Be sure that discipline rules and procedures are clear, firm, fair and consistent.

— Show interest in their personal lives outside the school.

— Ask them what kinds of learning environments have been most and least successful for them in the past and use this information to guide instruction.

In addition to teaching life-skills explicitly at elementary and secondary levels, students also benefit from co-ordinated, explicit, developmentally sensitive instruction in the prevention of specific problems, such as smoking, drug use, alcohol, pregnancy, violence and bullying. Different cultures will select and focus on preventing different problem behaviours. In a similar way, students benefit from explicit guidance in finding a healthy life style. Eating habits, sleeping patterns, study and work environments are among the areas that are important to promoting academic and social-emotional learning. Further, all students need to be taught and given opportunities to practice age-appropriate strategies for conflict resolution. Finally, schools should be attentive to difficult life events that befall students and try to provide them with support and coping strategies at those stressful moments.

Typically, such assistance is not given until students show problems that are the result of those difficult life events; unfortunately, during this time, many students are distracted from learning. Even when they are not actively disrupting class, they are not taking in all that their teachers are working so hard to provide. Providing social-emotional assistance to students facing difficult events is a sound prevention strategy that also promotes better academic learning. Students with special education needs must also receive social-emotional skill-building instruction and be included in related activities.

Students are required to learn many things, but without a sense of connection between and to those things, students are not likely to retain what they learn and use it in their lives. When their learning is presented in terms of understandable goals (goals that students can play a larger role in defining as they get older), students become more engaged and focused and less likely to exhibit behaviour problems. Learning experiences that co-ordinate and integrate different aspects of learning across subject areas and over time, as well as those that link to their lives outside of school in the present and future, are especially valuable. Students also benefit from learning problem-solving strategies that they can apply to new situations that face them. Instruction in reading that includes examining the problem-solving and decision-making processes used by various characters in stories is particularly enriching.

The same is true for history and current events instruction that allows students to focus on the different perspectives of individuals and groups involved and the problem-solving processes they used (or might have used). A similar approach can be used to help students understand how scientific and mathematical problem-solving occurs. When taught in this way, students find that, as they encounter new books, new civic situations and new group processes, they have strategies to apply that enhance their learning and performance and enable them to make better progress. Practical applications are given below:

— Ask students how they calm themselves down when they are very upset; remind them to use this strategy when they get into frustrating or difficult situations, or teach them a self-calming strategy.

— Have students set goals that include how they will get better at a particular area of study or schooling and how they will make a contribution to the classroom.

— Teach a problem-solving strategy for understanding fiction, history or current events that uses frameworks such as those illustrated in the following examples or related ones.

— For each person or group, name some different options or solutions to the problem that they thought might help them reach their goals.

— For each option or solution, picture all the things that might have happened next. Envision both long- and short-term consequences.

Instruction for academic and social-emotional learning should use varied modalities and approaches to reach the diverse styles and preferences of all learners.

Academic and social-emotional learning takes place best in different ways for different students. So, educational experiences marked by instruction that uses different modalities are most likely to reach all students and allow them to build their skills and feel that the classroom environment is suited to their preferred way of learning. Modalities include modelling, role-playing, art, dance, drama, working with materials and manipulatives, and digital media, computer technology, and the Internet. Also important for sound instruction are regular and constructive feedback, discussions that include open-ended questioning, and frequent reminders to use social-emotional skills in all aspects of school life. Practical applications are given below:

— Use a balance of teaching strategies, including asking open-ended questions, suggesting possible answers from which students might choose, checking with students to see if they understand what has been taught by asking them to repeat it to you or to a classmate, role-playing and lecturing.

— Vary instruction so that sometimes students are working in a large group, in small groups, in pairs, by themselves, at the computer, or on the Internet, working with digital media

— Provide opportunities for cross-age tutoring.

— Create learning centres so that students can move around and have different learning experiences over the course of a day. The centres can be related to Howard Gardner's concept of multiple intelligences, so that some can be very tactile and hands-on, others can involve writing, others can.16 relate to art or music, and others can provide opportunities to use to dramatic or imaginative play.

— Allow students to create exhibitions of what they learn in different subject areas that can be shared with other students, parents and members of the community.

— Bring in experts and other individuals in the community to share knowledge, skills, customs and stories with students.

Properly conducted community service, which begins at the earliest level of schooling and continues throughout all subsequent years, provides an opportunity for students to learn life-skills, integrate them, apply them, reflect upon them and then demonstrate them. This process solidifies their learning and also helps to create a climate in which others are more likely to engage in community service. Service experiences usually help students to encounter other people, ideas and circumstances in ways that broaden their sense of perspective and build empathic understanding and caring connections to the world around them. For many young people, community service provides an opportunity to nourish a universal need to be a generous and contributing member of important groups to which one belongs. This helps prepare students for their eventual roles in the larger society, as well as work and family groups of which they will be a part. Further, it helps nurture the spirit of students to see themselves as part of a larger world, with sets of ideals and beliefs that are important to living a fulfilled life.

6

Challenges of Higher Education

Challenges of Adult Literacy Programmes

In programmes that are learner-centred, guiding principles are the product of dialogue among representatives of all the stakeholder groups. A guiding principle for a community-wide adult literacy programme might be: 'Instructional methods and reading materials should affirm and build on the learners' life experiences.' Guiding principles for a nationwide or statewide programme might be: 'Supporting agencies should work together rather than compete with each other to implement and manage the programme.' Another guiding principle might be that, 'At each level and at each place of implementation, priority should be given to identifying and utilizing resources that are already available, rather than depending on outside resources to sustain the programme.'

A programme's goals describe in general terms what the stakeholders hope will happen in the future as a result of the literacy programme – its intended long-term consequences for the learners, the community, the education system, and for the nation as a whole. They describe an ideal future but are realistic so that stakeholders will be encouraged as they see themselves making progress.

Goals for learner-centred literacy programmes are congruent with national policies and plans and also with the educational goals of the prospective learners – their reasons for wanting to be literate. In a city-wide literacy programme for out-of-school or unemployed youth, for example, a goal formulated by the learners might be that they will have the knowledge, skills and motivation to find and keep gainful employment.

An additional goal of the programme – this one formulated by the programme's sponsors –might be that the crime rate among the city's youth will be reduced. A goal for a state-sponsored transitional literacy programme for new immigrants might be that the immigrant-learners will become an integral part of their new society (a goal of the sponsors) and also become fluent in the language of their new country (an additional goal of the learners).

The process of setting goals begins by seeking agreement among stakeholders at each level of implementation about why the programme is needed – the problems it is meant to solve – and achieving a consensus regarding the overall purpose it will serve. At national and sub-national levels, goal-setting might be the focus of early planning sessions involving representatives of the different groups who will implement, manage and support the programme at that level, together with representatives of the prospective learners. At local level, a community's goals for literacy might be formulated through formal meetings and informal discussions with the prospective learners, community leaders, and with local government agencies and NGOs.

Objectives describe the specific targets that are to be reached within the period of time covered in the programme plan. They are the explicit statements on which the programme will be periodically assessed in the process of achieving the programme's long-term goals. Objectives are flexible so that they can be adjusted if assessment reveals that they are unrealistic or that they are not serving the purposes for which they were planned.

An objective for a community literacy programme for out-of-school youth might relate to the number of learners that will complete the course in the first two years. At sub-national level, an objective might state the number of teachers that will be trained within a specific time period or the number of training centres that will be established. A national-level objective might list the number of states or provinces in which literature production centres will be established in the first three years. Whether planning takes place at national, sub-national, or local levels, the process of formulating objectives requires knowledge of the resources and activities that are necessary for the programme to be sustained, as well as awareness of the resources that are already available and the activities that are already taking place.

Decisions about the size and scope of a literacy programme are influenced by the needs and goals of the learners and by the political, economic and sociocultural context in which the programme will take place. Three common approaches are the mass campaign and large-scale and small-scale projects.

Mass campaigns are usually initiated by the government and depend on sustained and intensive government leadership at national, sub-national and local levels, usually with the support of relevant NGOs. The goal of a campaign is to make large numbers of people literate within a specified time-frame in order to consolidate large-scale social and/or political changes. Vast human and material resources are mobilized. Decision-making is centralized, although day-to-day management may be localized. Curricula and instructional materials focus on issues that the government considers important, although there may be flexibility in adapting the ideas to local contexts.

Viet Nam's literacy programme is an example of a mass campaign, actually three separate campaigns, initiated between 1954 and the late 1970s. The purpose of the campaigns was to promote national unity and economic growth through a more literate populace. Teacher-training workshops stressed patriotism as well as instructional strategies. The government provided full-time instructors and learning materials but village co-operatives were expected to take responsibility for funding first- and second-level classes. Decisions made at the national level were carried out by volunteers in local communities. All three campaigns were implemented in the midst of armed conflict and economic embargoes and without outside funding or support.

Nicaragua's literacy crusade was also intended to develop a new and unified national identity. The programme was initiated by the new government in 1980 but planning and decision-making were to be more decentralized. A National Co-ordinating Commission consisting of 25 ministerial, political, military, educational, cultural, religious, and 'mass' or local organizations was established within the Department of Education to set overall policy and facilitate implementation.

Parallel co-ordinating commissions were also established at departmental and municipal or local levels. Most of the actual planning for implementation took place at the municipal level. And it was in the municipalities that organizations worked together most co-operatively and that participation of the intended beneficiaries was greatest.

An advantage of the campaign approach is that government power and resources are put at the disposal of the literacy programme. Governments have the means of establishing a favourable political climate and mobilizing resources and popular support that usually are not available to smaller programmes.

A disadvantage of the campaign approach is that maintaining the programme over a long period of time requires a level of political and economic commitment that few governments are able or willing to sustain. Another potential problem is that a mass campaign, with its top-down approach to decision-making, might discourage the level of 'grass-roots' initiative and ownership that is necessary if the literacy programme is to survive when government support declines. A third potential disadvantage is that a mass campaign can be a tool for political indoctrination rather than for promoting equity. Finally, the mass campaign approach is ill-suited to multilingual and/or multicultural contexts. Centralized curricula and materials are ineffective if learners do not understand the language of instruction and if the content of the lessons does not relate to their own educational goals.

Large-scale projects also cover multiple political, geographic, and/or sociocultural areas, but they lack the intensity and unifying focus of mass campaigns. Primary responsibility for large-scale projects may rest either with a government agency or with one or more NGOs, or the programme may be under the joint sponsorship of a government agency and an NGO working in co-operation.

Overall goals and objectives may be established by the sponsoring agencies but because there is less control from the 'top', decisions are more easily adapted to sub-national and local contexts. Decisions about the language of instruction and content of the lessons, for example, may be left to local communities.

An example of a large-scale project is the national Literacy and Awareness Programme in Papua New Guinea, established by the government in 1989 to support NGOs and communities that had been conducting their own small-scale projects for decades. Responsibility for the smaller projects remained mostly with the groups that had originally initiated them.

Government support involved developing curriculum guidelines and prototype reading materials that could be adapted to different language and cultural situations, sponsoring training workshops, and allocating grants to NGOs and communities for teacher training and literature production.

An advantage of large-scale projects that are established in response to grass-roots' initiatives is that they build on infrastructures already in place at sub-national and local levels. The decentralized structure tends to reduce top-down control, leaving decisions about individual programmes to the people who know best what is needed and what will work in their situation. Curricula and reading materials, for example, can be modified to fit the educational goals of the learners.

A possible disadvantage is that a large-scale programme needs the ongoing co-ordination and support of a central agency. If the programme is dependent on the voluntary involvement of NGOs, it may be endangered if the NGOs leave or lose their funding. Decentralized control may also result in duplication of efforts if, for example, each of the supporting NGOs produce their own curriculum frameworks or teaching guides or establish their own materials production centres. Finally, the use of multiple languages can complicate the development of reading and teaching materials and may place a burden on limited human and material resources.

Small-scale projects are geared to a specific audience (a single language group or dialect, a single community, or a single interest group within a community) and serve a specific purpose (health education, family planning, income generation, etc.). They are usually sponsored by an NGO that also takes responsibility for training teachers and providing instructional and reading materials.

The Adivasi adult literacy programme in Andhra Pradesh Province in India is an example of a small-scale project. Integrated with a local development programme, its purpose is to help people become literate in their mother tongue in order to facilitate their transition to Telegu, the regional language, and improve their economic conditions. Local institutions take responsibility for managing and supervising the programme, developing curriculum and reading materials, and recruiting and training personnel.

Small-scale projects usually originate outside the bureaucracy and in close co-operation with the learners. They tend to be more flexible than large-scale projects or campaigns and are able to respond more rapidly to the changing needs of the people they serve. The most obvious disadvantage of small-scale projects is that they reach relatively few people. And because of their narrow support base, small projects are endangered if local infrastructures have not been firmly established and local people have not been equipped to maintain them.

In multilingual contexts, choosing a language for literacy, or for education in general, is a complex task that must take into account a multitude of social, cultural, economic and political factors. Some governments choose to use a single language in their campaigns or large projects in order to promote national unity or to ease the burden of producing literacy materials and training teachers. Others contend that using a single language serves a 'gate keeping' function: only minority language speakers who are willing to sacrifice their traditional languages and cultures are able to move successfully through the education system. Some who advocate mother tongue for early education also contend that too great a cognitive burden is placed on learners who "are expected to learn in a foreign language from teachers who are speaking a foreign language, using materials written in a foreign language, about concepts that are foreign to everyone's personal experience". Until the 1980s, large-scale mother-tongue literacy programmes in multilingual societies, with or without later transfer to a dominant language, were rare.

Relatively few governments had developed language and literacy policies that supported multilingualism and fewer still had made the commitment in time and resources that were required to develop and maintain literacy programmes in multiple languages. Among the exceptions were pre-primary education programmes in Namibia and Papua New Guinea.

The intent of the programmes in these two countries was to teach children in their local language for the first three years of school, after which they moved into primary grades in which English was the language of instruction. These nationwide programmes for children could serve as models for large-scale adult literacy programmes elsewhere if sponsoring agencies are prepared to make the commitment that is required for such efforts.

Another issue for planners to consider relates to the type of classes that will be established to serve the specific needs of the learners and build on the abilities they already possess. Four general types of classes can be identified, based on four general stages of literacy.

Basic literacy classes are for people who have had little or no previous formal or non-formal education but whose personal and occupational goals require literacy and numeracy. Curriculum, instructional methods, and reading materials build on the learners' well-developed understanding of their language and culture and begin immediately to encourage them to be involved actively in the affairs of the world around them.

In fluency classes, readers who have achieved a basic level of proficiency consolidate and expand their uses of reading, writing and numeracy to meet their expanding educational goals. Fluency classes might also be established to help more literate adults move into the formal education system or into vocational training programmes by preparing them for entrance examinations or introducing them to the kinds of reading materials they will be expected to use in the ongoing education programme.

In bilingual or multilingual contexts, transitional classes are for people who have become proficient readers in their mother tongue and now want to transfer their literacy skills into a second (or third) language. Labelling this type of literacy class 'transitional' assumes that the learners already speak the second language and are now ready to learn to read and write in it.

Post-literacy educational opportunities enable learners to continue their education in the formal or vocational systems or through special interest classes, reading clubs, and other educational opportunities in their local communities. Equally important to adults who have reached the post-literacy stage is the variety of reading materials that are interesting and relevant to them.

Decisions about the type of classes that will be established are best when they are based on prospective learners' own assessments of their ability to use literacy to achieve their goals. For example, out-of-school youth who had attained a basic reading ability in primary school may have relapsed into semi-literacy once they left the formal system.

Fluency classes could help them to regain and expand on what they had learned previously in order to prepare them for further education or help them learn specific skills for employment. In multilingual situations, transition classes might be appropriate if community members who are already literate in their mother tongue, want to become literate also in their second language.

The Adivasi people of India learned to read and write in their mother tongue in order to ease their transition to literacy in Telegu, the regional language. In other cases, people who are already literate in their second language want to transfer back to their mother tongue.

The Government of Paraguay, for example, initiated special literacy classes in the formal education system for Guarani-speaking students who had been required to learn to read and write in Spanish, the language of education, but still were most comfortable using Guarani, their mother tongue

At the local level, educational differences among the learners also influence the way classes are organized. A women's group, for example, might choose to divide itself into two separate classes if some members have achieved a measure of fluency while others are still at the basic literacy stage. On the other hand, the two groups might choose to stay together so that the more advanced readers can tutor the beginners. Decisions about the way to divide and/or organize their classes, then, would be based on the abilities, attitudes and goals of the women themselves.

The guiding principles, goals and objectives, established through dialogue among all the stakeholders, will, hopefully, influence decision-making throughout the life of the programme. Decisions relating to the size and scope of the literacy programme, the language(s) that will be used, and the type(s) of literacy classes that will be established will affect later decisions about other components of the programme such as teacher training and materials production. These preliminary decisions, and the manner in which they are made, will also affect the way the programme is perceived by the multiple stakeholders and, therefore, the degree to which it is accepted by them.

STRATEGIES FOR PROGRAMME IMPLEMENTATION

Most strategies for literacy include six component plans:

— *Preliminary research*: collecting information that will be used to plan the programme.

— *Promotion*: generating and nurturing interest and a sense of ownership for the programme among the intended beneficiaries and supporters.

— *Recruitment and training*: identifying the personnel that will be needed for the literacy effort, developing criteria for recruitment, and planning pre-service and in-service training.

— *Curriculum development*: defining educational goals and intended learning outcomes, developing curricula and teachers' guides, and, at community level, planning the content of the lessons.

— *Materials development and production*: identifying topics that are of interest to the learners; developing infrastructures or support systems for writing and illustrating reading materials and for producing and distributing them to local communities.

— *Evaluation*: determining if the literacy programme is achieving its objectives, if it actually is serving the needs of the intended beneficiaries, and, therefore, if it is in the process of achieving its long-term goals.

These six strategic elements are common to most literacy programmes, regardless of their size or location. Whether for a state-run transitional literacy programme for immigrants in London, a community-based literacy programme sponsored by a local women's group in Kenya, or a mass literacy campaign in Nicaragua, a literacy programme strategy would include, for example, a plan for promotion or mobilization – for informing the public of the programme and encouraging their participation in it. These same six strategic elements are also common across levels of implementation and administration.

Using promotion again as an example, a large-scale literacy programme needs to be promoted among government departments, funding agencies and supporting NGOs at sub-national, national and international levels, as well as among potential learners and supporters at the local level. But while the six general strategic elements are common to most successful literacy programmes, the manner in which they are implemented is specific to each context. An 'action plan' for each element might include the following components:

1) identifying the activities that will be carried out to implement the plan in that context;
2) establishing the time-frame for completing each activity;
3) identifying the people who will be responsible for each activity and the resources that will be needed; and
4) identifying the factors that might hinder successful completion of the activity and the possible means for overcoming these problems.

Let us describe the basic strategic elements necessary for implementing sustainable literacy programmes. Each element is examined in relation to its purposes and to the issues and questions that should be considered in planning for its implementation and maintenance.

Research needs

Preliminary research involves identifying, collecting and interpreting the information that will be needed to make planning decisions. Preliminary research requires two kinds of expertise: the technical expertise of the education specialists and the sociocultural expertise of the people who will be responsible for the local programmes. The research team might use one or more methods for gathering information, depending on the research objectives, the time and resources available, and on the type of relationship that planners want to begin developing with the different stakeholders:

— *Informal discussions*: Informal discussions with the intended beneficiaries of the programme can be the means for identifying the learners' needs and goals on which curriculum and reading materials will be based. Before beginning a basic education programme among poor people in rural Colombia, staff from the Ministry of Education met with community members to identify their immediate and long-term education goals and to determine what educational activities would best respond to their concerns and expectations. This information formed the basis for the plan for that area.

— *Formal meetings*. Formal meetings with relevant government and non-government agencies can be used to promote the programme as well as to gather information for planning. In Papua New Guinea, the local co-ordinator of a mother-tongue literacy programme met with district and provincial education officers to inform them of the programme, learn from them what government resources might be available for it, and encourage them to participate in planning and decision-making.

— *Survey instruments*. Different survey instruments can be prepared for different populations. Questionnaires can be mailed to literate individuals and interview forms can be used in individual and group interviews. Their purpose might be to collect information for a literacy database and to learn about people's attitudes and perceptions with regard to the literacy programme Group interviews have an added benefit in that responses can be used to stimulate further discussion and problem-solving by the respondents.

— *Mass media.* Electronic and print media can be used for research and for promoting the literacy programme. For example, radio broadcasts or newspaper articles dramatizing or discussing the potential benefits of literacy can conclude with an invitation to listeners or readers to send information to programme sponsors about literacy needs in their community and about literacy programmes that have already been established in their areas.

Promotion of literacy development programmes

Literacy-for-development programmes are people-centred: they consider intended beneficiaries as partners in rather than targets of development and are a product of ongoing collaboration among the different groups of stakeholder. The purpose of promotion, then, is first to encourage the non-literate public to think critically about the specific ways that literacy might benefit them and the problems it might help them solve, and secondly to encourage people's active participation in planning and maintaining the programme. This approach to development may be especially important in situations in which intended beneficiaries have been left out of decision-making in the past. Promotion serves specifically to:

— Provide preliminary information about the literacy programme and about what will be necessary to establish and maintain it.

— Invite representatives of each of the stakeholder groups –donors, government officials, NGOs, and prospective learners – to work together in planning the programme for their respective areas and begin identifying and/or developing the infrastructures that will be necessary to sustain it.

— Encourage stakeholders to begin identifying resources that can be used for implementation and maintenance and inform them of any additional outside assistance that will be available.

The possibilities for promotion are limited only by the ingenuity of the planners in making use of available resources. At local level, for example, skits can be performed at public gatherings. Schools can hold contests in which students draw pictures illustrating the value of literacy and winning entries can be posted around the community. Literate people in the community can write to government agencies, NGOs, businesses, and other potential supporters and donors to invite their involvement. At sub-national and national levels, radio stations can broadcast programmes about literacy, provide air time for listeners to call in with questions, and make regular announcements about literacy classes that are being planned. Newspapers can publish articles and stories. Formal ceremonies at national, sub-national and local levels can be held to inaugurate the literacy effort.

Recruiting of literacy personnel

Recruiting for a literacy programme involves identifying the activities that will take place in implementing and maintaining the programme, determining the qualifications that will be needed by the personnel responsible for these activities, and securing the services of people with those qualifications. Training involves helping these people gain the motivation, knowledge and competencies to function creatively and effectively in their positions.

The process of establishing qualifications and selecting people for the different positions is influenced by the programme's guiding principles, goals and objectives and by the context in which the different activities will take place. At each level of implementation, personnel for learner-centred literacy programmes require special personal attributes in addition to their technical and professional qualifications. They should be resourceful in adapting ideas and information to their specific situations and respected by the people with whom they work. They should appreciate the social, cultural and linguistic backgrounds of the different groups of learners and be committed to helping individuals and communities achieve their educational goals. While specific activities will vary, strategies for recruitment include several components:

— Identifying the activities for which personnel will be required at each level of implementation.

— Determining the criteria for recruiting personnel for each position at each level, based on a realistic assessment of the people that might be available.

— Identifying the financial and/or other support that different personnel will require and projecting the ability to provide that support. The amount of funding available will influence the degree to which the programme must rely on volunteers who may or may not be available.

— Planning the method of recruitment. At national and sub-national levels, procedures for recruitment follow the policies and practices of the respective government departments and NGOs.

Recruiting personnel at local level begins by informing community members of the essential qualifications for people in each position and asking them to identify people that have these qualifications and are acceptable to the community in general.

Training as an ongoing process. Training for learner-centred adult literacy programmes has both a formal component and an informal component. Ideally, formal and informal training share several general characteristics:

— Trainees participate in identifying what they need to learn and in assessing their own learning progress.

— Trainees and trainers have mutually supportive relationships.

— Adult learning characteristics are emphasized, especially as they differ from those of children.

— Trainees are encouraged to adapt what they have learned so that it is appropriate in their local situation.

— Training of trainers is a priority. Experienced teachers who have demonstrated special skills and sensitivity are encouraged and equipped to become trainers.

Formal and informal training for learner-centred literacy builds on the knowledge and experiences of the trainees as well as on the expertise of the trainer and encourages dialogue in which each facilitates the other's learning. A mutually supportive training process provides a model for trainees to follow later in their own classrooms. Helping teacher trainees to see themselves as facilitators and co-learners can be a long and difficult process, especially for those whose previous learning experiences emphasized knowledge as a product transferred from teacher to passive students rather than generated through participatory activities.

Trainees need ongoing opportunities to observe experienced teachers who demonstrate the desired attitudes and behaviour in their classroom and to practice under their tutelage. Ideally, then, the training process for new teachers would involve:

(1) several weeks observing an experienced teacher in a classroom situation;
(2) attending a training workshop;
(3) practice-teaching under the experienced teacher; and
(4) attending in-service training workshops on a regular basis to meet specific training needs as they arise.

Curriculum and instructional methods

In programmes that consider learning to be a self-directed, participatory process, curriculum and instructional methods are designed to help learners to achieve their personal goals for literacy. Decisions about curriculum and instruction, therefore, take into account general characteristics of adult learners:

— They possess a great deal of experience and knowledge relating to a variety of topics, are aware of their own problems, and have their own educational goals.

— They do not learn the same way as children do and do not want to be taught the same way as children are taught.

— They have many responsibilities and do not want to be involved in activities that they feel are a waste of time.

— They may be uninterested in individualized learning and uncomfortable in competitive situations or, conversely, they may enjoy competition and learn best on their own.

— They may lack self-esteem because of their inability to use print media, because they have had previous unsuccessful school experiences, because of their low social status or – if they are members of an ethnic minority – because of the low status of their language and culture.

The process of curriculum development, begins by learning about the learners themselves and identifying what they want to learn. During the planning phase, efforts are made to determine the prospective learners' educational goals, the reasons why they want to become literate. Women in a rural village in Asia, for example, might want to read, write and calculate so that they can start and maintain an income-generating project. These women's educational goals would be to be able to keep business records and to maintain their own bank accounts.

Although there are many differing definitions of curriculum, the term here refers to the organized collection of intended learning outcomes – the knowledge, skills, attitudes, and behaviours that will enable adult 'learners' to achieve their educational goals Intended learning outcomes for the rural Asian women would be the specific knowledge and skills relating to reading, writing and numeracy that will be necessary for them to keep business records and maintain bank accounts. Implied in this definition of curriculum is the possibility that the set of intended learning outcomes may be inadequate – that even though the learners gain the knowledge and skills prescribed in the curriculum, they still may be unable to meet their educational goals.

Curriculum development requires ongoing evaluation of learning outcomes to see if the curriculum truly is enabling learners to achieve their educational goals. If the intended learning outcomes are achieved but the educational goals have not been reached, the curriculum needs to be revised. If the educational goals answer the question 'why' and the curriculum answers the question 'what', the instructional method answers the question 'how'. The instructional method includes all the planned learning activities that are used to achieve the intended learning outcomes.

The approach that literacy providers take to curriculum and instruction is influenced by their own perceptions of 'literacy'. On the one hand are those who consider literacy to be a technology that literate people use for their own purposes. Based on that point of view, becoming literate is an educational process, but not necessarily a political one.

Curriculum and instructional methods are meant to help adult learners acquire gradually the technical skills and behaviours that the providers consider essential to reading and writing fluency. The assumption is that having gained the essential technical skills, the learners will be able to use the skills for their own specific purposes.

An alternative approach to literacy is based on the assumption that the process by which people learn to read, write and calculate influences the way they will use reading, writing and numeracy in their lives. Those who take this approach argue that curriculum and instructional methods should grow out of the learners' social context and immediately begin encouraging them to think about the ways they can use literacy to solve the problems they have identified and to achieve their personal goals.

Curricula and instructional methods that are meant, for example, to help adult learners improve their income-earning potential would be different from those meant to help them gain access to their religion's sacred writings or to communicate their community's needs more effectively to governmental agencies. Planning for curriculum development. If there are not enough specialists to prepare a curriculum for each group of learners, curriculum frameworks developed at sub-national, national and international levels can be adapted to the educational goals of the different learning groups.

A curriculum framework is a pattern or outline that helps teachers to organize their curriculum under different topics – health, community life, and culture, for example – that are of general relevance to the adult learners in that area. The topics and curriculum content can then be adapted to each group of learners. The process for developing, adapting, using and revising a curriculum framework for adult literacy might include the following steps:

— In national or sub-national workshops, curriculum specialists and experienced teachers develop a curriculum framework for adult literacy classes built around general topics of national or regional interest that can be modified to meet the educational goals of the individual groups of learners.

— In dialogue with the prospective learners, teacher-trainees in local communities identify the learners' educational goals and the specific topics that are interesting to them.

— At pre-service training workshops, teacher-trainees become familiar with the purpose, content and instructional method associated with the curriculum framework and then modify the framework to their learner-identified topics.

— Trainees practise teaching the lessons they have prepared to other participants. This practice teaching helps them to become familiar with the curriculum and enables them to identify and correct problems with their instructional methods.

— In the learners' communities, the curriculum is tested in pilot classes and revised as necessary.

Developing learning materials

Adults generally do not learn to read because someone tells them they should. They do so because they have certain goals and they believe that literacy will help them achieve those goals. If literacy does indeed serve their purposes, they will continue to use it as a resource. If it does not, they are likely to lose interest and, eventually, whatever abilities they had gained in reading and writing. Unfortunately, this point is often overlooked by planners at international as well as national, sub-national, and local levels. A common factor in the poor long-term survival rate of literacy programmes is that planners did not foresee the ongoing need for a variety of interesting and relevant reading materials in the languages of the readers. Self-sustaining infrastructures for literature development (writing, illustrating, and editing books, games, posters, etc.) and production (printing or duplicating the materials using offset press, photocopiers, duplicators, or silk-screen printers) are essential for ongoing literacy. Four general types of materials can be identified:

— Materials that introduce the reading process. Reading materials for early literacy classes help new readers to become familiar with print literature and to begin to experience the ways that literacy can help them to achieve their educational goals. Stories about familiar topics and experiences may be limited in length and complexity, but not so much that language becomes stilted and unnatural. Functional materials such as banking deposit and withdrawal slips or business order forms can also be introduced at this stage if the materials are relevant to the learners' educational goals and in a language they understand, and if the learners are already familiar with the contexts in which the materials are used.

— Materials that help learners to gain fluency. The purpose of materials at this stage is to help learners to increase their confidence in using print media and challenge them to expand their uses of reading and writing to meet their daily needs and to be active participants in the development process. New ideas are introduced as materials increase in length and language complexity.

— Materials that help people to transfer reading and writing from their first to their second language. Materials at this stage assume that readers already speak and understand the new language. Dictionaries, phrase books, books of legends, songs, poetry, and stories in their first and second languages are needed for readers at this level.

— Materials for lifelong education. Once they have achieved fluency in their spoken languages, adult learners are able to use the printed word for a multitude of purposes that require access to an increasing variety of literature. Unfortunately, it is at this point that the system often breaks down, especially in minority language groups without a long written tradition. Planning infrastructures for literature production that will continue to provide readers with relevant and challenging reading materials are essential for meeting the needs of this reading audience. A common tendency in materials production for adult literacy programmes, especially those that are centrally initiated and controlled, is to focus on functional topics or on topics that promote civic consciousness and national unity – topics that are considered important to the central planners. But as people living in a community, learners have other reasons for reading in addition to their functional and civic needs.

Developing and producing reading materials for adult learners living in a variety of contexts and speaking a variety of languages is a challenging task, but experiences in several countries indicate that it can be done. In addition to materials produced at central production facilities, a variety of technologies makes it possible for communities to produce their own reading materials.

VISION OF EDUCATION FOR THE 21ST CENTURY

Education for sustainable development is an emerging but dynamic concept that encompasses a new vision of education that seeks to empower people of all ages to assume responsibility for creating a sustainable future. Education will shape the world of tomorrow — it is the most effective means that society possesses for confronting the challenges of the future. Progress increasingly depends upon educated minds: upon research, invention, innovation and adaptation. Educated minds and instincts are needed not only in laboratories and research institutes, but also in every walk of life. While education is not the whole answer to every problem, in its broadest sense, education must be a vital part of all efforts to imagine and create new relations among people and to foster greater respect for the needs of the environment.

Since 1992, an international consensus has emerged that achieving sustainable development is essentially a process of learning. At major UN conferences of the 1990s, including those on human rights in Vienna (1993), population and development in Cairo (1994), small island developing states in Barbados (1994), social development in Copenhagen (1995), women in Beijing (1995), food security in Rome (1996), and human settlements in Istanbul (1996), the critical role of education was stressed. Just as we learnt to live unsustainably, we now need to learn our way out — to learn how to live sustainably. Sustainable development requires active and knowledgeable citizens and caring and informed decision makers capable of making the right choices about the complex and interrelated economic, social and environmental issues human society is facing.

To achieve this requires the broader process of social change known as social learning, or what the OECD calls 'enhancing societal capacity for the environment'. This involves not only specific education and training programmes but also the use of policy and legislation as opportunities for teaching and encouraging new forms of personal, community and corporate behaviour.

Social learning also involves reflection – often stimulated by religious leaders and the media - on the appropriateness of the mental models and assumptions that have traditionally guided thinking and behaviour. From such processes of social learning we have come to realise that sustainable development is a catalytic vision rather than a neatly defined, technical concept. Indeed, we have learnt that:

— Sustainable development is perhaps more a moral precept than a scientific concept, linked as much with notions of peace, human rights and fairness as with theories of ecology or global warning.

— While sustainable development involves the natural sciences, policy and economics, it is primarily a matter of culture: it is concerned with the values people cherish and with the ways in which we perceive our relationship with others and with the natural world.

— Sustainable development requires us to acknowledge the interdependent relationship between people and the natural environment. This interdependence means that no single social, economic, political or environmental objective be pursued to the detriment of others. The environment cannot be protected in a way that leaves half of humanity in poverty. Likewise there can be no long-term development on a depleted planet.

These principles remind us that sustainable development is grounded in four interdependent systems:

— Biophysical systems which provide the life support systems for all life, human and non-human;

— Economic systems which provide a continuing means of livelihood (jobs and money) for people;.

— Social systems which provide ways for people to live together peacefully, equitably and with respect for human rights and dignity; and

— Political systems through which power is exercised fairly and democratically to make decisions about the way social and economic systems use the biophysical environment.

This holistic view supports four inter-related principles for sustainable living:

— Conservation to ensure that natural systems can continue to provide life support systems for all living things, including the resources that sustain the economic system.

— Peace and Equity to encourage people to live cooperatively and in harmony with each other and have their basic needs satisfied in a fair and equitable way.

— Appropriate Development to ensures that people can support themselves in a long-term way

— Inappropriate development ignores the links between the economy and the other systems in the environment.

— Democracy to ensure that people have a fair and equal say over how natural, social and economic systems should be managed.

Linking social, economic, political and environmental concerns is a crucial aspect of sustainable development.

Creating such links demands a deeper, more ambitious way of thinking about education, one that retains a commitment to critical analysis while fostering creativity and innovation. It demands that education promotes a system of ethics and values that is sensitive to cultural identity, multicultural dialogue, democratic decision-making and the appropriate use and management of natural resources. All countries have sought to respond to the challenge of social learning, within the limits of their resources.

Increased scientific understanding of the scale, severity and interlocking nature of sustainable development issues over the last two decades has led to heightened levels of environmental and social reporting in the mass media, public awareness of issues, and public support for environmental campaigns. Governments and their citizens now expect that schools and other institutions of social learning will help prepare young people to respond positively to the opportunities offered by wide public understanding of, and support, for sustainable development. The potential of education is enormous. Seen as social learning for sustainability, education can increase concern over unsustainable practices and increase our capacity to confront and master change. Education not only informs people, it can change them. As a means for personal enlightenment and for cultural renewal, education is not only central to sustainable development, it is humanity's best hope and most effective means in the quest to achieve sustainable development.

Education and Sustainable Future

Education not only provides scientific and.technical skills, it also provides the motivation, justification, and social support for pursuing and applying them. For this reason, society must be deeply concerned that much of current education falls far short of what is required. Improving the quality and coverage of education and reorienting its goals to recognize the importance of sustainable development must be among society's highest priorities. Clarifying the concept of education for sustainable development was a major challenge for educators during the last decade.

The broad scope of Chapter 36 of Agenda 21 generated extensive debate over such issues as: the meanings of sustainable development in educational settings, the appropriate balance of peace, human rights, citizenship, social equity, ecological and development themes in already over-crowded curricula, and ways of integrating the humanities, the social sciences and the arts into what had up-to-now been seen and practised as a branch of science education.

Some argued that educating for sustainable development ran the risk of indoctrination while others wondered whether asking schools to take a lead in the transition to sustainable development was asking too much of teachers. These debates were compounded by the desire of many, predominantly environmental, NGOs to contribute to educational planning without the requisite understanding of how education systems work, how educational change and innovation takes place, and of relevant curriculum development, professional development and pedagogical principles. Not realising that effective educational change takes time, others were critical of governments for not acting more quickly.

The Commission on Sustainable Development assisted in overcoming the inertia of these debates by establishing priorities through a special Work Programme on education in 1996 and which was revised in 1998.Consequently, many international, regional and national initiatives have contributed to an expanded and refined understanding of the meaning of education for sustainable development. For example, Education International, the major umbrella group of teachers' unions and associations in the world, has issued a declaration and action plan to promote sustainable development through education. Similarly, statements and guidelines in support of reorienting education towards sustainable development have been issued by regional councils of Ministers of Education and/or Environment in the European Union, APEC, OAS, SADC, and the South Pacific.

Many regional strategic or action plans have been developed. A common call in all of these is the need for an integrated approach through which all government ministries (eg education, health, environment, finance, agriculture, industry and consumer affairs, etc.) collaborate in developing a shared understanding of and commitment to policies, strategies and programmes of education for sustainable development.

International conservation organisations such as WWF and IUCN are also actively promoting the integration of education into sustainable development at local community, national and eco-regional scales. In addition, many individual governments have established committees, panels, advisory councils and curriculum development projects to discuss education for sustainable development, develop policy and appropriate support structures, programmes and resources, and fund local initiatives. Indeed, the roots of education for sustainable development are firmly planted in the environmental education efforts of such groups.

Along with global education, development education, peace education, citizenship education, human rights education, and multicultural and anti-racist education that have all been significant, environmental education has been particularly significant. In its brief thirty-year history, contemporary environmental education has steadily striven towards goals and outcomes similar and comparable to those inherent in the concept of sustainability.

In the early 1970s, the emerging environmental education movement was given a powerful boost by the United Nations Conference on the Human Environment held in Stockholm in 1972, which recommended that environmental education be recognized and promoted in all countries. This recommendation led to.the launching in 1975 by UNESCO and the UN Environment Programme (UNEP) of the International Environmental Education Programme (IEEP), which continued until 1995. The influence of the IEEP —and the national and international activities that it inspired — have been widely felt and is reflected in many of the educational innovations carried out in the last two decades. That work was inspired largely by the guiding principles of environmental education laid down by the Intergovernmental Conference on Environmental Education held in Tbilisi in 1977. The vision and objectives in the Tbilisi Declaration integrated a broad spectrum of environmental, social, ethical, economic and cultural outcomes of education - all of which are central to education for sustainable development. Its basic principles were successfully translated into educational policies around the world and, with greater difficulty, into schoolroom practice in many countries.

The international community now strongly believes that we need to foster — through education — the values, behaviour and lifestyles required for a sustainable future. Education for sustainable development has come to be seen as a process of learning how to make decisions that consider the long-term future of the economy, ecology and social well-being of all communities. Building the capacity for such futures-oriented thinking is a key task of education.

This represents a new vision of education, a vision that helps students better understand the world in which they live, addressing the complexity and inter-connectedness of problems such as poverty, wasteful consumption, environmental degradation, urban decay, population growth, gender inequality, health, conflict and the violation of human rights that threaten our future. This vision of education emphasises a holistic, interdisciplinary approach to developing the knowledge and skills needed for a sustainable future as well as changes in values, behaviour, and lifestyles. This requires us to reorient education systems, policies and practices in order to empower everyone, young and old, to make decisions and act in culturally appropriate and locally relevant ways to redress the problems that threaten our common future. In this way, people of all ages can become empowered to develop and evaluate alternative visions of a sustainable future and to fulfil these visions through working creatively with others. Seeking sustainable development through education requires educators to:

— place an ethic for living sustainably, based upon principles of social justice, democracy, peace and ecological integrity, at the centre of society's concerns

— encourage a meeting of disciplines, a linking of knowledge and of expertise, to create understandings that are more integrated and contextualized

— encourage lifelong learning, starting at the beginning of life and grounded in life — one based on a passion for a radical transformation of the moral character of society

— develop to the maximum the potential of all human beings throughout their lives so that they can achieve self-fulfilment and full self-expression with the collective achievement of a viable future

— value aesthetics, the creative use of the imagination, an openness to risk and flexibility, and a willingness to explore new options

— encourage new alliances between the State and civil society in promoting citizens' emancipation and the practice of democratic principles

— mobilize society in a concerted effort so as to eliminate poverty and all forms of violence and injustice

— encourage a commitment to the values for peace in such a way as to promote the creation of new lifestyles and living patterns

— identify and pursue new human projects in the context of local sustainability within a planetary consciousness and a personal and communal awareness of global responsibility.

— create realistic hope in which the possibility of change and the real desire for change are accompanied by a concerted, active participation in change, at the appropriate time, in favour of a sustainable future for all.

There are over 60 million teachers in the world – and each one is a key agent for bringing about the changes in lifestyles and systems that we need. But, education is not confined to the classrooms of formal education. As an approach to social learning, education for sustainable development also encompasses the wide range of learning activities in basic and post-basic education, technical and vocational training and tertiary education, and both non-formal and informal learning by both young people and adults within their families and workplaces and in the wider community.

Deciding how education should contribute to sustainable development is a major task. In coming to decisions about what approaches to education will be locally relevant and culturally appropriate, countries, educational institutions and their communities may take heed of the following key lessons learnt from discussion and debate about education and sustainable development over the past decade.

— Education for sustainable development must explore the economic, political and social implications of sustainability by encouraging learners to reflect critically on their own areas of the world, to identify non-viable elements in their own lives and to explore the tensions among conflicting aims.

— Development strategies suited to the particular circumstances of various cultures in the pursuit of shared development goals will be crucial. Educational approaches must take into account the experiences of indigenous cultures and minorities, acknowledging and facilitating their original and important contributions to the process of sustainable development.

— The movement towards sustainable development depends more on the development of our moral sensitivities than on the growth of our scientific understanding — important as that is. Education for sustainable development cannot be concerned only with disciplines that improve our understanding of nature, despite their undoubted value. Success in the struggle for sustainable development requires an approach to education that strengthens our engagement in support of other values and the awareness that we share a common destiny with others.

— Ethical values are the principal factor in social cohesion and, at the same time, the most effective agent of change and transformation. Ultimately, sustainability will depend on changes in behaviour and lifestyles, changes which will need to be motivated by a shift in values and rooted in the cultural and moral precepts upon which behaviour is based. Without change of this kind, even the most enlightened legislation, the cleanest technology, the most sophisticated research will not succeed in steering society towards the long-term goal of sustainability.

— Changes in lifestyle will need to be accompanied by the development of an ethical awareness, whereby the inhabitants of rich countries discover within their cultures the source of a new and active solidarity, which will make possible to eradicate the widespread poverty that now besets 80% of the world's population as well as the environmental degradation and other problems linked to it.

— Ethical values are shaped through education, in the broadest sense of the term. Education is also essential in enabling people to use their ethical values to make informed and ethical choices. Fundamental social changes, such as those required to move towards sustainability, come about either because people sense an ethical imperative to change or because leaders have the political will to lead in that direction and sense that the people will follow them.

— The effectiveness of education for sustainable development must ultimately be measured by the degree to which it changes the attitudes and behaviours of people, both in their individual roles, including those of producers and consumers, and in carrying out their collective responsibilities and duties as citizens.

Basic Education for All

Basic education provides the foundation for all future education and learning. Its goal, as concerns those in the pre-school and primary school-age population, whether enrolled in school or not, is to produce children who are happy with themselves and with others, who find learning exciting and develop inquiring minds, who begin to build up a storehouse of knowledge about the world and, more importantly, an approach to seeking knowledge that they can use and develop throughout their lives.

Basic education is also integral to lifelong learning, especially in increasing the level adult literacy. Millions more attend only briefly — often for a year or less — then leave without the most essential elements of a basic education or the skills to make their way in an increasingly complex and knowledge-based world. These will join the nearly 900 million adults, the majority of whom are women, who cannot read. Those denied an education suffer enormous social and economic disadvantage.

They are amongst those with the poorest health, lowest housing standards, and poorest employment prospects in the world. In fact, they have less of nearly everything in life, except children. In Peru, for example, women with ten or more years of education bear an average of 2.5 children whereas women with no education have an average of 7.4 children.

In other countries, the difference is less extreme, but still sizeable. Nearly everywhere, higher levels of education — especially for girls and women — reduces the average size of families while contributing to the health, well-being and education of children. However, this is not the only way education impacts upon sustainability. Education is essential for mobilizing minds and communities in the struggle for sustainable development.

Education for All (EFA)The World Conference on Education for All (Jomtien, Thailand, 1990) marked a new start in the global quest to universalize basic education and eradicate illiteracy. The Jomtien Conference also marked the beginning of a broader vision of basic education to include, as well as literacy and numeracy, the general knowledge, skills, values and attitudes that they require to survive, develop their capacities, live and work in dignity, improve the quality of their lives, make informed decisions and continue learning.

The Education for All (EFA) Year 2000 Assessment was the end-of-decade review of the objectives agreed in Jomtien. This was the most in-depth evaluation of basic education ever undertaken. National assessments, sample surveys, case studies, a series of fourteen thematic studies, and data on eighteen statistical indicators quantified progress in more than 180 countries. The Assessment revealed that none of the EFA targets set at Jomtien were met in their entirety —most notably, the fundamental goal of achieving 'universal access to, and completion of' basic education by 2000'. However, many successes were noted:

— The number of children enrolled in school rose from an estimated 599 million in 1990 to 681 million in 1998, nearly twice the average increase during the preceding decade. Eastern Asia and the Pacific, as well as Latin America and the Caribbean are now close to, and China and India have made substantial progress towards, achieving universal primary education. Developing.countries as a whole have achieved a net-enrolment ratio in primary education in excess of 80 per cent.

— The importance of early childhood education is now recognised, and the idea that education begins at birth has taken root in many societies. As a result, the number of children in pre-school education rose by 5 per cent in the past decade.

— More people are now entering secondary education and the rate of completion for upper secondary education is rising steeply with each successive age group. Worldwide, secondary education enrolment has expanded ten-fold over the past fifty years, from 40 million in 1950 to more than 400 million today. Over the same period, tertiary education enrolments increased nearly fourteen fold from 6.5 million in 1950 to 88.2 million in 1997.

— The number of literate adults grew significantly over the past decade, from an estimated 2.7 billion in 1990 to 3.3 billion in 1998. The overall global adult literacy rate now stands at 85 per cent for men, 74 per cent for women. More than 50% of the world's adult population has now attended primary school. However, an estimated 880 million adults cannot read or write, and in the least developed countries one out of every two individuals falls into this category. Two-thirds of illiterate adults are women — exactly the same proportion as ten years ago.

— A few countries have made progress in reducing inequalities of educational opportunity as reflected by gender, disability, ethnicity, urban versus rural location and working children.

Positive trends in primary education mask disparity of access both between and within many countries, and disparities in educational quality can remain even when access rates are high. People in poor, rural and remote communities, ethnic minorities and indigenous populations have shown little or no progress over the past decade. And the gender gap persists. Despite the concerns noted, these improvements represent a substantial contribution to building capacity for sustainable development.

In 2000, ten years after Jomtien, the World Education Forum (Dakar, Senegal) confirmed the World Declaration on Education for All, and agreed to six new goals in the Dakar Framework for Action

— To expand and improve comprehensive early childhood care and education, especially for the most vulnerable and disadvantaged children;
— To ensure that by 2015 all children, particularly girls, children in difficult circumstances and those belonging to ethnic minorities, have access to and complete free and compulsory primary education of good quality;
— To ensure that the learning needs of all young people are met through equitable access to appropriate learning and life skills programmes;
— To achieve a 50 per cent improvement in levels of adult literacy by 2015, especially for women as well as equitable access to basic and continuing education for adults;
— To eliminate gender disparities in primary and secondary education by 2005 and achieve gender equality by 2015 with a focus on ensuring full and equal access to and achievement in basic education of good quality;
— To improve all aspects of the quality of education and ensure excellence of all, so that recognized and measurable learning outcomes are achieved by all, especially in literacy, numeracy and essential life skills.

These goals make the links between basic education and sustainable development very clear. Indeed, the Dakar Framework for Action states, 'Education is ... the key to sustainable development and peace and stability with and among countries, and thus an indispensable means for effective participation in the societies and economies of the twenty-first century'

UNESCO was nominated to orchestrate global efforts to achieve EFA by 2015, and is building partnerships with governments, civil society groups, regional organisations and international agencies. A key component of this is the International Decade For Literacy which strongly links education to the crucial task of poverty alleviation.

The following principles learned from successful EFA activities over the past decade are being integrated into regional and national EFA action plans:

— EFA goals are attainable provided that the problems of educational access are addressed first and adequately.
— Redressing inequalities and disparities in access, quality and learning outcomes should be the cornerstone of national educational policy-making, planning and implementation
— Increased attention should be given to curriculum planning and the provision of adequate and relevant learning materials for improved teaching and learning processes.
— The content of education, as well as processes of teaching and learning, need to be more learner-centred and less controlled by syllabuses, textbooks and examination requirements. This makes the school curriculum relevant, and also helps students become self-motivators, self-learners and critical thinkers.
— School effectiveness and learning outcomes can be improved through developing a culture of maintenance, discipline, stewardship, care and self-esteem, democratic management, school-community partnerships, and a commitment to responsibility, professionalism and excellence.

— The home environment has a major impact on learning outcomes. Parental education and home learning support are vital to learners, providing health and nutrition, moral values and codes of conduct, positive attitudes to education, and support for the school's requirements of learners.

— Systematic and continuous assessment, monitoring and evaluation schemes are needed to understand the dynamics of educational change and to help stakeholders develop appropriate responses.

A special audience of basic education are the millions of young people and adults living in emergency and post-conflict situations where the education system has been destabilised, disorganised or destroyed due to human-made crises such as civil strife and war or natural disasters such as flood and drought. The number of such people is not inconsiderable. At the end of 1999, the UNHCR recognised that there were over 15 million refugees in the world;other estimates placed the number of internally displaced persons at between 20 million and 50 million.These data mean that up to one per cent of the world's population has been displaced by conflict or other disasters, have returned home under difficult circumstances, or are otherwise attempting to rebuild their lives and communities without access to services such as education.

However, education is a vital way for students, their families and their communities to begin the trauma healing process, and to learn the skills and values needed for a more peaceful future and better governance at local and national levels. At its most basic level, this is education for sustainable development. Key lessons for education in emergency situations have been identified by UNHCR and its partners in the Interagency Network Group for Education in Emergencies , including:

— A rapid response to educational reconstruction is vital.

— A community-based approach, e.g. through the involvement of local groups in conducting needs and skills assessments, can ensure high levels of participation in education.

— Existing capacity should be strengthened through providing resources and training for teacher, youth leaders and school management committees

— Attention needs to be paid to the emotional and physical needs of learners as well as cognitive ones, particularly focusing on the needs of special groups, such as the physically maimed or abused, mentally traumatised, former child soldiers, etc.

— Durable educational solutions are most often related to the curriculum and language of study in the country of origin, and should provide physical and social protection skills, sustain study skills, and develop survival and peace-building messages and skills.

7

Global Challenges of Higher Education

In this world of massive, continuing and unpredictable social and technological changes, education has taken on a particular significance as a means both of understanding and of coping with such complexity. In spite of the frequency with which we are exhorted to adjust to change, it is difficult to realize the quite staggering impact of its increasing rate of acceleration. Higher education is one of the most durable forms of education. Universities have a long history and one in which their continued survival and, frequently their flourishing, is a remarkable story. It is doubtful if they have been through more difficult times over their many centuries than at present.

Quality Challenges in Higher Education System

Quality has become a major concern in higher education. This is because meeting society's needs and expectations towards higher education depends ultimately on the quality of its staff, programmes and students, as well as its infrastructure and academic environment. The search for 'quality' has many facets and the principal objective of quality enhancement measures in higher education should be institutional as well as system-wide improvement.

The quality of higher education is a multidimensional concept. As stressed by Donald Ekong, one approaches it through the composite concept of 'quality assurance', which implies that 'All the policies, systems and processes are directed to ensuring the maintenance and enhancement of the quality of educational provision within an institution. A quality assurance system is the means by which an institution confirms to itself and to others that the conditions are in place for students to achieve the standards that the institution has set'.

The concept of quality assurance implies that quality can be understood as adaptation to what is required by the institution, i.e. that the goals set have been reached in a manner consistent with fixed quality criteria. This definition is still very relative and leaves the door open to different interpretations as to the level required, owing to the diversity of tasks and goals and also to the influence of contextual factors on the choice and practicability of performance criteria. These considerations and the analyses made at the regional conferences lead to the conclusion that 'quality is inseparable from social relevance', that is, it is a quest for solutions to society's needs and problems, particularly those connected with the building of a culture of peace and sustainable development. They also lead to the conclusion that quality is not centred exclusively on products but also on the processes initiated by the system when it operates as a coherent whole in order to ensure this social relevance.

Challenges of Staff Development

The chief wealth of leading-edge enterprises lies in the quality of their human capital, this is all the more true for higher education establishments, so complex and demanding are the tasks (education, research and services) required of them. On the part of teachers and researchers they demand not only particularly great ability but also involvement and ethical values meeting the requirements of a quality directed at social relevance. A quality assurance policy therefore means identifying the required skill and attitude profiles before laying down a policy of teacher and researcher selection based essentially on merit, and applying it rigorously. But this also means managing careers so that progressively evolving needs match the available skill and attitude profiles, which calls for policies for the continuous training of teachers and researchers and the appropriate back-up strategies.

A quality assurance policy also implies working to motivate staff. This starts with a policy of conferring on teachers a suitable social and financial status comparable with their opposite numbers in industry. This furthermore implies policies to counter certain imbalances and develop 'well-articulated policies, remove gender inequity in education and, more importantly, promote the advancement of women in the entire society. This should include measures implemented by the institutions of higher education themselves. We suggest that meaningful affirmative action be taken in all possible directions. Women's associations and networks should be fully supported. A systematic and coherent policy of gender research and case studies should be implemented and their findings widely published...' (Dakar, para. 45).

As a result of the various developments in society and the higher education institutions, staff quality is going to depend increasingly on two types of major change. The first change concerns the training of teachers, who are increasingly having to adopt more innovative and interactive teaching ideas and methods, to use the resources offered by the new IT and to encourage their students to use them. 'Teachers and professors ...must be offered a training that enables them to integrate the use of ITs to their teaching programmes. This training will prepare them to act as multipliers of the use of these technologies'. The second change concerns the introduction of incentives and structures requiring researchers to work in multidisciplinary teams focusing on thematic projects and thus to abandon their habits of working exclusively in solitary isolation.

Insufficient attention, and insufficient resources for research is one of the worrying problems which higher education must tackle and whose nature varies with the region. In the developing countries, the burdens of teaching and supervision are sometimes such that high-quality research is impossible and researcher status is an empty word or is useful only for demanding additional funds. In certain very-low-income countries, the living conditions of teachers/researchers are such that moonlighting takes up the bulk of the time of those doing research.

In the more developed countries, the problems are different: some teachers divest themselves of their teaching duties because research is better for their career and because scientific criteria are the main factors in appointments and promotions. Others have chosen to invest first and foremost in teaching for reasons of personal preference or because of difficulties in doing research, depending on the case. If such an investment is not properly recognized by the establishment in its career management, the establishment will find that it is harbouring a great many frustrated individuals who may have a negative effect on a high-quality research policy.

Higher education institutions are generally labour intensive organisations. The quality of the staff these institutions are central to their effectiveness. In business and the professions there is a wide recognition that the skills of their staff need to be continually strengthened and enhanced. In the face of challenges from national and international competitors the better companies are investing more resources in the continual training and retraining of employees at all levels. They focus not only on the competence of their staff, but also give time to stressing the need for commitment to the organisation's goals and to promoting a capacity to change. They are crucial to national aspirations for economic development and, if such capacity building aims are to be achieved, the institutions will have to make the most effective use of all their human resources. In some academic fields it is said that the total of human knowledge is doubling every five or ten years. It is thus almost impossible for an individual staff member to remain in touch with the subject without a conscious investment in scholarship and self-tuition. When these knowledge advances are allied to similar changes in pedagogy, learning materials development and the use of technology, the scale of self improvement required becomes massive.

For administrative and support staff there are equally rapid changes in management processes, techniques and technology. In considering any strategy for developing human resources an institution must consider all its staff; administrative and support personnel can play crucial roles in helping students to learn, and in enabling and facilitating an environment that favours learning. If non-academic staff are committed to the goals of an institution, they can be valuable partners in working with academic colleagues.

The boundaries between categories of staff are blurring, as graduates assume jobs that would previously have been taken by non-graduates. In libraries, computer centres and laboratories those jobs once labelled "non-professional" are being filled by people who will expect to be challenged and to have careers which allow them to continue learning. To deny them staff development would miss a massive opportunity for the institution. In developing countries one of the biggest problems is that of obtaining and then retaining staff.

In no country are higher education institutions immune from severe pressures and challenges. Not only do governments talk to one another about funding, but the growing globalisation of higher education imposes similar burdens and threats on every institution. Among the principal challenges which affect human resource development are the following:

a) *the growth in demand for higher education* is a world wide phenomenon whether one approaches it from the standpoint of an age participation ratio of 35% or of 5%. UNESCO has charted the expansion in student enrolments from 13 million in 1960 to 65 million in 1991. In many countries the rate of expansion has exceeded that of the economy, while the reluctance of some countries to contemplate cost sharing has posed a major problem for their public sector financing. In institutional terms the expansion of numbers has placed pressures on facilities of all kinds.

b) *financial constraints in all countries* mean that governments can no longer fund higher education to the same extent as previously. Apart from asking students and their parents to share the cost, their response has been to call for continued efficiency savings (or simple cuts) in institutional budgets, which has led throughout the world to more severe staff student ratios and heavier workloads for academic staff. Another government response is to expect institutions to generate more of their income from non-governmental sources such as industry or commerce. This places new demands on academic staff who are expected to master entrepreneurial skills in converting their specialist knowledge into market-oriented services. One irony of the situation is that institutional budgets for human resource development are often the first to be cut, just when they are most needed, in times of severe financial difficulty. In many countries the reduction in funding for state institutions is leading to a growth in higher education provision by the private sector.

c) *a focus on basic education* has persuaded many developing countries to limit their support for higher education. Many bilateral donors have followed the messages from Jomtien and reduced their funding for higher education. Within many countries the reputation and public image of universities and the students in them has not helped their cause of getting more finance from either government or industry.

d) *the government and public expectations of universities and other tertiary institutions are* that they will be able to serve wider audiences of students, at different levels, in different ways. Thus among the new expectations will be: an ability to handle a growing proportion of part time students (usually meaning longer hours for staff); willingness to teach a greater number of mature students; the assumption that an institution can serve regional populations using links to associated colleges or providers; an ability to offer distance learning and face to face tuition in "dual mode", that is using the same materials and the same staff; an expectation that institutions can instil a set of "general transferable skills" in all their graduates so that employers needs are more fully met that faculty are all outward-looking and sensitive to the needs of their community; that staff have technical competencies which can offer research and consultancy services to industry and commerce in the area. These expectations place a great onus on institutions to give much more formal consideration to the needs of their stakeholders in their strategic planning and to involve their communities in advising on their institution's development.

e) *A concern for quality* of the product has accompanied the expansion in numbers and the reduction in funding. There is an inevitable fear that "more means worse" and quality will suffer as mass higher education becomes a reality. Governments, parents and students are asking questions about the teaching/learning process and are expecting institutions and funding bodies to monitor the quality of the processes and their outcomes. This questioning adds new pressures to academic staff, not only through the new accountability and reporting procedures, but also through having to be more explicit about the way they conduct themselves and more formal in the way they evaluate the effectiveness of their work. They must also be alert to the different ways in which they can maintain quality with larger class or group sizes.

f) *Technological change affects all disciplines and expects staff members* to be alert to the latest innovations in teaching method and research support. It is evident that there are at least three sets of distinguishing factors: the age factor in which younger staff members feel more at home with technology; the discipline factor in which some academic subjects are more affected than others and the developing country factor in which the gulf between "technology haves" and "technology have-nots" is widening. Even though access to the Internet will eventually enable developing country universities to remedy some of the deficiencies in their library and information services, this will only partly help to close the gap.

g) *The importance of increasing women's participation* among staff and students presents institutions with a clear challenge. As regards students this will affect their admissions strategies, their student support services and sometimes their teaching practices. Thus, several categories of staff may need to be involved in the solution. An even harder challenge faces those seeking to achieve a higher involvement of women in the higher ranks of teachers, researchers or institutional management. Whether the blockages to change in these two areas are in attitudes or processes, the problem requires a strategic review, followed by firm action, if it is to be resolved.

h) *The demands of the labour market* are changing dramatically and inevitably affect those institutions which seek to be responsive to national or regional demand. Some industries in developed countries operate in a global market place and thus recruit on an international basis and compare one country's graduates with another's. It may be unwise to ignore global or regional perspectives in the curricula in any courses which aim to serve these industries. Patterns of employment are also changing; courses which once met national needs are now irrelevant. New offerings are required in areas such as telecommunications, tourism, health care, financial services, food technology and transportation studies. Students who fear unemployment after graduation will now be seeking the more vocational and relevant courses which enhance their chances of employment. In many countries they will also need to be taught how to create their own employment opportunities, when traditional employment is not available. All these changes require increasing adaptability among academic staff, particularly those in declining disciplines.

i) *Effective management demands new skills* within institutions which may not always be present among those who traditionally lead at either central or faculty level. There are widespread complaints within institutions about "new managerial cultures" driving out the old academic collegial spirit, yet the very complexity of the demands on senior institutional managers makes it essential for them to be fully professional. In seeking to achieve this they must learn to adapt commercial management techniques sensitively to the academic environment and never forget the mission of the institution they serve. The technical skills needed by today's institutional managers call into question some of the traditional management structures and job specifications. If it is thought that the answer rests in greater devolution to Deans and other middle level managers, this means that a large number of people in each institution will require management development support.

j) *Roles of people in higher educational institutions*: These daunting challenges are likely to have a considerable impact on the work and role of each of the main participants in institutions. All will be affected by a number of common changes and trends. There are seven:

— a need to be responsive and able to change (in line with the changing policies of governments, external demands and social pressures);

— a call for greater awareness of international perspectives in the content of courses;

— the demand for relevance in the curriculum from employers, governments and students;

— the need for more inter-institutional co-operation, in some cases with the burgeoning private sector;

— awareness of the institution's role in society and the need for it to contribute to national development or the local community;

— a growing emphasis on quality teaching as opposed to research as a worthwhile career goal for academic staff ;

— the increase in demand for postgraduate provision, particularly in those countries with relatively high participation rates in HE.

These have varying impacts on each category of person in an institution and we now review this in turn For institutional leaders, Rectors, Vice Presidents, Pro Vice Chancellors etc, the challenges are immense. They bear the brunt of decision making and strategic direction in new, very uncertain environments.

Leadership skills will be essential as will communications and persuasive skills in convincing academic colleagues of the need for changes to long established habits. The leadership role will centre on the management of change and on reconciling the essential need to adapt what are usually conservative institutions with the opposition and unease that such change will cause. Thus, the key roles for such leaders will include:

— providing strategic guidance and a vision of where the institution should be going;

— persuading external bodies such as business, donors and alumni to contribute funds to replace those which government has withdrawn;

— encouraging innovation and an entrepreneurial culture and ensuring that institutional processes support rather than hinder this;

— maintaining commitment to institutional goals in a community which is instinctively suspicious of such things.

Institutional managers such as deans and heads of departments are the Executive Head's partners in ensuring that change happens. They have a leadership role at the discipline level and a key part in implementing institutional change. They will share in the turmoils of managing institutions in transition: however, because their responsibilities are at a more detailed level they will need to have more tangible competencies. Among them will be the following:

- people management skills, such as team building and helping staff to develop themselves academically and professionally;
- numeracy and understanding of financial and cost issues;
- IT awareness;
- sensitivity to new developments in the external environment, such as competitive threats;
- customer consciousness;
- strategic awareness of the institution's position;
- understanding of how to use institutional decision making processes in a collegial environment.

Academic staff in their teaching role face probably the biggest set of challenges to their working patterns. They bear the ultimate burden of having to "do more with less", as student numbers increase without matching funding. They are being asked to teach a wider range of students (mature, disadvantaged, part time etc) in different ways involving new methods and technologies. Their accountabilities are being sharpened and made explicit, as quality reviews and assessments examine what they do. In this harsh environment a model teaching staff member would have the following competencies:

- awareness and understanding of the different ways in which students learn;
- knowledge, skills and attitudes relating to assessment and evaluation of students, in order to help students learn;
- commitment to scholarship in the discipline, maintaining professional standards and knowledge of current developments;
- awareness of IT applications to the discipline, both as regards access to materials and resources world-wide and as regards teaching technology;
- sensitivity to external "market" signals as regards the needs of those likely to employ graduates of the discipline;
- mastery of new developments in teaching and learning, including an awareness of the requirements of "dual mode" tuition with face to face and distance learning using similar materials;
- customer awareness, as regards the views and aspirations of stakeholders, including students; understanding of the impact that international and multi-cultural factors would have on the curricula;
- ability to teach a diverse range of students, from different age groups, socio-economic backgrounds, races etc, throughout a longer day;
- skills in handling larger numbers of students in formal lectures, seminars or workshops than hitherto, without the loss of quality;

— development of personal and professional "coping strategies"

This list of required competencies is unlikely to come together in any one person, so that there will be a tendency to encouraging staff to specialise in some of the skills and functions described.

Academic staff in their research role are also under pressure. Universities are increasingly basing their assessment of research quality on the ability of researchers to raise outside funding, as well as on the volume of research conducted and published. Funding is much more competitive than before and often open to international bidders. Research customers are becoming more demanding in the quality of the proposals they require and the final end products they expect. Among the skills which researchers now need are: proposal writing; networking and fund raising for projects; managing PhD students and researchers; project management, particularly relating to international partnership projects.

For academic support staff in libraries, resource and computer centres there are matching demands. The new technologies require mastery of new techniques and software in searching for information and a changed role in supporting users of these support services. The boundaries are blurring between the roles of teachers and those advising students on information retrieval. Both are helping the student to access knowledge held elsewhere and both are faced with calls for help over longer hours from a wider ability range of students. The UK's Dearing Report endorsed this finding "where communications and information technology has changed the nature of learning and teaching, there is a need to review and redefine the roles of academic and support staff within institutions".

For administrative staff there are also new competencies required: information technology skills are now taken for granted similar financial pressures mean that cost awareness and sensitivity to the need for value for money in all administrative processes have to be in the bloodstream customer sensitivity is a key skill, now that budgets are so often devolved to Deans or Schools and central administrators find that they have many academic clients to serve flexible working practices become essential as management costs are being continually trimmed.

Some of these are echoed for technical and manual staff who find themselves under equal pressures to be more cost effective, flexible in work practices, more technically alert and more sensitive to what their customers want. In addition, they are often now expected to work in a less secure environment due to threats of outsourcing or contracting out their services. As a reward for accepting this uncertainty they are sometimes being brought more into decision making and being asked to share in the corporate ethos of the institution.

In developing countries there are particular problems which affect the ability of staff at all levels to acquire the skills described. When even professorial staff are paid salaries so low that they are not enough to feed their families, it is not surprising that staff should spend much of their time on second and even third jobs. Retaining good staff in such circumstances is often only possible because the institution provides a house at a negligible rent, but finding funds and time for staff development is much harder. In addition, the pressures of survival limit the time that even the most professional staff members can devote to activities other than the basic teaching load. In small states there are unique staff development problems arising from the small size of higher education institutions. Limited human resource capacity in the country makes senior staff very dependent on external partnerships for advice and information. Multi-skilling within institutions is unavoidable and there are inevitable shortages of specialist staff.

Training Needs

A response to the challenge is integrated and holistic. There are two other key principles which should be borne in mind: staff at all levels should be encouraged to expect to embark on lifelong learning, in their discipline and in the skills needed for their workplace and their role in their institution; any staff development programme must adopt multiple mechanisms for its delivery offering flexibility of access. In this model world institutions would have clear strategies covering staff development for all levels of staff at all stages of their career. These would be integrated with their human resource strategies so that selection and promotion criteria, career planning and staff appraisal processes were all influenced by the strategy.

Initial training for academic staff in institutions is not universal and after a generation of worthy campaigning by staff developers it is still unusual to find countries where it is even mandatory to have completed any training before being confirmed in an academic post. However, even here the pedagogical pressures have rarely provided what might be called a systematic, professional approach to personal development. There are exceptions to the dismal picture. India has 48 academic staff colleges, funded by the University Grants Committee, which offer initial training and limited mid career training to all university staff.

In the United Kingdom the recommendation in the Dearing Report to create an Institute of Learning and Teaching in Higher Education for all academic staff is being energetically pursued. Formal training for higher education staff was required in the former Soviet Union and Eastern Europe. In West European states such as

Great Britain, the Netherlands and Germany institutions have been making efforts to strengthen pedagogical training and the status of staff development programmes has increased. Some of the hopeful signs are: Laws passed in several German Laender to the effect that applicants for a professorship have to give evidence of their pedagogical skills; inclusion in staff contracts, in some institutions in Germany, Norway and Great Britain, of clauses binding new academic staff to attend staff development courses; The creation in France of a national plan for practice-oriented pedagogical training down to postgraduate applicants for teaching posts; The growing number of staff development units within universities; even though the norm is for non-mandatory courses, the numbers participating on them are increasing.

Continuing professional development (CPD) in the academic teaching profession has had as disappointing a history as initial training. Even though some regard it "an essential rather than a desirable objective, an obligation rather than an option - both a professional expectation and duty and a responsibility that institutions have for their staff", this view is rarely echoed by those allocating resources within institutions or at national level. Voluntary courses offered by an underfunded central support service are the normal approach to meeting this need.

The basis on which staff are employed is changing golbally.Several countries are abandoning universal tenure for academic staff in favour of term contracts and the jobs of many non-academic staff are subject to the threat of competitive tendering from external contractors. Many institutional managers find that employing part time contract staff is a cost-effective way of meeting their need for teaching skills. For teachers and researchers in particular one should ask, what is the continuing place of tenure and other forms of job security within the institution? Will increasing insecurity affect the willingness of the individual to adapt and change in line with the institution's requests?

Salaries and salary structures have in the past been based on civil service precedents. Yet now there is competition from private sector institutions of higher education with deeper pockets and differing reward systems. How realistic is it to consider relating pay to performance and what effect will this have on the demand for staff development? Can the state sector compete by stressing non-pay benefits such as the status of a professorial title? Will institutions be able to retain good people in this way? Is there not a case for devising incentive systems, as institutions' earnings from the commercial sector increase? If staff bring in extra income from non governmental sources, what share of it should they be able to retain?

If policies are generous to the individual in this respect, will it prove divisive within the institution if it favours staff in disciplines with high potential for such earning? The implications of the changes in the age profile and study mode of students are that working hours for all teaching staff in institutions will lengthen to stretch into evenings and weekends. This can be resourced by expecting existing staff to work in a different way or by using job-sharing, part time helpers or non-academic support staff. The culture within which academic staff operate has always favoured research excellence at the expense of teaching.

There is a large gap between the massive need for staff development and the present small level of activity, and this should lead some governments and institutions to plan an increase in their provision. In many cases they have much to learn about how to plan, develop, promote and then deliver staff development programmes. Inter-university Co-operation can play a major role in helping those at the beginning of the learning curve benefit from the greater experience of others. Such co-operation can be provided through national networks or professional associations of staff developers within a country or within a region; however, few countries have such organisations and therefore most institutions will need to seek an international network.

In recent years UNESCO's Networks for Staff Development have met this need, as they have brought together groups of those concerned with staff development in higher education institutions. Such networks have cost implications in the first instance, although their existence can bring operational economies by helping members to share resources and learn from each others' experience. Areas where such network co-operation can prove valuable are:

— advice on the staffing and structure of staff development units within institutions; support in developing and drafting strategies for staff development;

— advice on the training that staff developers need and the personal skills and competencies they should have;

— exchanges of course content on all aspects of improving the quality of teaching (but care must be taken to amend the content for cultural differences);

— joint development of staff development programmes;

— information on good practice in operating and managing a staff development unit;

— direct exchanges of staff between members ;

— supplying names of good training providers and feedback on their performance;

— advice on how to collaborate with other providers in the private and public sectors.

Once networks of this kind are created, they allow a variety of interactions between members: exchanges of materials, easy communications with each other, the opportunity to meet at network workshops, staff exchanges between members, jointly run activities, formal problem solving consultancy visits by one member to another etc. The great value of networks is that they provide an easy forum for peer review and debate; if this can include people from other cultures and environments, there will be the added bonus of the diversity from a range of international perspectives.

There have not matched the need and that much more has to be done if the human resource capacity of our higher education institutions is to be fully and effectively utilised. We now consider some suggestions for action by the various participants. The organisation able to adopt these proposals will vary according to where authority lies in each country.

For all the staff in institutions the issue is one of awareness of the need for continuing development. What is often lacking is the strong push by them for the development of training and development opportunities. In the absence of this demand training providers sometimes find that the courses they offer are undersubscribed.

For institutional managers there are several areas where action is needed: every institution should prepare a staff development plan as part of its human resource strategy. This should state clearly what policies are as regards the level of staff development and training which each staff member is entitled to. It should define the roles that categories of staff are expected to fulfil and the staff development needs of those roles ; institutions should review their institutional policies relating to selection and promotion criteria, confirmation of contracts after probation and award of tenure and consider whether they should be linked to the achievement of any staff development targets; consideration should be given to making participation in staff development a mandatory requirement before promotion or entry to certain posts.

This should apply to both academic and administrative staff; the head of the institution should give firm backing and support to staff development as an institutional priority and should ensure that it receives adequate funding; each institution should establish a central staff development unit to develop and monitor institutional staff development policies, provide a programme of short courses and workshops and report to the Governing Body on overall performance of the institution in this area; the institution should seek to create a culture where participation in staff development activities is a regular feature of life and is welcomed; responsibility for promoting staff development should be clearly defined; one model is for Heads of Departments to be given managerial responsibility for helping members of their staff develop their performance and effectiveness, using central institutional or external providers as necessary; institutions should consider setting targets for individuals to join in CPD for particular categories of staff and should consider making some training mandatory (eg: safety, customer service) for some jobs.

For governments and national funding agencies there are several ways they can achieve effective staff development strategies. If they are in a position to control such matters centrally, they should modify the national systems of recruitment and promotion in order to stress the importance of staff development by making it mandatory at certain stages. If institutions are responsible for such matters, governments can make it clear that staff development has their strong backing by asking to see human resource strategies as part of their reviews of institutional strategic planning. They could even consider penalising those institutions which have not given proper consideration to staff development activities in their planning and funding. They can also directly fund innovations in staff development.

Governments can also promote collaboration and co-operation in staff development by providing pump priming support for institutional units or for a national association/network of professionals involved. Another approach is to establish a staff development unit at national level, preferably with the backing of the national organisation of vice chancellors/rectors, to support universities' units and act as a forum for the discussion of staff development policies and mechanisms for collaboration. Ensuring that institutions have an adequate advisory and support service is a proper national function.

For international agencies and donors there are various options for support. The idea of continuing international Staff Development Networks has already been mentioned, but this assumes that countries and institutions are already committed to the idea of staff development. There may be an opinion-forming and educational function before this, in which agencies such as UNESCO or IIEP could run workshops for national policy makers in higher education on the issue of encouraging institutional staff development. Other possible interventions would be: sponsoring surveys of good practice and disseminating them through networks; organising an informal "network of networks" in staff development;

Promoting joint projects between new staff development units and experienced ones in different countries; helping staff in developing countries maintain their professional competence by funding participation at conferences and sabbaticals; funding a UNESCO chair in staff development in higher education; running workshops on specialist topics using international experts; providing consultancy advice to national staff development agencies in response to demand; sponsoring surveys of good practice outside higher education identifying ideas which might be imported; promoting the development of performance indicators or management statistics allowing institutions to compare their staff development activities with each other.

Challenges of Curriculum Development

An increasing number of factors have an impact on the need to modify curricula and can therefore affect their quality: the knowledge explosion and the burgeoning of new disciplines; the increasing need to adopt a multi- and trans-disciplinary approach in order to understand natural and societal phenomena; diversification and regionalization of education courses; the proliferation of short courses and the need to provide crossovers between the various short and long courses; the desire for greater social relevance in a changing world. These pressures compel higher education to adopt three major types of qualitative change in their curricula: changes in goals, in methods and in the structure of curricula as they relate to one another.

Basic training must not be viewed simply as the accumulation of knowledge but must be directed at acquiring skills, the chief ones for each student being: their ability to mobilize their knowledge and related skills in order to analyse complex situations, resolve the problems they pose, be capable of teamwork, be capable of providing logical justification for their choices and show foresight. Value education will develop the capability and habit of reacting as a bona fide committed intellectual and as a responsible and co-operative citizen in order to build sustainable development and a culture of peace. To ensure that such basic education and training are of high quality, it is important for them to be rooted in real-life settings and not to be just a formal exercise that has no meaning and is non-transferable. The place where training takes place and its immediate environment are the initial means of exercising the aforementioned skills and attitudes and thus of responding to the explicit or implicit demands of the environment.

The networking of physical or virtual exchanges provides more extensive possibilities, making it possible to attain universality through comparison with other contexts and thereby also to reach a better understanding of the specific features of local contexts. Students thus learn, together with the partner institutions, to pinpoint common goals and specific goals more accurately and to distinguish more clearly between what is transferable as such and what must be adapted.

. While the quality of curricula is contingent on the quality of goals, it is also highly dependent on the quality of teaching methods. As a result of mass education - without any proportional increase in resources - and the use of new technology, higher education faces the temptation to make greater use of transmissive teaching in large groups, which it is difficult to reconcile with the goals set out above. To meet the increasingly crucial challenge 'to respond to the mass phenomenon and not diminish, and even increase quality', this means a big effort of imagination by higher education. Methods which involve students more deeply in the management of their learning and the use of certain facilities offered by IT, whether in real time or at a distance, are routes which should be explored and cross-fertilized through exchanges of experience.

With increasing openness to training throughout life and in different places, curricula will have to adapt teaching methods to the characteristics of the population concerned: an adult with professional experience does not react in the same way as a young person just out of adolescence; an adult sent by his or her firm to acquire skills relating to a change of job does not have the motivation or needs of an unemployed adult who comes to study of his or her own volition in the hope of acquiring qualifications that will be useful. The increasing openness towards greater flexibility and lifelong learning schemes is leading, and will increasingly lead, higher education institutions to carry out a fundamental re-consideration of their curriculum structures so as to create a linkage, or an 'interstructuring', of curricula.

Against the background of a growing internationalization of curricula, higher education is being compelled to re-think the ways in which it organizes its curricula; it no longer does this in isolation but in conjunction with other institutions, and taking into account the increasing readiness to accept lifelong training. It is therefore necessary to continue the effort begun by the student and teacher exchange networks to define more explicit conditions for entering and leaving curricula and programmes that are open to exchanges.

Challenges of Higher Education Researches

Higher education is now regarded as an institution not only for developing knowledge and training young minds, but for disseminating and applying such knowledge as well. The 20th century will be remembered for its intellectual discoveries of relativity and quantum mechanics, and for the interpretation of the structure of DNA—discoveries that have enabled researchers to unravel some of nature's secrets and the fundamental behaviour of some of its life forms.

The university's utilitarian perception of its mission, now regarded with greater emphasis and urgency, has come about largely as a result of these breakthroughs of knowledge in the natural sciences. Among the consequences of these discoveries could be listed the fantastic development of information technology and high-tech industries, the increase in life-expectancy (chiefly because of advances in medical research and nutritional science), and increased food security (derived from genetic engineering research). In all these, the university has provided much of the leadership; with the partnership of government and its agents, industry and international agencies either as research collaborators or as funding bodies.

It is such achievements, such triumphs of science, higher educational institutions should pursue knowledge only for its own sake. Of course there will continue to be programmes of liberal education devoted entirely to scholarly study of the major works of other scholars to help clarify and possibly modify one's previously held convictions. Pure scholarship will remain with us because of the persistence of the cherished value of freedom of thought and enquiry, that intellectual value upon which the life of the university as a place of research and teaching depends.

But in recent times, the immense contributions that university research has made to the national economy ironically places in jeopardy the future funding of such work. The university itself appears to be moving away from its ancient tradition of pursuing pure inquiry for its own sake precisely because of the pressures felt from underfunding.

The current triumphs of research are due in large measure to the provision of adequate financial support from government, from the private sector (through its industries) and from international agencies. The successes of the newly emerging economies in South east Asia—the present economic crises notwithstanding—provide sufficient evidence that in a science and technology-driven economy, it is the university that must be the powerhouse of the "knowledge economy." Now governments everywhere are expecting the university to fulfill its role as a major agent of economic growth.

However, there is a price to pay for this. The injection of public funds into the university for research requires accountability that may be directed by an outside body and not by reliance upon the university's own evaluative procedures. This may impact negatively on a tenet the university holds so dear: respect for academic freedom and autonomy of choice in conducting one's own research. In the same way, industry in the private sector is accountable to its shareholders who are typically more interested in their profits than in the pursuit of knowledge for its own sake.

Shareholders are likely to favour programmes and projects that yield immediately applicable results. The effect is that basic research will be the loser. Going after government and industry-supported research could lead to long-term consequences that are not easy to predict. The challenge now is to work out ways of catering for the interests of both parties in the research partnership. There is also the problem of research conducted outside the university. The total government expenditure for research is often shared between the university and other specialised national research institutes or centres, while multinational industries have their own laboratories for research. The conduct of advanced research is no longer solely the preserve of the university.

Research results obtained in national research institutes as well as in industry may be classified and so may remain unknown to the research public, sometimes until two or more decades have passed. No longer is all knowledge readily disseminated to all those capable of benefiting from it. The freedom to pursue research and to publish one's results, the freedom to communicate among researchers and to disseminate such research information—these cherished rights—are thereby compromised with predictably morbid consequences for the educational training of the next generation of researchers.

Inadequate funding, leading to the need to generate additional income from other sources, is one reason for the university and its researchers to move toward applied research at the expense of basic research. The need for funding has yielded the marginalisation of research motivated by a sense of curiosity generating from the intuition and the sheer intellectual power of individual minds. Yet fostering such work remains one of the basic missions of any higher educational institution, perhaps all the more so during times of socio-economic crisis.

Prior to the demise of one of the superpowers, national agencies used to support basic research principally for its potential applications in the military and in commerce. But now they have less reason to invest in it. Yet everyone recognizes the economic and social benefits of basic research: it produces background knowledge, it develops research skills, new techniques, instruments and methods that in turn yield economic benefits over a much broader range of production sectors.Also there is a symbiotic relation between basic research and technology, with each moving ahead increasingly faster because of the impact that one has upon the other. Thus inadequate funding for basic research has an immediate deteriorating effect not only on higher educational institutions themselves but on national economies.

Curricula of some of the most advanced universities encourage too early a specialisation for the student. A science student specialises in the study of nature but not of man; student of the humanities concentrates upon man, to the complete neglect of nature. The result is the existence of what of the two cultures. Some policy makers are students of the humanities with little or no interest in how the technological gadgets that they regularly use came about. Similarly, some scientists are hardly conversant with the appreciation of poetry or art or music. The public will better appreciate the work of the researcher if he has been prepared with an understanding of that public in all its dimensions.

Indeed our educational system should be guided by the scientific worldview that has emerged in this century, that is, the Copenhagen interpretation of quantum mechanics that states that there exist several mutually exclusive but complementary approaches to reality, since nature and society are too subtle to be described from any single viewpoint. The education of the scientist should include training in the social sciences, and that of the social scientist should include training in the natural sciences, so that it is possible for them both to apply their fullest potentials to national life and development.

Development is closely linked to environmental change. Two major causative factors have been identified as responsible for the degradation of the environment, with serious implications for the future of planet Earth. These are the increased consumption patterns and life-styles of the affluent industrialised countries, and high population growth rates in the developing countries. Sustaining these life-styles and catering for the minimum needs of the global community have led to a considerable pressure on our natural resources.

So, in order not to compromise the needs of future generations, the challenge to the researcher whether at a higher educational institution or in industry is to either identify alternative sources of energy which are renewable and are environmentally-friendly or, if we are to live with non-renewable sources, to find ways of decreasing the carbon dioxide emitted by fossil fuels. How to achieve population stabilization has to be considered not only from a purely economic point of view but from human and cultural aspects as well. Happiness in some cultures means having many children while in others it is having one or none at all. All researchers, social and natural, basic and applied, have a role to play in our attempt to encourage a globally applicable plan for sustainable development.

Research on the management of the environment, is global and interdisciplinary. Fortunately, meaningful cooperation and collaboration is now possible because of information technology. We need to take advantage of this very useful technology. No doubt, the 21st century will raise even more problems but in the midst of difficulties lie challenges and opportunities. In all our deliberation, we need to ask ourselves what sort of human society we want to build in the next century; it must surely be one dominated by science and technology, but which engages the participation of all researchers.

To fulfil universities's role as a major agent of economic growth, governments should continue to fund basic research to levels. Governments of developing countries must create the necessary social environment that nurtures scholarship; they should also provide a reasonable percentage of their GNP to promote quality higher education and capacity-building in research, International organisations and researchers in the developed countries must help break the isolation often experienced by researchers working in developing countries, through such methods as creation of centres of excellence twinning and sandwich post-graduate programmes, Higher educational institutions and research institutes outside the higher educational set-up need to collaborate to promote the principle of universality of knowledge.

Higher educational institutions should ensure that the education of the researcher includes training in both the natural and social sciences, nature and society being too subtle to be described from one single viewpoint only, International organisations including International Council for Science (ICSU) and the International Social Science Council (ISSC), must prepare guidelines for their members concerning the ethics and responsibility in the conduct of their research.

Information technology has proven to be a powerful aid to the researcher; but its potential has yet to be fully exploited. Its recent forays into the higher education industry, through the establishment of the 'Virtual University', has led some to forecast the demise of the traditional university structure as it is presently constituted. This is because of the several advantages the 'virtual university' has over the traditional one: it encourages collaboration between universities and staff in distant locations; it affords the ready availability of first class libraries to students in varied institutions; and it is an excellent tool for cutting down costs.

The Internet is encouraging is the possibility of providing at lower cost the capacity to unite spatially disparate people. In this way, it enlarges the research community to include those outside one's physical neighbourhood, so that people with shared interests can interact while working in different places on the globe.

Currently, questions are being raised concerning the desirability and even the purpose of some of the research carried out in higher educational institutions. For although these institutions provide the technical tools of civilisation, they do not at present provide any guidance for their use. They are neither interested in ultimate ends nor can they predict ultimate consequences.

Typically, researchers are now faced with questions concerning the consequences of their work: what will be the consequences of biochemical weapons research for future generations, or of nuclear waste disposal, or of human cloning and other genetic experiments? How can our planet be saved from the current as well as for the future generations? Here we are dealing not just with technological and ecological questions but with moral dilemmas as well. The university cannot remain wholly indifferent to all values other than its cherished prizes of the search for truth and for funds, important though these quests may be. The "good members of society", duly trained by the university, should "go into life conscious of the deeper issues at stake and of the values involved in them."

Truth and its applications must be pursued with responsibility, and it is for this reason that ICSU has created a Committee on Responsibility and Ethics in Science, charged with the duty of helping to find solutions to problems concerning ethics and responsibility in the conduct of science. ICSU aims to ensure that the contributions science makes to humanity will be for our common well-being and for humane social progress. For, without such ethical vigilance, the distrust that some of the public currently has about science will most likely intensify at great cost to the progress of science. It is the challenge of the researcher to ensure that the two values of freedom and responsibility in the conduct of research are kept in their proper perspective, if the researcher is not to encourage the rejection of progress or modernity as an item of reactionary dogma.

The economic progress that industrialised nations have enjoyed was hastened because of the existence of the relevant indigenous capability in a social environment that nurtured scholarship. The gap between the developed and the developing worlds, which is widening at an increasing pace, will be narrowed only if the necessary infrastructure and local supports for high education and research exist within the developing world.

While most governments of the developing countries are facing serious economic crises, in the long run it will be to their advantage if a reasonable percentage of their GNP provides the resources necessary for the promotion of quality higher education and capacity-building in research. The advanced countries can also contribute in the effort to create an indigenous base for research by helping to equip researchers of the developing world for full participation in knowledge-based socio-economic development. Working as a researcher in a less than sound environment, with few exceptions, means working in complete isolation.

Bibliography

Bond, David/Graham Feletti (eds.), *The Challenge of Problem-based Learning*. London 1991.

Botkin, J.W., *No Limits to Learning*, Pergamon Press, Oxford, 1979

Boud, D./G. Feletti, *The Challenge of Problem-based Learnbing*, Kogan Page, Londong 1991

Bull, P., *Body Movement and Interpersonal Communication*, John Wiley & Sons 1983.

Collings/Ellswoorth, *An experiment with a project curriculum*, London/New York 1923.

Creese, R., "Project-based Manufacturing Engineering Program", *Industrial Education*, December 1987.

Enemark, S., "Facing the Educational Challenges of the Future", *FIG XX International Congress*, Melbourne 1994.

de Graaff, E./P. Bouhuijr (eds), "Implementation of problem-based learning in higher Education", *Thesis*, Amterdam 1993.

Lames, W.K., "Development of Creative Problem Solving", *The Technology Teacher*, Virginia, 1990.

Kjersdam, F., "An Education to Catch the Challenge of the Future", *Key lecture*, SEFI, Copenhagen, 1993.

_____________., "Evaluation of Project-Organized Engineering Education", *European Journal of Engineering Education* vol. 18, No. 4, 1993

_____________., "Problem-oriented Higher Education for Engineering and Technology", *In: International Symposium on Higher Engineering Education*, Pergaman Press, Oxford 1990.

Lorentsen A./A. Kolmos (eds.), *Quality by Theory and Practice of Higher Education*, TNP-Series no. 6, AalborgU niversity, 1991.

Miller, A. H., "Student Assessment of Teaching in Higher Education", *In: Higher Education*, No.17, 1988.

Owen, W., "The Problem method", *The Journal of Educational Methods*, Yonkers 1921/22.

Pollard, A., "The Education and Training of Engineers for the 21st Century: A Forward Look", *Followship of Engineering*, London 1989.

Searle, J. R., *Speech Acts*, Cambridge 1969.

Slavin, R., *Learning to Cooperate*, Cooperating in Learning, New York 1986.

Vinther, O., "Project-organized curricula in engineering education", *SEFI-seminar*, Copenhagen, 1993

Index